# cram101

## Textbook Outlines

Outlines, Notes & Highlights for:

## Cram101 Textbook Reviews

Just The

**facts101**

Textbook Key Facts

Textbook Outlines, Highlights, and Practice Quizzes

# Psychology

## by Weiten, 9th Edition

All "Just the Facts101" Material Written or Prepared by Cram101 Publishing

Title Page

## LEARNING SYSTEM

*"Just the Facts101"* is a Cram101 publication and tool designed to give you all the facts from your textbooks. Visit Cram101.com for the full practice test for each of your chapters for virtually any of your textbooks.

Cram101 has built custom study tools specific to your textbook. We provide all of the factual testable information and unlike traditional study guides, we will never send you back to your textbook for more information.

*YOU WILL NEVER HAVE TO HIGHLIGHT A BOOK AGAIN!*

## Cram101 StudyGuides

All of the information in this StudyGuide is written specifically for your textbook. We include the key terms, places, people, and concepts... the information you can expect on your next exam!

## Want to take a practice test?

Throughout each chapter of this StudyGuide you will find links to cram101.com where you can select specific chapters to take a complete test on, or you can subscribe and get practice tests for up to 12 of your textbooks, along with other exclusive cram101.com tools like problem solving labs and reference libraries.

## Cram101.com

Only cram101.com gives you the outlines, highlights, and PRACTICE TESTS specific to your textbook. Cram101.com is an online application where you'll discover study tools designed to make the most of your limited study time.

By purchasing this book, you get 50% off the normal subscription free!. Just enter the promotional code **'DK73DW20111'** on the Cram101.com registration screen.

*www.Cram101.com*

Learning System

Psychology
Weiten, 9th

# CONTENTS

CHAPTER OUTLINE: KEY TERMS, PEOPLE, PLACES, CONCEPTS

_____ | Gamma-Aminobutyric acid

_____ | Popular psychology

_____ | Psyche

_____ | Principles of Psychology

_____ | Evolutionary leadership theory

_____ | Introspection

_____ | Natural selection

_____ | Structuralism

_____ | Animal mind

_____ | Psychoanalysis

_____ | Psychoanalytic theory

_____ | Verbal Behavior

_____ | Behaviorism

_____ | Nature versus nurture

_____ | Humanism

_____ | Applied psychology

_____ | Clinical psychology

_____ | Person-centered therapy

_____ | Self-concept

Mendelian inheritance

Personality Assessment Inventory

Cognition

Rating scale

Cultural diversity

Discrimination

Racism

Reproductive success

Ponzo illusion

Positive psychology

Case study

Cognitive psychology

Developmental psychology

Educational psychology

Experimental psychology

Health psychology

Personality psychology

Physiological psychology

Psychometrics

CHAPTER OUTLINE: KEY TERMS, PEOPLE, PLACES, CONCEPTS

Social psychology

Clinical neuropsychology

Counseling psychology

Psychiatry

School psychology

Empiricism

Skepticism

Heredity

Subjectivity

Behavior modification

Classical conditioning

Operant conditioning

Bounded rationality

Critical thinking

Mental rotation

# Chapter 1. The Evolution of Psychology

| | |
|---|---|
| Gamma-Aminobutyric acid | γ-Aminobutyric acid is the chief inhibitory neurotransmitter in the mammalian central nervous system. It plays a role in regulating neuronal excitability throughout the nervous system. In humans, GABA is also directly responsible for the regulation of muscle tone. |
| | Although chemically it is an amino acid, GABA is rarely referred to as such in the scientific or medical communities, because the term 'amino acid,' used without a qualifier, conventionally refers to the alpha amino acids, which GABA is not, nor is it ever incorporated into a protein. |
| | In spastic diplegia in humans, GABA absorption becomes impaired by nerves damaged from the condition's upper motor neuron lesion, which leads to hypertonia of the muscles signaled by those nerves that can no longer absorb GABA.Function Neurotransmitter |
| | In vertebrates, GABA acts at inhibitory synapses in the brain by binding to specific transmembrane receptors in the plasma membrane of both pre- and postsynaptic neuronal processes. This binding causes the opening of ion channels to allow the flow of either negatively charged chloride ions into the cell or positively charged potassium ions out of the cell. Depending on which ion channels open, the membrane potential is either hyperpolarized or depolarized. This action results in a negative change in the transmembrane potential, usually causing hyperpolarization. Two general classes of GABA receptor are known: $GABA_A$ in which the receptor is part of a ligand-gated ion channel complex, and $GABA_B$ metabotropic receptors, which are G protein-coupled receptors that open or close ion channels via intermediaries (G proteins). |
| | Neurons that produce GABA as their output are called GABAergic neurons, and have chiefly inhibitory action at receptors in the adult vertebrate. Medium Spiny Cells are a typical example of inhibitory CNS GABAergic cells. In contrast, GABA exhibits both excitatory and inhibitory actions in insects, mediating muscle activation at synapses between nerves and muscle cells, and also the stimulation of certain glands. In mammals, some GABAergic neurons, such as chandelier cells, are also able to excite their glutamatergic counterparts. |
| | $GABA_A$ receptors are ligand-activated chloride channels; that is, when activated by GABA, they allow the flow of chloride ions across the membrane of the cell. Whether this chloride flow is excitatory/depolarizing (makes the voltage across the cell's membrane less negative), shunting (has no effect on the cell's membrane) or inhibitory/hyperpolarizing (makes the cell's membrane more negative) depends on the direction of the flow of chloride. When net chloride flows out of the cell, GABA is excitatory or depolarizing; when the net chloride flows into the cell, GABA is inhibitory or hyperpolarizing. When the net flow of chloride is close to zero, the action of GABA is shunting. Shunting inhibition has no direct effect on the membrane potential of the cell; however, it minimises the effect of any coincident synaptic input essentially by reducing the electrical resistance of the cell's membrane (in essence, equivalent to Ohm's law). |

A developmental switch in the molecular machinery controlling concentration of chloride inside the cell - and, hence, the direction of this ion flow - is responsible for the changes in the functional role of GABA between the neonatal and adult stages. That is to say, GABA's role changes from excitatory to inhibitory as the brain develops into adulthood. Brain development

For the past two decades, the theory of excitatory action of GABA early in development was unquestioned based on experiments in vitro, on brain slices. The main observation was that in the hippocampus and neocortex of the mammalian brain, GABA has primarily excitatory effects, and is in fact the major excitatory neurotransmitter in many regions of the brain before the maturation of glutamateergic synapses.

However, this theory has been questioned based on results showing that in brain slices of immature mice incubated in artificial cerebrospinal fluid (ACSF) (modified in a way that takes into account the normal composition of the neuronal milieu in sucklings by adding an energy substrate alternative to glucose, beta-hydroxybutyrate) GABA action shifts from excitatory to inhibitory mode. This effect has been later repeated when other energy substrates, pyruvate and lactate, supplemented glucose in the slices' media. The effects of beta-hydroxybutyrate were later confirmed for pyruvate and for lactate. However it was argued that the concentrations of the alternative energy substrates used in these experiments were non-physiological and the GABA-shift was instead caused by changes in pH resulting from the substrates acting as 'weak acids'. These arguments were later rebutted by further findings showing that changes in pH even greater than that caused by energy substrates do not affect the GABA-shift described in the presence of energy substrate-fortified ACSF and that the mode of action of beta-hydroxybutyrate, pyruvate and lactate (assessed by measurement NAD(P)H and oxygen utilization) was energy metabolism-related.

In the developmental stages preceding the formation of synaptic contacts, GABA is synthesized by neurons and acts both as an autocrine (acting on the same cell) and paracrine (acting on nearby cells) signalling mediator.

GABA regulates the proliferation of neural progenitor cells the migration and differentiation the elongation of neurites and the formation of synapses.

GABA also regulates the growth of embryonic and neural stem cells. GABA can in?uence the development of neural progenitor cells via brain-derived neurotrophic factor (BDNF) expression. GABA activates the $GABA_A$ receptor, causing cell cycle arrest in the S-phase, limiting growth. Beyond the nervous system

GABAergic mechanisms have been demonstrated in various peripheral tissues and organs including, but not restricted to the intestine, stomach, pancreas, Fallopian tube, uterus, ovary, testis, kidney, urinary bladder, lung, and liver.

# Chapter 1. The Evolution of Psychology

In 2007, an excitatory GABAergic system was described in the airway epithelium. The system activates following exposure to allergens and may participate in the mechanisms of asthma. GABAergic systems have also been found in the testis and in the eye lens. Structure and conformation

GABA is found mostly as a zwitterion, that is, with the carboxy group deprotonated and the amino group protonated. Its conformation depends on its environment. In the gas phase, a highly folded conformation is strongly favored because of the electrostatic attraction between the two functional groups. The stabilization is about 50 kcal/mol, according to quantum chemistry calculations. In the solid state, a more extended conformation is found, with a trans conformation at the amino end and a gauche conformation at the carboxyl end. This is due to the packing interactions with the neighboring molecules. In solution, five different conformations, some folded and some extended, are found as a result of solvation effects. The conformational flexibility of GABA is important for its biological function, as it has been found to bind to different receptors with different conformations. Many GABA analogues with pharmaceutical applications have more rigid structures in order to control the binding better. History

Gamma-aminobutyric acid was first synthesized in 1883, and was first known only as a plant and microbe metabolic product.

| Popular psychology | The term popular psychology refers to concepts and theories about human mental life and behavior that are purportedly based on psychology and that attain popularity among the general population. The concept is closely related to the human potential movement of the 1950s and '60s. |
|---|---|

The term 'pop psychologist' can be used to describe authors, consultants, lecturers and entertainers who are widely perceived as being psychologists, not because of their academic credentials, but because they have projected that image or have been perceived in that way in response to their work.

**Psyche**

In psychology the psyche ( ) is the totality of the human mind, conscious and unconscious. Psychology is the scientific or objective study of the psyche. The word has a long history of use in psychology and philosophy, dating back to ancient times, and has been one of the fundamental concepts for understanding human nature from a scientific point of view.

**Principles of Psychology**

The Principles of Psychology is a monumental text in the history of psychology, written by William James and published in 1890.

There were four methods in James' psychology: analysis (i.e. the logical criticism of precursor and contemporary views of the mind), introspection (i.e.

the psychologist's study of his own states of mind), experiment (e.g. in hypnosis or neurology), and comparison (the use of statistical means to distinguish norms from anomalies).

Analytical arguments of the Principles

There were five chief targets of the critical/analytical arguments of the volume: innatism (typified by Immanuel Kant); associationism (by Jeremy Bentham); materialism (by Herbert Spencer); spiritualism (by scholastic theology); and metaphysical idealism (by Georg Wilhelm Friedrich Hegel).

| | |
|---|---|
| Evolutionary leadership theory | Evolutionary leadership theory analyses leadership from an evolutionary perspective. Evolutionary psychology assumes that our thinking, feeling and doing are the product of innate psychological mechanisms. These mechanisms have evolved because they enable people to effectively deal with situations that (directly or indirectly) are important for survival and reproduction (reproductive success). |
| Introspection | Introspection is the self-examination of one's conscious thoughts and feelings. In psychology, the process of introspection relies exclusively on the purposeful and rational self-observation of one's mental state; however, introspection is sometimes referenced in a spiritual context as the examination of one's soul. Introspection is closely related to the philosophical concept of human self-reflection, and is contrasted with external observation. |
| Natural selection | Natural selection is the process by which traits become more or less common in a population due to consistent effects upon the survival or reproduction of their bearers. It is a key mechanism of evolution. The natural genetic variation within a population of organisms may cause some individuals to survive and reproduce more successfully than others in their current environment. |
| Structuralism | Structuralism is a theoretical paradigm that emphasizes that elements of culture must be understood in terms of their relationship to a larger, overarching system or 'structure.' Alternately, as summarized by philosopher Simon Blackburn, Structuralism is 'the belief that phenomena of human life are not intelligible except through their interrelations. These relations constitute a structure, and behind local variations in the surface phenomena there are constant laws of abstract culture'.<br><br>Structuralism originated in the early 1900s, in the structural linguistics of Ferdinand de Saussure and the subsequent Prague, Moscow and Copenhagen schools of linguistics. |
| Animal mind | The question of animal minds asks whether it is meaningful to describe a non-human animal as having a mind. |

# Chapter 1. The Evolution of Psychology

Discussion of this subject is frequently confused by the fact that some schools of philosophy and psychology (e.g. radical behaviorism) would question whether one should ascribe mind to anyone else (or even to oneself). Such an approach would naturally deny the existence of animal minds.

| | |
|---|---|
| Psychoanalysis | Psychoanalysis is a body of ideas developed by Austrian neurologist Sigmund Freud and continued by others. It is primarily devoted to the study of human psychological functioning and behavior, although it can also be applied to societies. Psychoanalysis has three main components:•a method of investigation of the mind and the way one thinks;•a systematized set of theories about human behavior;•a method of treatment of psychological or emotional illness.<br><br>Under the broad umbrella of psychoanalysis, there are at least 22 theoretical orientations regarding human mentation and development. |
| Psychoanalytic theory | Psychoanalytic theory refers to the definition and dynamics of personality development which underlie and guide psychoanalytic and psychodynamic psychotherapy. First laid out by Sigmund Freud, psychoanalytic theory has undergone many refinements since his work . Psychoanalytic theory came to full prominence as a critical force in the last third of the twentieth century as part of 'the flow of critical discourse after the 1960's. |
| Verbal Behavior | Verbal Behavior is a 1957 book by psychologist B. F. Skinner, in which he analyzes human behavior, encompassing what is traditionally called language, linguistics, or speech. For Skinner, verbal behavior is simply behavior subject to the same controlling variables as any other operant behavior, although Skinner differentiates between verbal behavior which is mediated by other people, and that which is mediated by the natural world. The book Verbal Behavior is almost entirely theoretical, involving little experimental research in the work itself. |
| Behaviorism | Behaviorism also called the learning perspective (where any physical action is a behavior), is a philosophy of psychology based on the proposition that all things that organisms do--including acting, thinking and feeling--can and should be regarded as behaviors. The behaviorist school of thought maintains that behaviors as such can be described scientifically without recourse either to internal physiological events or to hypothetical constructs such as the mind. Behaviorism comprises the position that all theories should have observational correlates but that there are no philosophical differences between publicly observable processes (such as actions) and privately observable processes (such as thinking and feeling). |
| Nature versus nurture | The nature versus nurture debate concerns the relative importance of an individual's innate qualities ('nature,' i.e. nativism, or innatism) versus personal experiences ('nurture,' i.e. empiricism or behaviorism) in determining or causing individual differences in physical and behavioral traits. |

'Nature versus nurture' in its modern sense was coined by the English Victorian polymath Francis Galton in discussion of the influence of heredity and environment on social advancement, although the terms had been contrasted previously, for example by Shakespeare (in his play, The Tempest: 4.1). Galton was influenced by the book On the Origin of Species written by his cousin, Charles Darwin.

| | |
|---|---|
| Humanism | Humanism is an approach in study, philosophy, world view, or practice that focuses on human values and concerns, attaching prime importance to human rather than divine or supernatural matters. According to Greg M. Epstein, 'Humanism today can be categorized as a movement, a philosophy of life or worldview, or ... [a] lifestance.' In philosophy and social science, humanism is a perspective which affirms some notion of human nature, and is contrasted with anti-humanism. |

Secular humanism is a secular ideology which espouses reason, ethics, and justice, whilst specifically rejecting supernatural and religious dogma as a basis of morality and decision-making.

| | |
|---|---|
| Applied psychology | The basic premise of applied psychology is the use of psychological principles and theories to overcome problems in other areas, such as mental health, business management, education, health, product design, ergonomics, and law. Applied psychology includes the areas of clinical psychology, counseling psychology, industrial and organizational psychology, occupational health psychology, human factors, forensic psychology, engineering psychology, as well as many other areas such as school psychology, sports psychology and community psychology. In addition, a number of specialized areas in the general field of psychology have applied branches (e.g., applied social psychology, applied cognitive psychology). |
| Clinical psychology | Clinical psychology is an integration of science, theory and clinical knowledge for the purpose of understanding, preventing, and relieving psychologically-based distress or dysfunction and to promote subjective well-being and personal development. Central to its practice are psychological assessment and psychotherapy, although clinical psychologists also engage in research, teaching, consultation, forensic testimony, and program development and administration. In many countries, clinical psychology is a regulated mental health profession. |
| Person-centered therapy | Person-centered therapy is also known as person-centered psychotherapy, person-centered counselling, client-centered therapy and Rogerian psychotherapy. Person centered therapy is a form of talk-psychotherapy developed by psychologist Carl Rogers in the 1940s and 1950s. It is one of the most widely used models in mental health and psychotherapy. |

# Chapter 1. The Evolution of Psychology

| | |
|---|---|
| Self-concept | Self-concept is a multi-dimensional construct that refers to an individual's perception of 'self' in relation to any number of characteristics, such as academics (and nonacademics), gender roles and sexuality, racial identity, and many others. Each of these characteristics is a research domain (i.e. Academic Self-Concept) within the larger spectrum of self-concept although no characteristics exist in isolation as one's self-concept is a collection of beliefs about oneself. While closely related with self-concept clarity (which 'refers to the extent to which self-knowledge is clearly and confidently defined, internally consistent, and temporally stable'), it presupposes but is distinguishable from self-awareness, which is simply an individual's awareness of their self. |
| Mendelian inheritance | Mendelian inheritance, hereditary characteristics from parent organisms to their offspring; it underlies much of genetics. They were initially derived from the work of Gregor Johann Mendel published in 1865 and 1866 which was 're-discovered' in 1900, and were initially very controversial. When they were integrated with the chromosome theory of inheritance by Thomas Hunt Morgan in 1915, they became the core of classical genetics. |
| Personality Assessment Inventory | Personality Assessment Inventory PhD, is a multi-scale test of psychological functioning that assesses constructs relevant to personality and psychopathology evaluation (e.g., depression, anxiety, aggression) in various contexts including psychotherapy, crisis/evaluation, forensic, personnel selection, pain/medical, and child custody assessment. The PAI has 22 non-overlapping scales, providing a comprehensive overview of psychopathology in adults. The PAI contains four kinds of scales: 1) validity scales, which measure the respondent's approach to the test, including faking good or bad, exaggeration, or defensiveness; 2) clinical scales, which correspond to psychiatric diagnostic categories; 3) treatment consideration scales, which assess factors that may relate to treatment of clinical disorders or other risk factors but which are not captured in psychiatric diagnoses (e.g., suicidal ideation); and 4) interpersonal scales, which provide indicators of interpersonal dimensions of personality functioning. |
| Cognition | Cognition is the scientific term for 'the process of thought'. Usage of the term varies in different disciplines; for example in psychology and cognitive science, it usually refers to an information processing view of an individual's psychological functions. Other interpretations of the meaning of cognition link it to the development of concepts; individual minds, groups, and organizations. |
| Rating scale | A rating scale is a set of categories designed to elicit information about a quantitative or a qualitative attribute. In the social sciences, common examples are the Likert scale and 1-10 rating scales in which a person selects the number which is considered to reflect the perceived quality of a product.<br><br>A rating scale is a method that requires the rater to assign a value, sometimes numeric, to the rated object, as a measure of some rated attribute. |

CHAPTER HIGHLIGHTS & NOTES: KEY TERMS, PEOPLE, PLACES, CONCEPTS

| | |
|---|---|
| Cultural diversity | Cultural diversity is the quality of diverse or different cultures, as opposed to monoculture, as in the global monoculture, or a homogenization of cultures, akin to cultural decay. For example, before Hawaii was conquered by Europeans, the culturally diverse Hawaiian culture existed in the world, and contributed to the world's cultural diversity. Now Hawaii has been westernized; the vast majority of its culture has been replaced with Western or American culture. |
| Discrimination | Discrimination is the cognitive and sensory capacity or ability to see fine distinctions and perceive differences between objects, subjects, concepts and patterns, or possess exceptional development of the senses. Used in this way to identify exceptional discernment since the 17th century, the term began to be used as an expression of derogatory racial prejudice in the 1830s from Thomas D. Rice's performances as 'Jim Crow'. |
| Racism | Racism is generally understood as either belief that different racial groups are characterized by intrinsic characteristics or abilities and that some such groups are therefore naturally superior to others or as practices that discriminate against members of particular racial groups, for example by perpetuating unequal access to resources between groups. <br><br> The definition of racism is controversial both because there is little scholarly agreement about what the word 'race' means, and because there is also little agreement about what does and doesn't constitute discrimination. Some definitions would have it that any assumption that a person's behavior would be influenced by their racial categorization is racist, regardless of how seemingly benign such assumptions might be. |
| Reproductive success | Reproductive success is defined as the passing of genes onto the next generation in a way that they too can pass those genes on. In practice, this is often a tally of the number of offspring produced by an individual. A more correct definition, which incorporates inclusive fitness, is the relative production of fertile offspring by a genotype. |
| Ponzo illusion | The Ponzo illusion is a geometrical-optical illusion that was first demonstrated by the Italian psychologist Mario Ponzo (1882-1960) in 1913. He suggested that the human mind judges an object's size based on its background. He showed this by drawing two identical lines across a pair of converging lines, similar to railway tracks. The upper line looks longer because we interpret the converging sides according to linear perspective as parallel lines receding into the distance. |
| Positive psychology | Positive psychology is a recent branch of psychology whose purpose was summed up in 2000 by Martin Seligman and Mihaly Csikszentmihalyi: 'We believe that a psychology of positive human functioning will arise that achieves a scientific understanding and effective interventions to build thriving in individuals, families, and communities.' Positive psychologists seek 'to find and nurture genius and talent', and 'to make normal life more fulfilling', not simply to treat mental illness. |

# Chapter 1. The Evolution of Psychology

|  |  |
|---|---|
|  | The emerging field of Positive Psychology is intended to complement, not to replace traditional psychology.

By scientifically studying what has gone right, rather than wrong in both individuals and societies, Positive Psychology hopes to achieve a renaissance of sorts. |
| Case study | A case study is a research method common in social science. It is based on an in-depth investigation of a single individual, group, or event. Case studies may be descriptive or explanatory. |
| Cognitive psychology | Cognitive psychology is a subdiscipline of psychology exploring internal mental processes. It is the study of how people perceive, remember, think, speak, and solve problems.

Cognitive psychology is radically different from previous psychological approaches in two key ways. |
| Developmental psychology | Developmental psychology is the scientific study of systematic psychological, emotional, and perceptional changes that occur in human beings over the course of their life span. Originally concerned with infants and children, the field has expanded to include adolescence, adult development, aging, and the entire life span. This field examines change across a broad range of topics including motor skills and other psycho-physiological processes; cognitive development involving areas such as problem solving, moral understanding, and conceptual understanding; language acquisition; social, personality, and emotional development; and self-concept and identity formation. 3 major contexts to consider when analysing child psychology are: social context, cultural context, and socioeconomic context. |
| Educational psychology | Educational psychology is the study of how humans learn in educational settings, the effectiveness of educational interventions, the psychology of teaching, and the social psychology of schools as organizations. Educational psychology is concerned with how students learn and develop, often focusing on subgroups such as gifted children and those subject to specific disabilities. Researchers and theorists are likely to be identified in the US and Canada as educational psychologists, whereas practitioners in schools or school-related settings are identified as school psychologists. |
| Experimental psychology | Experimental psychology refers to work done by those who apply experimental methods to the study of behavior and the processes that underlie it. Experimental psychologists employ human participants and animal subjects to study a great many topics, including, among others sensation & perception, memory, cognition, learning, motivation, emotion; developmental processes, social psychology, and the neural substrates of all of these. |

| | |
|---|---|
| Health psychology | Health psychology is concerned with understanding how biological, psychological, environmental, and cultural factors are involved in physical health and illness. Health psychologists work alongside other medical professionals in clinical settings, work on behavior change in public health promotion, teach at universities, and conduct research. Although its early beginnings can be traced to the kindred field of clinical psychology, four different divisions within health psychology and one allied field have developed over time. |
| Personality psychology | Personality psychology is a branch of psychology that studies personality and individual differences. Its areas of focus include:•Constructing a coherent picture of the individual and his or her major psychological processes•Investigating individual differences--how people are unique•Investigating human nature--how people are alike

'Personality' can be defined as a dynamic and organized set of characteristics possessed by a person that uniquely influences his or her cognitions, emotions, motivations, and behaviors in various situations. The word 'personality' originates from the Latin persona, which means mask. |
| Physiological psychology | Physiological psychology is a subdivision of behavioral neuroscience (biological psychology) that studies the neural mechanisms of perception and behavior through direct manipulation of the brains of nonhuman animal subjects in controlled experiments. Unlike other subdivisions within biological psychology, the main focus of physiological psychological research is the development of theories that describe brain-behavior relationships rather than the development of research that has translational value. It is sometimes alternatively called psychophysiology, and in recent years also cognitive neuroscience. |
| Psychometrics | Psychometrics is the field of study concerned with the theory and technique of psychological measurement, which includes the measurement of knowledge, abilities, attitudes, personality traits, and educational measurement. The field is primarily concerned with the construction and validation of measurement instruments such as questionnaires, tests, and personality assessments.

It involves two major research tasks, namely: (i) the construction of instruments and procedures for measurement; and (ii) the development and refinement of theoretical approaches to measurement. |
| Social psychology | Social psychology (sociology), known as sociological social psychology, and sometimes as psychological sociology, is an area of sociology that focuses on social actions and on interrelations of personality, values, and mind with social structure and culture. Some of the major topics in this field are sociocultural change, social inequality and prejudice, leadership and intra-group behavior, social exchange, group conflict, impression formation and management, conversation structures, socialization, social constructionism, social norms and deviance, identity and roles, and emotional labor. |

# Chapter 1. The Evolution of Psychology

| | |
|---|---|
| Clinical neuropsychology | Clinical neuropsychology is a sub-field of psychology concerned with the applied science of brain-behaviour relationships. Clinical neuropsychologists use this knowledge in the assessment, diagnosis, treatment, and or rehabilitation of patients across the lifespan with neurological, medical, neurodevelopmental and psychiatric conditions, as well as other cognitive and learning disorders. Assessment is primarily by way of neuropsychological tests, but also includes patient history, qualitative observation and may draw on findings from neuroimaging and other diagnostic medical procedures. |
| Counseling psychology | Counseling psychology is a psychological specialty that encompasses research and applied work in several broad domains: counseling process and outcome; supervision and training; career development and counseling; and prevention and health. Some unifying themes among counseling psychologists include a focus on assets and strengths, person-environment interactions, educational and career development, brief interactions, and a focus on intact personalities. In the United States, the premier scholarly journals of the profession are the Journal of Counseling Psychology and The Counseling Psychologist. |
| Psychiatry | Psychiatry is the medical specialty devoted to the study and treatment of mental disorders. These mental disorders include various affective, behavioural, cognitive and perceptual abnormalities. The term was first coined by the German physician Johann Christian Reil in 1808, and literally means the 'medical treatment of the mind' . |
| School psychology | School psychology is a field that applies principles of clinical psychology and educational psychology to the diagnosis and treatment of children's and adolescents' behavioral and learning problems. School psychologists are educated in psychology, child and adolescent development, child and adolescent psychopathology, education, family and parenting practices, learning theories, and personality theories. They are knowledgeable about effective instruction and effective schools. |
| Empiricism | Empiricism is a theory of knowledge that asserts that knowledge comes only or primarily from sensory experience. One of several views of epistemology, the study of human knowledge, along with rationalism, idealism and historicism, empiricism emphasizes the role of experience and evidence, especially sensory perception, in the formation of ideas, over the notion of innate ideas or traditions.<br><br>Empiricism in the philosophy of science emphasizes evidence, especially as discovered in experiments. |
| Skepticism | Skepticism, but generally refers to any questioning attitude towards knowledge, facts, or opinions/beliefs stated as facts, or doubt regarding claims that are taken for granted elsewhere. |

The word may characterize a position on a single matter, as in the case of religious skepticism, which is 'doubt concerning basic religious principles (such as immortality, providence, and revelation)', but philosophical skepticism is an overall approach that requires all information to be well supported by evidence. Skeptics may even doubt the reliability of their own senses.

| | |
|---|---|
| Heredity | Heredity is the passing of traits to offspring (from its parent or ancestors). This is the process by which an offspring cell or organism acquires or becomes predisposed to the characteristics of its parent cell or organism. Through heredity, variations exhibited by individuals can accumulate and cause some species to evolve. |
| Subjectivity | Subjectivity refers to the subject and his or her perspective, feelings, beliefs, and desires. In philosophy, the term is usually contrasted with objectivity.<br><br>Subjectivity may refer to the specific discerning interpretations of any aspect of experiences. |
| Behavior modification | Behavior modification is the use of empirically demonstrated behavior change techniques to increase or decrease the frequency of behaviors, such as altering an individual's behaviors and reactions to stimuli through positive and negative reinforcement of adaptive behavior and/or the reduction of behavior through its extinction, punishment and/or satiation. Most behavior modification programs currently used are those based on Applied behavior analysis (ABA), formerly known as the experimental analysis of behavior which was pioneered by B. F. Skinner. |
| Classical conditioning | Introduction<br><br>Classical conditioning is a form of learning in which one stimulus comes to signal the occurrence of a second stimulus. This is often brought about by pairing the two stimuli, as in Pavlov's classic experiments. Pavlov presented dogs with a ringing bell followed by food. |
| Operant conditioning | Operant conditioning is the use of a behavior's antecedent and/or its consequence to influence the occurrence and form of behavior. Operant conditioning is distinguished from classical conditioning (also called respondent conditioning) in that operant conditioning deals with the modification of 'voluntary behavior' or operant behavior. Operant behavior 'operates' on the environment and is maintained by its consequences, while classical conditioning deals with the conditioning of reflexive (reflex) behaviors which are elicited by antecedent conditions. |
| Bounded rationality | Bounded rationality is the idea that in decision-making, rationality of individuals is limited by the information they have, the cognitive limitations of their minds, and the finite amount of time they have to make a decision. It was proposed by Herbert A. Simon as an alternative basis for the mathematical modeling of decision making, as used in economics and related disciplines; it complements rationality as optimization, which views decision-making as a fully rational process of finding an optimal choice given the information available. |

# Chapter 1. The Evolution of Psychology

| Critical thinking | Critical thinking is thinking that questions assumptions. It is a way of deciding whether a claim is always true, sometimes true, partly true, or false. Critical thinking can be traced in Western thought to the Socratic method of Ancient Greece and in the East, to the Buddhist kalama sutta and Abhidharma. |
| --- | --- |
| Mental rotation | Mental rotation is the ability to rotate mental representations of two-dimensional and three-dimensional objects. |
| | Mental rotation is somewhat localized to the right cerebral hemisphere. It is thought to take place largely in the same areas as perception. |

1. _____ is generally understood as either belief that different racial groups are characterized by intrinsic characteristics or abilities and that some such groups are therefore naturally superior to others or as practices that discriminate against members of particular racial groups, for example by perpetuating unequal access to resources between groups.

   The definition of _____ is controversial both because there is little scholarly agreement about what the word 'race' means, and because there is also little agreement about what does and doesn't constitute discrimination. Some definitions would have it that any assumption that a person's behavior would be influenced by their racial categorization is racist, regardless of how seemingly benign such assumptions might be.

   a. Rankism
   b. Racism
   c. Reverse discrimination
   d. Reverse racism

2. . γ-Aminobutyric acid is the chief inhibitory neurotransmitter in the mammalian central nervous system. It plays a role in regulating neuronal excitability throughout the nervous system. In humans, GABA is also directly responsible for the regulation of muscle tone.

   Although chemically it is an amino acid, GABA is rarely referred to as such in the scientific or medical communities, because the term 'amino acid,' used without a qualifier, conventionally refers to the alpha amino acids, which GABA is not, nor is it ever incorporated into a protein.

   In spastic diplegia in humans, GABA absorption becomes impaired by nerves damaged from the condition's upper motor neuron lesion, which leads to hypertonia of the muscles signaled by those nerves that can no longer absorb GABA.Function Neurotransmitter

   In vertebrates, GABA acts at inhibitory synapses in the brain by binding to specific transmembrane receptors in the plasma membrane of both pre- and postsynaptic neuronal processes.

## Chapter 1. The Evolution of Psychology

*Visit Cram101.com for full Practice Exams*

. This binding causes the opening of ion channels to allow the flow of either negatively charged chloride ions into the cell or positively charged potassium ions out of the cell. Depending on which ion channels open, the membrane potential is either hyperpolarized or depolarized. This action results in a negative change in the transmembrane potential, usually causing hyperpolarization. Two general classes of GABA receptor are known: $GABA_A$ in which the receptor is part of a ligand-gated ion channel complex, and $GABA_B$ metabotropic receptors, which are G protein-coupled receptors that open or close ion channels via intermediaries (G proteins).

Neurons that produce GABA as their output are called GABAergic neurons, and have chiefly inhibitory action at receptors in the adult vertebrate. Medium Spiny Cells are a typical example of inhibitory CNS GABAergic cells. In contrast, GABA exhibits both excitatory and inhibitory actions in insects, mediating muscle activation at synapses between nerves and muscle cells, and also the stimulation of certain glands. In mammals, some GABAergic neurons, such as chandelier cells, are also able to excite their glutamatergic counterparts.

$GABA_A$ receptors are ligand-activated chloride channels; that is, when activated by GABA, they allow the flow of chloride ions across the membrane of the cell. Whether this chloride flow is excitatory/depolarizing (makes the voltage across the cell's membrane less negative), shunting (has no effect on the cell's membrane) or inhibitory/hyperpolarizing (makes the cell's membrane more negative) depends on the direction of the flow of chloride. When net chloride flows out of the cell, GABA is excitatory or depolarizing; when the net chloride flows into the cell, GABA is inhibitory or hyperpolarizing. When the net flow of chloride is close to zero, the action of GABA is shunting. Shunting inhibition has no direct effect on the membrane potential of the cell; however, it minimises the effect of any coincident synaptic input essentially by reducing the electrical resistance of the cell's membrane (in essence, equivalent to Ohm's law). A developmental switch in the molecular machinery controlling concentration of chloride inside the cell - and, hence, the direction of this ion flow - is responsible for the changes in the functional role of GABA between the neonatal and adult stages. That is to say, GABA's role changes from excitatory to inhibitory as the brain develops into adulthood. Brain development

For the past two decades, the theory of excitatory action of GABA early in development was unquestioned based on experiments in vitro, on brain slices. The main observation was that in the hippocampus and neocortex of the mammalian brain, GABA has primarily excitatory effects, and is in fact the major excitatory neurotransmitter in many regions of the brain before the maturation of glutamateergic synapses.

However, this theory has been questioned based on results showing that in brain slices of immature mice incubated in artificial cerebrospinal fluid (ACSF) (modified in a way that takes into account the normal composition of the neuronal milieu in sucklings by adding an energy substrate alternative to glucose, beta-hydroxybutyrate) GABA action shifts from excitatory to inhibitory mode. This effect has been later repeated when other energy substrates, pyruvate and lactate, supplemented glucose in the slices' media. The effects of beta-hydroxybutyrate were later confirmed for pyruvate and for lactate. However it was argued that the concentrations of the alternative energy substrates used in these experiments were non-physiological and the GABA-shift was instead caused by changes in pH resulting from the substrates acting as 'weak acids'. These arguments were later rebutted by further findings showing that changes in pH even greater than that caused by energy substrates do not affect the GABA-shift described in the presence of energy substrate-fortified ACSF and that the mode of action of beta-hydroxybutyrate, pyruvate and lactate (assessed by measurement NAD(P)H and oxygen utilization) was energy metabolism-related.

In the developmental stages preceding the formation of synaptic contacts, GABA is synthesized by neurons and acts both as an autocrine (acting on the same cell) and paracrine (acting on nearby cells) signalling mediator.

GABA regulates the proliferation of neural progenitor cells the migration and differentiation the elongation of neurites and the formation of synapses.

GABA also regulates the growth of embryonic and neural stem cells. GABA can in?uence the development of neural progenitor cells via brain-derived neurotrophic factor (BDNF) expression. GABA activates the GABA$_A$ receptor, causing cell cycle arrest in the S-phase, limiting growth. Beyond the nervous system

GABAergic mechanisms have been demonstrated in various peripheral tissues and organs including, but not restricted to the intestine, stomach, pancreas, Fallopian tube, uterus, ovary, testis, kidney, urinary bladder, lung, and liver.

In 2007, an excitatory GABAergic system was described in the airway epithelium. The system activates following exposure to allergens and may participate in the mechanisms of asthma. GABAergic systems have also been found in the testis and in the eye lens. Structure and conformation

GABA is found mostly as a zwitterion, that is, with the carboxy group deprotonated and the amino group protonated. Its conformation depends on its environment. In the gas phase, a highly folded conformation is strongly favored because of the electrostatic attraction between the two functional groups. The stabilization is about 50 kcal/mol, according to quantum chemistry calculations. In the solid state, a more extended conformation is found, with a trans conformation at the amino end and a gauche conformation at the carboxyl end. This is due to the packing interactions with the neighboring molecules. In solution, five different conformations, some folded and some extended, are found as a result of solvation effects. The conformational flexibility of GABA is important for its biological function, as it has been found to bind to different receptors with different conformations. Many GABA analogues with pharmaceutical applications have more rigid structures in order to control the binding better. History

_____ was first synthesized in 1883, and was first known only as a plant and microbe metabolic product.

a. Clinical Neurochemistry
b. Gamma-Aminobutyric acid
c. Dopaminergic
d. False neurotransmitter

3. _____ is an integration of science, theory and clinical knowledge for the purpose of understanding, preventing, and relieving psychologically-based distress or dysfunction and to promote subjective well-being and personal development. Central to its practice are psychological assessment and psychotherapy, although clinical psychologists also engage in research, teaching, consultation, forensic testimony, and program development and administration. In many countries, _____ is a regulated mental health profession.

a. Mental health counselor
b. Educational psychology
c. Industrial and organizational psychology
d. Clinical psychology

4. . _____ is the use of a behavior's antecedent and/or its consequence to influence the occurrence and form of behavior.

# Chapter 1. The Evolution of Psychology

_____ is distinguished from classical conditioning (also called respondent conditioning) in that _____ deals with the modification of 'voluntary behavior' or operant behavior. Operant behavior 'operates' on the environment and is maintained by its consequences, while classical conditioning deals with the conditioning of reflexive (reflex) behaviors which are elicited by antecedent conditions.

a. Operant conditioning chamber

b. Operant conditioning

c. Acceptance and commitment therapy

d. Aversion therapy

5.  _____ is the scientific term for 'the process of thought'. Usage of the term varies in different disciplines; for example in psychology and cognitive science, it usually refers to an information processing view of an individual's psychological functions. Other interpretations of the meaning of _____ link it to the development of concepts; individual minds, groups, and organizations.

a. Basic category

b. Cognition

c. Beat induction

d. Beck's cognitive triad

1. b
2. b
3. d
4. b
5. b

*You can take the complete Chapter Practice Test*

**for Chapter 1. The Evolution of Psychology**
on all key terms, persons, places, and concepts.

*Online 99 Cents*

*http://www.epub3.2.20111.1.cram101.com/*

**Use www.Cram101.com for all your study needs**

**including Cram101's online interactive problem solving labs in**

**chemistry, statistics, mathematics, and more.**

# Chapter 2. The Research Enterprise in Psychology

_____ Personality Assessment Inventory

_____ Empiricism

_____ Critical thinking

_____ Poggendorff illusion

_____ Affirmative action

_____ Operational definition

_____ Data collection

_____ Statistic

_____ Survey research

_____ Common sense

_____ Peer review

_____ Confounding

_____ Extraneous variable

_____ Random assignment

_____ Subjectivity

_____ Case study

_____ Naturalistic observation

_____ Animal mind

_____ Interpersonal psychotherapy

CHAPTER OUTLINE: KEY TERMS, PEOPLE, PLACES, CONCEPTS

Mass index

Central tendency

Descriptive statistics

Median

Spinal cord

Standard deviation

Ponzo illusion

Prediction

Gamma-Aminobutyric acid

Meta-analysis

Self-esteem

Placebo

Sampling bias

Halo effect

Meditation

Social desirability bias

Ethics

Skepticism

Popular psychology

| | Review article |
|---|---|
| | Anecdotal evidence |

| Personality Assessment Inventory | Personality Assessment Inventory PhD, is a multi-scale test of psychological functioning that assesses constructs relevant to personality and psychopathology evaluation (e.g., depression, anxiety, aggression) in various contexts including psychotherapy, crisis/evaluation, forensic, personnel selection, pain/medical, and child custody assessment. The PAI has 22 non-overlapping scales, providing a comprehensive overview of psychopathology in adults. The PAI contains four kinds of scales: 1) validity scales, which measure the respondent's approach to the test, including faking good or bad, exaggeration, or defensiveness; 2) clinical scales, which correspond to psychiatric diagnostic categories; 3) treatment consideration scales, which assess factors that may relate to treatment of clinical disorders or other risk factors but which are not captured in psychiatric diagnoses (e.g., suicidal ideation); and 4) interpersonal scales, which provide indicators of interpersonal dimensions of personality functioning. |
|---|---|
| Empiricism | Empiricism is a theory of knowledge that asserts that knowledge comes only or primarily from sensory experience. One of several views of epistemology, the study of human knowledge, along with rationalism, idealism and historicism, empiricism emphasizes the role of experience and evidence, especially sensory perception, in the formation of ideas, over the notion of innate ideas or traditions.<br><br>Empiricism in the philosophy of science emphasizes evidence, especially as discovered in experiments. |
| Critical thinking | Critical thinking is thinking that questions assumptions. It is a way of deciding whether a claim is always true, sometimes true, partly true, or false. Critical thinking can be traced in Western thought to the Socratic method of Ancient Greece and in the East, to the Buddhist kalama sutta and Abhidharma. |
| Poggendorff illusion | The Poggendorff Illusion is a geometrical-optical illusion that involves the misperception of the position of one segment of a transverse line that has been interrupted by the contour of an intervening structure (here a rectangle). |

It is named after Poggendorff, the editor of the journal, who discovered it in the figures Johann Karl Friedrich Zöllner submitted when first reporting on what is now known as the Zöllner illusion, in 1860.

In the picture to the right, a straight black and red line is obscured by a grey rectangle.

| | |
|---|---|
| Affirmative action | Affirmative action refers to policies that take factors including 'race, color, religion, gender, sexual orientation or national origin' into consideration in order to benefit an underrepresented group 'in areas of employment, education, and business', usually justified as countering the effects of a history of discrimination.<br><br>The term 'affirmative action' was first used in the United States. It first appeared in Executive Order 10925, which was signed by President John F. Kennedy on 6 March 1961, and it was used to refer to measures to achieve non-discrimination. |
| Operational definition | An operational definition defines something (e.g. a variable, term, or object) in terms of the specific process or set of validation tests used to determine its presence and quantity. That is, one defines something in terms of the operations that count as measuring it. The term was coined by Percy Williams Bridgman and is a part of the process of operationalization. |
| Data collection | Data collection is a term used to describe a process of preparing and collecting data - for example as part of a process improvement or similar project. The purpose of data collection is to obtain information to keep on record, to make decisions about important issues, to pass information on to others. Primarily, data is collected to provide information regarding a specific topic. |
| Statistic | A statistic is a single measure of some attribute of a sample (e.g. its arithmetic mean value). It is calculated by applying a function (statistical algorithm) to the values of the items comprising the sample which are known together as a set of data.<br><br>More formally, statistical theory defines a statistic as a function of a sample where the function itself is independent of the sample's distribution; that is, the function can be stated before realisation of the data. |
| Survey research | Survey research This method was pioneered in the 1930s and 1940s by sociologist Paul Lazarsfeld. The initial use of the method was to examine the effects of the radio on political opinion formation of the United States. One of its early successes was the development of the theory of two-step flow of communication. |
| Common sense | Common sense, based on a strict construction of the term, consists of what people in common would agree on : that which they 'sense' as their common natural understanding. |

# Chapter 2. The Research Enterprise in Psychology

| | |
|---|---|
| | Some people (such as the authors of Merriam-Webster Online) use the phrase to refer to beliefs or propositions that -- in their opinion -- most people would consider prudent and of sound judgment, without reliance on esoteric knowledge or study or research, but based upon what they see as knowledge held by people 'in common'. Thus 'common sense' (in this view) equates to the knowledge and experience which most people already have, or which the person using the term believes that they do or should have. |
| Peer review | Peer review is a process of self-regulation by a profession or a process of evaluation involving qualified individuals within the relevant field. Peer review methods are employed to maintain standards, improve performance and provide credibility. In academia peer review is often used to determine an academic paper's suitability for publication. |
| Confounding | In statistics, a confounding variable (also confounding factor, lurking variable, a confound, or confounder) is an extraneous variable in a statistical model that correlates (positively or negatively) with both the dependent variable and the independent variable. The methodologies of scientific studies therefore need to control for these factors to avoid a false positive (Type I) error; an erroneous conclusion that the dependent variables are in a causal relationship with the independent variable. Such a relation between two observed variables is termed a spurious relationship. |
| Extraneous variable | Extraneous variables are variables other than the independent variable that may bear any effect on the behavior of the subject being studied. This only affects the people in the experiment, not the place the experiment is taking place in. Some examples are gender, ethnicity, social class, genetics, intelligence, age. |
| Random assignment | Random assignment is an experimental technique for assigning subjects to different treatments (or no treatment). The thinking behind random assignment is that by randomizing treatment assignment, then the group attributes for the different treatments will be roughly equivalent and therefore any effect observed between treatment groups can be linked to the treatment effect and is not a characteristic of the individuals in the group.

In experimental design, random assignment of participants in experiments or treatment and control groups help to ensure that any differences between and within the groups are not systematic at the outset of the experiment. |
| Subjectivity | Subjectivity refers to the subject and his or her perspective, feelings, beliefs, and desires. In philosophy, the term is usually contrasted with objectivity.

Subjectivity may refer to the specific discerning interpretations of any aspect of experiences. |
| Case study | A case study is a research method common in social science. |

| | It is based on an in-depth investigation of a single individual, group, or event. Case studies may be descriptive or explanatory. |
| --- | --- |
| Naturalistic observation | Naturalistic observation is a research tool in which a subject is observed in its natural habitat without any manipulation by the observer. During naturalistic observation researchers take great care to avoid interfering with the behavior they are observing by using unobtrusive methods. Naturalistic observation involves two main differences that set it apart from other forms of data gathering. |
| Animal mind | The question of animal minds asks whether it is meaningful to describe a non-human animal as having a mind.<br><br>Discussion of this subject is frequently confused by the fact that some schools of philosophy and psychology (e.g. radical behaviorism) would question whether one should ascribe mind to anyone else (or even to oneself). Such an approach would naturally deny the existence of animal minds. |
| Interpersonal psychotherapy | Interpersonal Psychotherapy is a time-limited treatment that encourages the patient to regain control of mood and functioning typically lasting 12-16 weeks. IPT is based on the common factors of psychotherapy: a 'treatment alliance in which the therapist empathically engages the patient, helps the patient to feel understood, arouses affect, presents a clear rationale and treatment ritual, and yields success experiences.'. Interpersonal Psychotherapy of Depression was developed in the New Haven-Boston Collaborative Depression Research Project by Gerald Klerman, MD, Myrna Weissman, PhD, and their colleagues for the treatment of ambulatory depressed, nonpsychotic, nonbipolar patients. |
| Mass index | The mass index is an indicator, developed by Donald Dorsey, used in technical analysis to predict trend reversals. It is based on the notion that there is a tendency for reversal when the price range widens, and therefore compares previous trading ranges (highs minus lows).<br><br>Mass index for a commodity is obtained by calculating its exponential moving average over a 9 day period and the exponential moving average of this average (a 'double' average), and summing the ratio of these two over a given amount of days (usually 25). |
| Central tendency | In statistics, the term central tendency relates to the way in which quantitative data tend to cluster around some value. A measure of central tendency is any of a number of ways of specifying this 'central value'. In practical statistical analyses, the terms are often used before one has chosen even a preliminary form of analysis: thus an initial objective might be to 'choose an appropriate measure of central tendency'. |

# Chapter 2. The Research Enterprise in Psychology

| | |
|---|---|
| Descriptive statistics | Descriptive statistics is the discipline of quantitatively describing the main features of a collection of data. Descriptive statistics are distinguished from inferential statistics , in that descriptive statistics aim to summarize a data set, rather than use the data to learn about the population that the data are thought to represent. This generally means that descriptive statistics, unlike inferential statistics, are not developed on the basis of probability theory. |
| Median | In probability theory and statistics, a median is described as the numeric value separating the higher half of a sample, a population, or a probability distribution, from the lower half. The median of a finite list of numbers can be found by arranging all the observations from lowest value to highest value and picking the middle one. If there is an even number of observations, then there is no single middle value; the median is then usually defined to be the mean of the two middle values. |
| Spinal cord | The spinal cord is a long, thin, tubular bundle of nervous tissue and support cells that extends from the brain (the medulla oblongata specifically). The brain and spinal cord together make up the central nervous system (CNS). The spinal cord begins at the occipital bone and extends down to the space between the first and second lumbar vertebrae; it does not extend the entire length of the vertebral column. |
| Standard deviation | Standard deviation is a widely used measurement of variability or diversity used in statistics and probability theory. It shows how much variation or 'dispersion' there is from the 'average' (mean, or expected/budgeted value). A low standard deviation indicates that the data points tend to be very close to the mean, whereas high standard deviation indicates that the data are spread out over a large range of values. |
| Ponzo illusion | The Ponzo illusion is a geometrical-optical illusion that was first demonstrated by the Italian psychologist Mario Ponzo (1882-1960) in 1913. He suggested that the human mind judges an object's size based on its background. He showed this by drawing two identical lines across a pair of converging lines, similar to railway tracks. The upper line looks longer because we interpret the converging sides according to linear perspective as parallel lines receding into the distance. |
| Prediction | A prediction is a statement about the way things will happen in the future, often but not always based on experience or knowledge. While there is much overlap between prediction and forecast, a prediction may be a statement that some outcome is expected, while a forecast may cover a range of possible outcomes. <br><br> Although guaranteed information about the information is in many cases impossible, prediction is necessary to allow plans to be made about possible developments; Howard H. Stevenson writes that prediction in business '... is at least two things: Important and hard.' |

| | |
|---|---|
| Gamma-Aminobutyric acid | γ-Aminobutyric acid is the chief inhibitory neurotransmitter in the mammalian central nervous system. It plays a role in regulating neuronal excitability throughout the nervous system. In humans, GABA is also directly responsible for the regulation of muscle tone.

Although chemically it is an amino acid, GABA is rarely referred to as such in the scientific or medical communities, because the term 'amino acid,' used without a qualifier, conventionally refers to the alpha amino acids, which GABA is not, nor is it ever incorporated into a protein.

In spastic diplegia in humans, GABA absorption becomes impaired by nerves damaged from the condition's upper motor neuron lesion, which leads to hypertonia of the muscles signaled by those nerves that can no longer absorb GABA.Function Neurotransmitter

In vertebrates, GABA acts at inhibitory synapses in the brain by binding to specific transmembrane receptors in the plasma membrane of both pre- and postsynaptic neuronal processes. This binding causes the opening of ion channels to allow the flow of either negatively charged chloride ions into the cell or positively charged potassium ions out of the cell. Depending on which ion channels open, the membrane potential is either hyperpolarized or depolarized. This action results in a negative change in the transmembrane potential, usually causing hyperpolarization. Two general classes of GABA receptor are known: $GABA_A$ in which the receptor is part of a ligand-gated ion channel complex, and $GABA_B$ metabotropic receptors, which are G protein-coupled receptors that open or close ion channels via intermediaries (G proteins).

Neurons that produce GABA as their output are called GABAergic neurons, and have chiefly inhibitory action at receptors in the adult vertebrate. Medium Spiny Cells are a typical example of inhibitory CNS GABAergic cells. In contrast, GABA exhibits both excitatory and inhibitory actions in insects, mediating muscle activation at synapses between nerves and muscle cells, and also the stimulation of certain glands. In mammals, some GABAergic neurons, such as chandelier cells, are also able to excite their glutamatergic counterparts.

$GABA_A$ receptors are ligand-activated chloride channels; that is, when activated by GABA, they allow the flow of chloride ions across the membrane of the cell. Whether this chloride flow is excitatory/depolarizing (makes the voltage across the cell's membrane less negative), shunting (has no effect on the cell's membrane) or inhibitory/hyperpolarizing (makes the cell's membrane more negative) depends on the direction of the flow of chloride. When net chloride flows out of the cell, GABA is excitatory or depolarizing; when the net chloride flows into the cell, GABA is inhibitory or hyperpolarizing. When the net flow of chloride is close to zero, the action of GABA is shunting. Shunting inhibition has no direct effect on the membrane potential of the cell; however, it minimises the effect of any coincident synaptic input essentially by reducing the electrical resistance of the cell's membrane (in essence, equivalent to Ohm's law). |

A developmental switch in the molecular machinery controlling concentration of chloride inside the cell - and, hence, the direction of this ion flow - is responsible for the changes in the functional role of GABA between the neonatal and adult stages. That is to say, GABA's role changes from excitatory to inhibitory as the brain develops into adulthood. Brain development

For the past two decades, the theory of excitatory action of GABA early in development was unquestioned based on experiments in vitro, on brain slices. The main observation was that in the hippocampus and neocortex of the mammalian brain, GABA has primarily excitatory effects, and is in fact the major excitatory neurotransmitter in many regions of the brain before the maturation of glutamateergic synapses.

However, this theory has been questioned based on results showing that in brain slices of immature mice incubated in artificial cerebrospinal fluid (ACSF) (modified in a way that takes into account the normal composition of the neuronal milieu in sucklings by adding an energy substrate alternative to glucose, beta-hydroxybutyrate) GABA action shifts from excitatory to inhibitory mode. This effect has been later repeated when other energy substrates, pyruvate and lactate, supplemented glucose in the slices' media. The effects of beta-hydroxybutyrate were later confirmed for pyruvate and for lactate. However it was argued that the concentrations of the alternative energy substrates used in these experiments were non-physiological and the GABA-shift was instead caused by changes in pH resulting from the substrates acting as 'weak acids'. These arguments were later rebutted by further findings showing that changes in pH even greater than that caused by energy substrates do not affect the GABA-shift described in the presence of energy substrate-fortified ACSF and that the mode of action of beta-hydroxybutyrate, pyruvate and lactate (assessed by measurement NAD(P)H and oxygen utilization) was energy metabolism-related.

In the developmental stages preceding the formation of synaptic contacts, GABA is synthesized by neurons and acts both as an autocrine (acting on the same cell) and paracrine (acting on nearby cells) signalling mediator.

GABA regulates the proliferation of neural progenitor cells the migration and differentiation the elongation of neurites and the formation of synapses.

GABA also regulates the growth of embryonic and neural stem cells. GABA can in?uence the development of neural progenitor cells via brain-derived neurotrophic factor (BDNF) expression. GABA activates the $GABA_A$ receptor, causing cell cycle arrest in the S-phase, limiting growth. Beyond the nervous system

GABAergic mechanisms have been demonstrated in various peripheral tissues and organs including, but not restricted to the intestine, stomach, pancreas, Fallopian tube, uterus, ovary, testis, kidney, urinary bladder, lung, and liver.

In 2007, an excitatory GABAergic system was described in the airway epithelium. The system activates following exposure to allergens and may participate in the mechanisms of asthma. GABAergic systems have also been found in the testis and in the eye lens. Structure and conformation

GABA is found mostly as a zwitterion, that is, with the carboxy group deprotonated and the amino group protonated. Its conformation depends on its environment. In the gas phase, a highly folded conformation is strongly favored because of the electrostatic attraction between the two functional groups. The stabilization is about 50 kcal/mol, according to quantum chemistry calculations. In the solid state, a more extended conformation is found, with a trans conformation at the amino end and a gauche conformation at the carboxyl end. This is due to the packing interactions with the neighboring molecules. In solution, five different conformations, some folded and some extended, are found as a result of solvation effects. The conformational flexibility of GABA is important for its biological function, as it has been found to bind to different receptors with different conformations. Many GABA analogues with pharmaceutical applications have more rigid structures in order to control the binding better. History

Gamma-aminobutyric acid was first synthesized in 1883, and was first known only as a plant and microbe metabolic product.

| | |
|---|---|
| Meta-analysis | In statistics, a meta-analysis combines the results of several studies that address a set of related research hypotheses. In its simplest form, this is normally by identification of a common measure of effect size, for which a weighted average might be the output of a meta-analyses. Here the weighting might be related to sample sizes within the individual studies. |
| Self-esteem | Self-esteem is a term in psychology to reflect a person's overall evaluation or appraisal of his or her own worth. Self-esteem encompasses beliefs (for example, 'I am competent', 'I am worthy') and emotions such as triumph, despair, pride and shame . 'The self-concept is what we think about the self; self-esteem, the positive or negative evaluation of the self, is how we feel about it'. |
| Placebo | A placebo is a sham or simulated medical intervention. Sometimes patients given a placebo treatment will have a perceived or actual improvement in a medical condition, a phenomenon commonly called the placebo effect.<br><br>In medical research, placebos are given as control treatments and depend on the use of measured deception. |
| Sampling bias | In statistics, sampling bias is when a sample is collected in such a way that some members of the intended population are less likely to be included than others. |

# Chapter 2. The Research Enterprise in Psychology

| | |
|---|---|
| | It results in a biased sample, a non-random sample of a population in which all individuals, or instances, were not equally likely to have been selected. If this is not accounted for, results can be erroneously attributed to the phenomenon under study rather than to the method of sampling. |
| Halo effect | The halo effect is a cognitive bias in which our judgments of a person's character can be influenced by our overall impression of them. It can be found in a range of situations--from the courtroom to the classroom and in everyday interactions. The halo effect was given its name by psychologist Edward Thorndike and since then, several researchers have studied the halo effect in relation to attractiveness, and its bearing on the judicial and educational systems. |
| Meditation | Meditation is any form of a family of practices in which practitioners train their minds or self-induce a mode of consciousness to realize some benefit.<br><br>Meditation is generally an inwardly oriented, personal practice, which individuals do by themselves. Prayer beads or other ritual objects are commonly used during meditation. |
| Social desirability bias | Social desirability bias is the tendency of respondents to answer questions in a manner that will be viewed favorably by others. It can take the form of over-reporting good behavior or under-reporting bad behavior. The tendency poses a serious problem with conducting research with self-reports, especially questionnaires. |
| Ethics | Ethics, is a branch of philosophy that involves systematizing, defending, and recommending concepts of right and wrong behavior.<br><br>It is also a common term to refer to or define e.g. code of conduct, honourable behaviours, virtues, just actions, etc. Ethics may be either externally imposed (by e.g. society, professional organizations, schools, law enforcement, etc). |
| Skepticism | Skepticism, but generally refers to any questioning attitude towards knowledge, facts, or opinions/beliefs stated as facts, or doubt regarding claims that are taken for granted elsewhere. The word may characterize a position on a single matter, as in the case of religious skepticism, which is 'doubt concerning basic religious principles (such as immortality, providence, and revelation)', but philosophical skepticism is an overall approach that requires all information to be well supported by evidence. Skeptics may even doubt the reliability of their own senses. |
| Popular psychology | The term popular psychology refers to concepts and theories about human mental life and behavior that are purportedly based on psychology and that attain popularity among the general population. The concept is closely related to the human potential movement of the 1950s and '60s. |

# Chapter 2. The Research Enterprise in Psychology

| | |
|---|---|
| Review article | Review articles are an attempt to summarize the current state of understanding on a topic. They analyze or discuss research previously published by others, rather than reporting new experimental results.<br><br>They come in the form of systematic reviews and literature reviews and are a form of secondary literature. |
| Anecdotal evidence | The expression anecdotal evidence refers to evidence from anecdotes. Because of the small sample, there is a larger chance that it may be true but unreliable due to cherry-picked or otherwise non-representative samples of typical cases.<br><br>Anecdotal evidence is considered dubious support of a claim; it is accepted only in lieu of more solid evidence. |

1. _____ is a research tool in which a subject is observed in its natural habitat without any manipulation by the observer. During _____ researchers take great care to avoid interfering with the behavior they are observing by using unobtrusive methods. _____ involves two main differences that set it apart from other forms of data gathering.

   a. Naturalistic observation
   b. Psychomotor vigilance task
   c. PsyScope
   d. Rat Park

2. A _____ is a sham or simulated medical intervention. Sometimes patients given a _____ treatment will have a perceived or actual improvement in a medical condition, a phenomenon commonly called the _____ effect.

   In medical research, _____s are given as control treatments and depend on the use of measured deception.

   a. Cosmic pluralism
   b. Cultural Theory of risk
   c. Peace Ecology
   d. Placebo

3. . An _____ defines something (e.g. a variable, term, or object) in terms of the specific process or set of validation tests used to determine its presence and quantity. That is, one defines something in terms of the operations that count as measuring it. The term was coined by Percy Williams Bridgman and is a part of the process of operationalization.

   a. Operationalization
   b. Opinion poll

c. Operational definition

d. Assessment centre

4. A _____ is a single measure of some attribute of a sample (e.g. its arithmetic mean value). It is calculated by applying a function (statistical algorithm) to the values of the items comprising the sample which are known together as a set of data.

More formally, statistical theory defines a _____ as a function of a sample where the function itself is independent of the sample's distribution; that is, the function can be stated before realisation of the data.

a. Statistical parameter

b. Statistical population

c. Statistic

d. Sufficient statistic

5. The question of _____s asks whether it is meaningful to describe a non-human animal as having a mind.

Discussion of this subject is frequently confused by the fact that some schools of philosophy and psychology (e.g. radical behaviorism) would question whether one should ascribe mind to anyone else (or even to oneself). Such an approach would naturally deny the existence of _____s.

a. Avian Brain Nomenclature Consortium

b. Animal mind

c. Web-based taxonomy

d. West American Digest System

**1.** a
**2.** d
**3.** c
**4.** c
**5.** b

---

*You can take the complete Chapter Practice Test*

**for Chapter 2. The Research Enterprise in Psychology**
on all key terms, persons, places, and concepts.

*Online 99 Cents*

*http://www.epub3.2.20111.2.cram101.com/*

**Use www.Cram101.com for all your study needs**

**including Cram101's online interactive problem solving labs in**

**chemistry, statistics, mathematics, and more.**

# Chapter 3. The Biological Bases of Behavior

CHAPTER OUTLINE: KEY TERMS, PEOPLE, PLACES, CONCEPTS

Case study

Personality Assessment Inventory

Soma

Electroconvulsive therapy

Information processing

Nervous system

Axon

Glial cell

Multiple sclerosis

Neurotransmitter

Ponzo illusion

Action potential

All-or-none law

Cell membrane

Synaptic vesicle

Reuptake

Synaptic pruning

Acetylcholine

Endorphin

_____ Gamma-Aminobutyric acid

_____ Memory loss

_____ Norepinephrine

_____ Serotonin

_____ L-DOPA

_____ Parkinsonism

_____ Curare

_____ Dopamine

_____ Ames room

_____ Long-term potentiation

_____ Morphine

_____ Stimulant

_____ Brain damage

_____ Autonomic nervous system

_____ Nerve fiber

_____ Sensory receptor

_____ Somatic nervous system

_____ Spinal cord

_____ Mendelian inheritance

CHAPTER OUTLINE: KEY TERMS, PEOPLE, PLACES, CONCEPTS

Popular psychology

Cerebrospinal fluid

Fight or flight response

Meditation

Transcranial magnetic stimulation

Flynn effect

Hippocampus

Sexual arousal

Area studies

Poggendorff illusion

Brainstem

Cerebellum

Cerebral cortex

Cerebrum

Drunk driving

Mesencephalon

Pituitary gland

Reticular formation

Amygdala

Corpus callosum

Hypothalamus

Thalamus

James-Lange theory

Endocrine system

Hormone

Limbic system

Olfactory bulb

Pleasure center

Cerebral hemisphere

Medial forebrain bundle

Occipital lobe

Parietal lobe

Temporal lobe

Visual cortex

Visual processing

Prefrontal cortex

Mirror neuron

Motor cortex

Motor skill

Primary auditory cortex

Social class

Dentate gyrus

Neurogenesis

Visual field

Verbal Behavior

Gonadotropin

Gonad

Insulin

Oxytocin

Social behavior

Stress hormone

Puberty

Chromosomal crossover

Mutation

Zygote

Phenotype

Dizygotic twins

_____ | Heredity

_____ | Psychoanalytic theory

_____ | Cystic fibrosis

_____ | Epigenetics

_____ | Muscular dystrophy

_____ | Natural selection

_____ | Gene pool

_____ | Reproductive success

_____ | Metaphor

_____ | Empiricism

_____ | Rating scale

_____ | Cognitive style

_____ | Handedness

_____ | Critical period

_____ | Neural development

_____ | Mozart effect

| Case study | A case study is a research method common in social science. It is based on an in-depth investigation of a single individual, group, or event. Case studies may be descriptive or explanatory. |
|---|---|
| Personality Assessment Inventory | Personality Assessment Inventory PhD, is a multi-scale test of psychological functioning that assesses constructs relevant to personality and psychopathology evaluation (e.g., depression, anxiety, aggression) in various contexts including psychotherapy, crisis/evaluation, forensic, personnel selection, pain/medical, and child custody assessment. The PAI has 22 non-overlapping scales, providing a comprehensive overview of psychopathology in adults. The PAI contains four kinds of scales: 1) validity scales, which measure the respondent's approach to the test, including faking good or bad, exaggeration, or defensiveness; 2) clinical scales, which correspond to psychiatric diagnostic categories; 3) treatment consideration scales, which assess factors that may relate to treatment of clinical disorders or other risk factors but which are not captured in psychiatric diagnoses (e.g., suicidal ideation); and 4) interpersonal scales, which provide indicators of interpersonal dimensions of personality functioning. |
| Soma | The soma is the bulbous end of a neuron, containing the cell nucleus. There are many different specialized types of neurons, and their sizes vary from as small as about 30 micrometres to over 10 millimetre for some of the largest neurons of invertebrates. The soma contains many organelles, including granules called Nissl granules, which are composed largely of rough endoplasmic reticulum and free polyribosomes. The cell nucleus is a key feature of the soma. The nucleus is the source of most of the RNA that is produced in neurons. |
| Electroconvulsive therapy | Electroconvulsive therapy formerly known as electroshock, is a psychiatric treatment in which seizures are electrically induced in anesthetized patients for therapeutic effect. Its mode of action is unknown. Today, ECT is most often recommended for use as a treatment for severe depression that has not responded to other treatment, and is also used in the treatment of mania and catatonia. |
| Information processing | Within the field of cognitive psychology, information processing is an approach to the goal of understanding human thinking. It arose in the 1940s and 1950s. The essence of the approach is to see cognition as being essentially computational in nature, with mind being the software and the brain being the hardware. The information processing approach in psychology is closely allied to the Computational theory of mind in philosophy ; it is also related, though not identical, to cognitivism in psychology and functionalism in philosophy. |
| Nervous system | The nervous system is an organ system containing a network of specialized cells called neurons that coordinate the actions of an animal and transmit signals between different parts of its body. In most animals the nervous system consists of two parts, central and peripheral. |

# Chapter 3. The Biological Bases of Behavior

| | |
|---|---|
| Axon | An axon is a long, slender projection of a nerve cell, or neuron, that conducts electrical impulses away from the neuron's cell body or soma.<br><br>An axon is one of two types of protoplasmic protrusions that extrude from the cell body of a neuron, the other type being dendrites. Axons are distinguished from dendrites by several features, including shape (dendrites often taper while axons usually maintain a constant radius), length (dendrites are restricted to a small region around the cell body while axons can be much longer), and function (dendrites usually receive signals while axons usually transmit them). |
| Glial cell | Glial cells are non-neuronal cells that maintain homeostasis, form myelin, and provide support and protection for the brain's neurons. In the human brain, there is roughly one glia for every neuron with a ratio of about two neurons for every three glia in the cerebral gray matter. |
| Multiple sclerosis | Multiple sclerosis is an inflammatory disease in which the fatty myelin sheaths around the axons of the brain and spinal cord are damaged, leading to demyelination and scarring as well as a broad spectrum of signs and symptoms. Disease onset usually occurs in young adults, and it is more common in females. It has a prevalence that ranges between 2 and 150 per 100,000. multiple sclerosis was first described in 1868 by Jean-Martin Charcot. |
| Neurotransmitter | Neurotransmitters are endogenous chemicals which transmit signals from a neuron to a target cell across a synapse. Neurotransmitters are packaged into synaptic vesicles clustered beneath the membrane on the presynaptic side of a synapse, and are released into the synaptic cleft, where they bind to receptors in the membrane on the postsynaptic side of the synapse. Release of neurotransmitters usually follows arrival of an action potential at the synapse, but may also follow graded electrical potentials. |
| Ponzo illusion | The Ponzo illusion is a geometrical-optical illusion that was first demonstrated by the Italian psychologist Mario Ponzo (1882-1960) in 1913. He suggested that the human mind judges an object's size based on its background. He showed this by drawing two identical lines across a pair of converging lines, similar to railway tracks. The upper line looks longer because we interpret the converging sides according to linear perspective as parallel lines receding into the distance. |
| Action potential | In physiology, an action potential is a short-lasting event in which the electrical membrane potential of a cell rapidly rises and falls, following a consistent trajectory. Action potentials occur in several types of animal cells, called excitable cells, which include neurons, muscle cells, and endocrine cells, as well as in some plant cells. In neurons, they play a central role in cell-to-cell communication. |
| All-or-none law | The all-or-none law is the principle that the strength by which a nerve or muscle fiber responds to a stimulus is not dependent on the strength of the stimulus. |

|  | If the stimulus is any strength above threshold, the nerve or muscle fiber will give a complete response or otherwise no response at all. |
|---|---|
|  | It was first established by the American physiologist Henry Pickering Bowditch in 1871 for the contraction of heart muscle. |
| Cell membrane | The cell membrane is a biological membrane that separates the interior of all cells from the outside environment. The cell membrane is selectively-permeable to ions and organic molecules and controls the movement of substances in and out of cells. It consists of the phospholipid bilayer with embedded proteins. |
| Synaptic vesicle | In a neuron, synaptic vesicles store various neurotransmitters that are released at the synapse. The release is regulated by a voltage-dependent calcium channel. Vesicles are essential for propagating nerve impulses between neurons and are constantly recreated by the cell. |
| Reuptake | Reuptake, is the reabsorption of a neurotransmitter by a neurotransmitter transporter of a pre-synaptic neuron after it has performed its function of transmitting a neural impulse. |
|  | Reuptake is necessary for normal synaptic physiology because it allows for the recycling of neurotransmitters and regulates the level of neurotransmitter present in the synapse and controls how long a signal resulting from neurotransmitter release lasts. Because neurotransmitters are too large and hydrophilic to diffuse through the membrane, specific transport proteins are necessary for the reabsorption of neurotransmitters. |
| Synaptic pruning | In neuroscience, synaptic pruning, neuronal pruning or axon pruning refer to neurological regulatory processes, which facilitate a change in neural structure by reducing the overall number of neurons and synapses, leaving more efficient synaptic configurations. Pruning is a process that is a general feature of mammalian neurological development. Pruning starts near the time of birth and is completed by the time of sexual maturation in humans. |
| Acetylcholine | The chemical compound acetylcholine is a neurotransmitter in both the peripheral nervous system (PNS) and central nervous system (CNS) in many organisms including humans. Acetylcholine is one of many neurotransmitters in the autonomic nervous system (ANS) and the only neurotransmitter used in the motor division of the somatic nervous system. (Sensory neurons use glutamate and various peptides at their synapses). Acetylcholine is also the principal neurotransmitter in all autonomic ganglia. |
| Endorphin | Endorphins ('endogenous morphine') are endogenous opioid peptides that function as neurotransmitters. They are produced by the pituitary gland and the hypothalamus in vertebrates during exercise, excitement, pain, consumption of spicy food, love and orgasm, and they resemble the opiates in their abilities to produce analgesia and a feeling of well-being. |

| Gamma-Aminobutyric acid | γ-Aminobutyric acid is the chief inhibitory neurotransmitter in the mammalian central nervous system. It plays a role in regulating neuronal excitability throughout the nervous system. In humans, GABA is also directly responsible for the regulation of muscle tone. |
|---|---|
| | Although chemically it is an amino acid, GABA is rarely referred to as such in the scientific or medical communities, because the term 'amino acid,' used without a qualifier, conventionally refers to the alpha amino acids, which GABA is not, nor is it ever incorporated into a protein. |
| | In spastic diplegia in humans, GABA absorption becomes impaired by nerves damaged from the condition's upper motor neuron lesion, which leads to hypertonia of the muscles signaled by those nerves that can no longer absorb GABA.Function Neurotransmitter |
| | In vertebrates, GABA acts at inhibitory synapses in the brain by binding to specific transmembrane receptors in the plasma membrane of both pre- and postsynaptic neuronal processes. This binding causes the opening of ion channels to allow the flow of either negatively charged chloride ions into the cell or positively charged potassium ions out of the cell. Depending on which ion channels open, the membrane potential is either hyperpolarized or depolarized. This action results in a negative change in the transmembrane potential, usually causing hyperpolarization. Two general classes of GABA receptor are known: $GABA_A$ in which the receptor is part of a ligand-gated ion channel complex, and $GABA_B$ metabotropic receptors, which are G protein-coupled receptors that open or close ion channels via intermediaries (G proteins). |
| | Neurons that produce GABA as their output are called GABAergic neurons, and have chiefly inhibitory action at receptors in the adult vertebrate. Medium Spiny Cells are a typical example of inhibitory CNS GABAergic cells. In contrast, GABA exhibits both excitatory and inhibitory actions in insects, mediating muscle activation at synapses between nerves and muscle cells, and also the stimulation of certain glands. In mammals, some GABAergic neurons, such as chandelier cells, are also able to excite their glutamatergic counterparts. |
| | $GABA_A$ receptors are ligand-activated chloride channels; that is, when activated by GABA, they allow the flow of chloride ions across the membrane of the cell. Whether this chloride flow is excitatory/depolarizing (makes the voltage across the cell's membrane less negative), shunting (has no effect on the cell's membrane) or inhibitory/hyperpolarizing (makes the cell's membrane more negative) depends on the direction of the flow of chloride. When net chloride flows out of the cell, GABA is excitatory or depolarizing; when the net chloride flows into the cell, GABA is inhibitory or hyperpolarizing. When the net flow of chloride is close to zero, the action of GABA is shunting. Shunting inhibition has no direct effect on the membrane potential of the cell; however, it minimises the effect of any coincident synaptic input essentially by reducing the electrical resistance of the cell's membrane (in essence, equivalent to Ohm's law). |

A developmental switch in the molecular machinery controlling concentration of chloride inside the cell - and, hence, the direction of this ion flow - is responsible for the changes in the functional role of GABA between the neonatal and adult stages. That is to say, GABA's role changes from excitatory to inhibitory as the brain develops into adulthood. Brain development

For the past two decades, the theory of excitatory action of GABA early in development was unquestioned based on experiments in vitro, on brain slices. The main observation was that in the hippocampus and neocortex of the mammalian brain, GABA has primarily excitatory effects, and is in fact the major excitatory neurotransmitter in many regions of the brain before the maturation of glutamateergic synapses.

However, this theory has been questioned based on results showing that in brain slices of immature mice incubated in artificial cerebrospinal fluid (ACSF) (modified in a way that takes into account the normal composition of the neuronal milieu in sucklings by adding an energy substrate alternative to glucose, beta-hydroxybutyrate) GABA action shifts from excitatory to inhibitory mode. This effect has been later repeated when other energy substrates, pyruvate and lactate, supplemented glucose in the slices' media. The effects of beta-hydroxybutyrate were later confirmed for pyruvate and for lactate. However it was argued that the concentrations of the alternative energy substrates used in these experiments were non-physiological and the GABA-shift was instead caused by changes in pH resulting from the substrates acting as 'weak acids'. These arguments were later rebutted by further findings showing that changes in pH even greater than that caused by energy substrates do not affect the GABA-shift described in the presence of energy substrate-fortified ACSF and that the mode of action of beta-hydroxybutyrate, pyruvate and lactate (assessed by measurement NAD(P)H and oxygen utilization) was energy metabolism-related.

In the developmental stages preceding the formation of synaptic contacts, GABA is synthesized by neurons and acts both as an autocrine (acting on the same cell) and paracrine (acting on nearby cells) signalling mediator.

GABA regulates the proliferation of neural progenitor cells the migration and differentiation the elongation of neurites and the formation of synapses.

GABA also regulates the growth of embryonic and neural stem cells. GABA can in?uence the development of neural progenitor cells via brain-derived neurotrophic factor (BDNF) expression. GABA activates the $GABA_A$ receptor, causing cell cycle arrest in the S-phase, limiting growth. Beyond the nervous system

GABAergic mechanisms have been demonstrated in various peripheral tissues and organs including, but not restricted to the intestine, stomach, pancreas, Fallopian tube, uterus, ovary, testis, kidney, urinary bladder, lung, and liver.

In 2007, an excitatory GABAergic system was described in the airway epithelium. The system activates following exposure to allergens and may participate in the mechanisms of asthma. GABAergic systems have also been found in the testis and in the eye lens. Structure and conformation

GABA is found mostly as a zwitterion, that is, with the carboxy group deprotonated and the amino group protonated. Its conformation depends on its environment. In the gas phase, a highly folded conformation is strongly favored because of the electrostatic attraction between the two functional groups. The stabilization is about 50 kcal/mol, according to quantum chemistry calculations. In the solid state, a more extended conformation is found, with a trans conformation at the amino end and a gauche conformation at the carboxyl end. This is due to the packing interactions with the neighboring molecules. In solution, five different conformations, some folded and some extended, are found as a result of solvation effects. The conformational flexibility of GABA is important for its biological function, as it has been found to bind to different receptors with different conformations. Many GABA analogues with pharmaceutical applications have more rigid structures in order to control the binding better. History

Gamma-aminobutyric acid was first synthesized in 1883, and was first known only as a plant and microbe metabolic product.

| Memory loss | Memory loss can be partial or total and it is normal when it comes with aging. Sudden memory loss is usually a result of brain trauma and it may be permanent or temporary. When it is caused by medical conditions such as Alzheimer's disease, the memory loss is gradual and tends to be permanent. |

| Norepinephrine | Norepinephrine is a catecholamine with multiple roles including as a hormone and a neurotransmitter. |

As a stress hormone, norepinephrine affects parts of the brain, such as the amygdala, where attention and responses are controlled. Along with epinephrine, norepinephrine also underlies the fight-or-flight response, directly increasing heart rate, triggering the release of glucose from energy stores, and increasing blood flow to skeletal muscle. It increases the brain's oxygen supply. Norepinephrine can also suppress neuroinflammation when released diffusely in the brain from the locus ceruleus.

| Serotonin | Serotonin is a monoamine neurotransmitter. Biochemically derived from tryptophan, serotonin is primarily found in the gastrointestinal (GI) tract, platelets, and in the central nervous system (CNS) of animals including humans. It is a well-known contributor to feelings of well-being; therefore it is also known as a 'happiness hormone' despite not being a hormone. |

L-DOPA

L-DOPA (L-3,4-dihydroxyphenylalanine) is a chemical that is made and used as part of the normal biology of some animals and plants. Some animals including humans make it via biosynthesis from the amino acid L-tyrosine. L-DOPA is the precursor to the neurotransmitters dopamine, norepinephrine (noradrenaline), and epinephrine (adrenaline) collectively known as catecholamines. L-DOPA can be manufactured and in its pure form is sold as a psychoactive drug with the INN levodopa; trade names include Sinemet, Parcopa, Atamet, Stalevo, Madopar, Prolopa, etc).. As a drug it is used in the clinical treatment of Parkinson's disease and dopamine-responsive dystonia.

L-DOPA crosses the protective blood-brain barrier, whereas dopamine itself cannot. Thus, L-DOPA is used to increase dopamine concentrations in the treatment of Parkinson's disease and dopamine-responsive dystonia. This treatment was originally developed by George Cotzias and his coworkers. Once L-DOPA has entered the central nervous system, it is converted into dopamine by the enzyme aromatic L-amino acid decarboxylase, also known as DOPA decarboxylase (DDC). Pyridoxal phosphate (vitamin B6) is a required cofactor in this reaction, and may occasionally be administered along with L-DOPA, usually in the form of pyridoxine.

Besides the central nervous system, L-DOPA is also converted into dopamine from within the peripheral nervous system. The resulting hyperdopaminergia causes many of the adverse side effects seen with sole L-DOPA administration. In order to bypass these effects, it is standard clinical practice to co-administer (with L-DOPA) a peripheral DOPA decarboxylase inhibitor (DDCI) such as carbidopa (medicines combining L-DOPA and carbidopa are branded as Lodosyn, Sinemet, Parcopa, Atamet, Stalevo) or with a benserazide (combination medicines are branded Madopar, Prolopa), to prevent the peripheral synthesis of dopamine from L-DOPA. Co-administration of pyridoxine without a DDCI accelerates the peripheral decarboxylation of L-DOPA to such an extent that it negates the effects of L-DOPA administration, a phenomenon that historically caused great confusion.

In addition, L-DOPA, co-administered with a peripheral DDCI, has been investigated as a potential treatment for restless leg syndrome. However, studies have demonstrated 'no clear picture of reduced symptoms'.

There are two types of response seen with administration of L-DOPA:•Short-duration response, which is related to the half-life of the drug•Longer-duration response, which depends on the accumulation of effects over at least two weeks. This response is evident only in early therapy, as the inability of the brain to store dopamine is not yet a concern.Dietary supplements

Herbal extracts containing L-DOPA are available. The most common plant source of L-DOPA marketed in this manner is Mucuna pruriens (Velvet Bean). Biological role

L-DOPA is produced from the amino acid L-tyrosine by the enzyme tyrosine hydroxylase (TH).

It is also the precursor for the monoamine or catecholamine neurotransmitters dopamine, norepinephrine (noradrenaline), and epinephrine (adrenaline). Dopamine is formed by the decarboxylation of L-DOPA.

L-DOPA can be directly metabolized by catechol-O-methyl transferase (COMT) to 3-O-methyldopa (3-OMD), and then further to vanillactic acid (VLA). This metabolic pathway is non-existent in the healthy body, but becomes important after peripheral L-DOPA administration in patients with PD or in the rare cases of patients with aromatic L-amino acid decarboxylase (AADC) enzyme deficiency.

The prefix L- references its property of levorotation (compared with dextrorotation or D-DOPA).

L-Phenylalanine, L-tyrosine, and L-DOPA, are all precursors to the biological pigment melanin. The enzyme tyrosinase catalyzes the oxidation of L-DOPA to the reactive intermediate dopaquinone, which reacts further, eventually leading to melanin oligomers. Side effects

The side effects of L-DOPA may include, but not limited to:•Hypotension, especially if the dosage is too high•Arrhythmias, although these are uncommon•Nausea, which is often reduced by taking the drug with food, although protein interferes with drug absorption•Gastrointestinal bleeding•Disturbed respiration, which is not always harmful, and can actually benefit patients with upper airway obstruction•Hair loss•Disorientation and confusion•Extreme emotional states, particularly anxiety, but also excessive libido•Vivid dreams and/or insomnia•Auditory and/or visual hallucinations•Effects on learning; there is some evidence that it improves working memory, while impairing other complex functions•Somnolence and narcolepsy•A condition similar to stimulant psychosis

Although there are many adverse effects associated with L-DOPA, in particular psychiatric ones, it has fewer than other antiparkinsonian agents, such as anticholinergics and dopamine receptor agonists.

More serious are the effects of chronic levodopa administration in the treatment of Parkinson disease, which include:•End-of-dose deterioration of function•On/off oscillations•Freezing during movement•Dose failure (drug resistance)•Dyskinesia at peak dose•Possible serotonin depletion: Recent studies have demonstrated that use of L-DOPA without simultaneously giving proper levels of serotonin precursors depletes serotonin•Possible dopamine dysregulation: The long-term use of L-DOPA in PD has been linked to the so-called dopamine dysregulation syndrome.

Clinicians will try to avoid these side effects by limiting L-DOPA doses as much as possible until absolutely necessary.

| Parkinsonism | Parkinsonism is a neurological syndrome characterized by tremor, hypokinesia, rigidity, and postural instability. The underlying causes of parkinsonism are numerous, and diagnosis can be complex. While the neurodegenerative condition Parkinson's disease (PD) is the most common cause of parkinsonism, a wide-range of other etiologies may lead to a similar set of symptoms, including some toxins, a few metabolic diseases, and a handful of non-PD neurological conditions. |
|---|---|
| Curare | Curare /kju?'r??ri?/ is a common name for various arrow poisons originating from South America. The three main types of curare are:•tubocurare. It is a mono-quaternary alkaloid, an isoquinoline derivative.•calebas curare•pot curare.

Of these three types, some formulas belonging to the calebas curare are the most toxic, relative to their LD values. History

Curare was used as a paralyzing poison by South American indigenous people. |
| Dopamine | Dopamine, a simple organic chemical in the catecholamine family, plays a number of important physiological roles in the bodies of animals. Its name derives from its chemical structure, which consists of an amine group ($NH_2$) linked to a catechol structure called dihydroxyphenethylamine, the decarboxyalted form of dihydroxyphenylalanine (acronym DOPA). In the brain, dopamine functions as a neurotransmitter--a chemical released by nerve cells to send signals to other nerve cells. |
| Ames room | An Ames room is a distorted room that is used to create an optical illusion. Probably influenced by the writings of Hermann Helmholtz, it was invented by American ophthalmologist Adelbert Ames, Jr. in 1934, and constructed in the following year. |
| Long-term potentiation | In neuroscience, long-term potentiation is a long-lasting enhancement in signal transmission between two neurons that results from stimulating them synchronously. It is one of several phenomena underlying synaptic plasticity, the ability of chemical synapses to change their strength. As memories are thought to be encoded by modification of synaptic strength, LTP is widely considered one of the major cellular mechanisms that underlies learning and memory. |
| Morphine | Morphine ( ; MS Contin, MSIR, Avinza, Kadian, Oramorph, Roxanol, Kapanol) is a potent opiate analgesic drug that is used to relieve severe pain. It was first isolated in 1804 by Friedrich Sertürner, first distributed by him in 1817, and first commercially sold by Merck in 1827, which at the time was a single small chemists' shop. It was more widely used after the invention of the hypodermic needle in 1857. It took its name from the Greek god of dreams Morpheus . |
| Stimulant | Stimulants (also referred to as psychostimulants) are psychoactive drugs which induce temporary improvements in either mental or physical function or both. |

# Chapter 3. The Biological Bases of Behavior

|  |  |
|---|---|
|  | Examples of these kinds of effects may include enhanced alertness, wakefulness, and locomotion, among others. Due to their effects typically having an 'up' quality to them, stimulants are also occasionally referred to as 'uppers'. |
| Brain damage | Brain damage is the destruction or degeneration of brain cells. Brain injuries occur due to a wide range of internal and external factors. A common category with the greatest number of injuries is traumatic brain injury (TBI) following physical trauma or head injury from an outside source, and the term acquired brain injury (ABI) is used in appropriate circles, to differentiate brain injuries occurring after birth from injury due to a disorder or congenital malady. |
| Autonomic nervous system | The autonomic nervous system is the part of the peripheral nervous system that acts as a control system functioning largely below the level of consciousness, and controls visceral functions. The Autonomic nervous system affects heart rate, digestion, respiration rate, salivation, perspiration, diameter of the pupils, micturition (urination), and sexual arousal. Whereas most of its actions are involuntary, some, such as breathing, work in tandem with the conscious mind. |
| Nerve fiber | A nerve fiber is a threadlike extension of a nerve cell and consists of an axon and myelin sheath (if present) in the nervous system. There are nerve fibers in the central nervous system and peripheral nervous system. A nerve fiber may be myelinated and/or unmyelinated. |
| Sensory receptor | In a sensory system, a sensory receptor is a sensory nerve ending that responds to a stimulus in the internal or external environment of an organism. In response to stimuli the sensory receptor initiates sensory transduction by creating graded potentials or action potentials in the same cell or in an adjacent one. Functions<br><br>The sensory receptors involved in taste and smell contain receptor molecules that bind to specific chemicals. |
| Somatic nervous system | The somatic nervous system is the part of the peripheral nervous system associated with the voluntary control of body movements via skeletal muscles. The SoNS consists of efferent nerves responsible for stimulating muscle contraction, including all the non sensory neurons connected with skeletal muscles and skin.<br><br>The somatic nervous system controls all voluntary muscular systems within the body, with the exception of reflex arcs. |
| Spinal cord | The spinal cord is a long, thin, tubular bundle of nervous tissue and support cells that extends from the brain (the medulla oblongata specifically). The brain and spinal cord together make up the central nervous system (CNS). |

| | |
|---|---|
| Mendelian inheritance | Mendelian inheritance, hereditary characteristics from parent organisms to their offspring; it underlies much of genetics. They were initially derived from the work of Gregor Johann Mendel published in 1865 and 1866 which was 're-discovered' in 1900, and were initially very controversial. When they were integrated with the chromosome theory of inheritance by Thomas Hunt Morgan in 1915, they became the core of classical genetics. |
| Popular psychology | The term popular psychology refers to concepts and theories about human mental life and behavior that are purportedly based on psychology and that attain popularity among the general population. The concept is closely related to the human potential movement of the 1950s and '60s. |
| | The term 'pop psychologist' can be used to describe authors, consultants, lecturers and entertainers who are widely perceived as being psychologists, not because of their academic credentials, but because they have projected that image or have been perceived in that way in response to their work. |
| Cerebrospinal fluid | Cerebrospinal fluid Liquor cerebrospinalis, is a clear, colorless, bodily fluid, that occupies the subarachnoid space and the ventricular system around and inside the brain and spinal cord. |
| | The CSF occupies the space between the arachnoid mater (the middle layer of the brain cover, meninges) and the pia mater (the layer of the meninges closest to the brain). It constitutes the content of all intra-cerebral (inside the brain, cerebrum) ventricles, cisterns, and sulci, as well as the central canal of the spinal cord. |
| Fight or flight response | The fight or flight response was first described by Walter Bradford Cannon. |
| | His theory states that animals react to threats with a general discharge of the sympathetic nervous system, priming the animal for fighting or fleeing. This response was later recognized as the first stage of a general adaptation syndrome that regulates stress responses among vertebrates and other organisms. |
| Meditation | Meditation is any form of a family of practices in which practitioners train their minds or self-induce a mode of consciousness to realize some benefit. |
| | Meditation is generally an inwardly oriented, personal practice, which individuals do by themselves. Prayer beads or other ritual objects are commonly used during meditation. |
| Transcranial magnetic stimulation | Transcranial magnetic stimulation is a noninvasive method to cause depolarization or hyperpolarization in the neurons of the brain. |

# Chapter 3. The Biological Bases of Behavior

|  | |
|---|---|
| | Transcranial magnetic stimulation uses electromagnetic induction to induce weak electric currents using a rapidly changing magnetic field; this can cause activity in specific or general parts of the brain with minimal discomfort, allowing the functioning and interconnections of the brain to be studied. A variant of Transcranial magnetic stimulation, repetitive transcranial magnetic stimulation has been tested as a treatment tool for various neurological and psychiatric disorders including migraines, strokes, Parkinson's disease, dystonia, tinnitus, depression and auditory hallucinations. |
| Flynn effect | The Flynn effect is the name given to a substantial and long-sustained increase in intelligence test scores measured in many parts of the world. When intelligence quotient (IQ) tests are initially standardized using a sample of test-takers, by convention the average of the test results is set to 100 and their standard deviation is set to 15 or 16 IQ points. When IQ tests are revised, they are again standardized using a new sample of test-takers, usually born more recently than the first. |
| Hippocampus | The hippocampus is a major component of the brains of humans and other mammals. It belongs to the limbic system and plays important roles in long-term memory and spatial navigation. Like the cerebral cortex, with which it is closely associated, it is a paired structure, with mirror-image halves in the left and right sides of the brain. In humans and other primates, the hippocampus is located inside the medial temporal lobe, beneath the cortical surface. It contains two main interlocking parts: Ammon's horn and the dentate gyrus. |
| Sexual arousal | Sexual arousal, is the arousal of sexual desire, during or in anticipation of sexual activity. Things that precipitate human sexual arousal are called erotic stimuli, or colloquially known as turn-ons. There are many potential stimuli, both physical or mental, which can cause a person to become sexually aroused. |
| Area studies | Area studies are interdisciplinary fields of research and scholarship pertaining to particular geographical, national/federal, or cultural regions. The term exists primarily as a general description for what are, in the practice of scholarship, many heterogeneous fields of research, encompassing both the social sciences and the humanities. Typical area studies programs involve history, political science, sociology, cultural studies, languages, geography, literature, and related disciplines. |
| Poggendorff illusion | The Poggendorff Illusion is a geometrical-optical illusion that involves the misperception of the position of one segment of a transverse line that has been interrupted by the contour of an intervening structure (here a rectangle). It is named after Poggendorff, the editor of the journal, who discovered it in the figures Johann Karl Friedrich Zöllner submitted when first reporting on what is now known as the Zöllner illusion, in 1860. |

| | |
|---|---|
| Brainstem | In vertebrate anatomy the brainstem is the posterior part of the brain, adjoining and structurally continuous with the spinal cord. The brain stem provides the main motor and sensory innervation to the face and neck via the cranial nerves. Though small, this is an extremely important part of the brain as the nerve connections of the motor and sensory systems from the main part of the brain to the rest of the body pass through the brain stem. |
| Cerebellum | The cerebellum is a region of the brain that plays an important role in motor control. It is also involved in some cognitive functions such as attention and language, and probably in some emotional functions such as regulating fear and pleasure responses. Its movement-related functions are the most clearly understood, however. |
| Cerebral cortex | The cerebral cortex is a sheet of neural tissue that is outermost to the cerebrum of the mammalian brain. It plays a key role in memory, attention, perceptual awareness, thought, language, and consciousness. It is constituted of up to six horizontal layers, each of which has a different composition in terms of neurons and connectivity. |
| Cerebrum | The cerebrum, together with the diencephalon, constitutes the forebrain. In humans, the cerebrum is the most superior region of the vertebrate central nervous system. However, in the majority of animals, the cerebrum is the most anterior region of the CNS as the anatomical position of animals is rarely in the upright position. |
| Drunk driving | Drunk driving is the act of operating or having care or control of a motor vehicle while under the influence of alcohol and/or drugs to the degree that mental and motor skills are impaired. It is illegal in Canada, and is punishable under multiple offences in the Criminal Code of Canada, and can also result in various types of driver's license suspensions. There are a number of powers given to police officer to assist in the enforcement of the offences, and there are a number of presumptions that assist in the prosecution of the offences. |
| Mesencephalon | In biological anatomy, the mesencephalon (or midbrain) comprises the tectum (or corpora quadrigemina), tegmentum, the ventricular mesocoelia (or 'iter'), and the cerebral peduncles, as well as several nuclei and fasciculi. Caudally the mesencephalon adjoins the pons (metencephalon) and rostrally it adjoins the diencephalon (Thalamus, hypothalamus, et al)..<br><br>During development, the mesencephalon forms from the middle of three vesicles that arise from the neural tube to generate the brain. |
| Pituitary gland | In vertebrate anatomy the pituitary gland, is an endocrine gland about the size of a pea and weighing 0.5 g (0.02 oz)., in humans. It is a protrusion off the bottom of the hypothalamus at the base of the brain, and rests in a small, bony cavity (sella turcica) covered by a dural fold (diaphragma sellae). |

# Chapter 3. The Biological Bases of Behavior

| | |
|---|---|
| Reticular formation | The reticular formation is a region in the pons that is involved in regulating the sleep-wake cycle and filtering incoming stimuli to discriminate irrelevant background stimuli. It is essential for governing some of the basic functions of higher organisms, and is one of the phylogenetically oldest portions of the brain.<br><br>The reticular formation consists of more than 100 small neural networks, with varied functions including the following:<br><br>1. Somatic motor control - Some motor neurons send their axons to the reticular formation nuclei, giving rise to the reticulospinal tracts of the spinal cord. |
| Amygdala | The amygdalae are almond-shaped groups of nuclei located deep within the medial temporal lobes of the brain in complex vertebrates, including humans. Shown in research to perform a primary role in the processing and memory of emotional reactions, the amygdalae are considered part of the limbic system.<br><br>The regions described as amygdala nuclei encompass several structures with distinct functional traits. |
| Corpus callosum | The corpus callosum, is a wide, flat bundle of neural fibers beneath the cortex in the eutherian brain at the longitudinal fissure. It connects the left and right cerebral hemispheres and facilitates interhemispheric communication. It is the largest white matter structure in the brain, consisting of 200-250 million contralateral axonal projections. |
| Hypothalamus | The Hypothalamus is a portion of the brain that contains a number of small nuclei with a variety of functions. One of the most important functions of the hypothalamus is to link the nervous system to the endocrine system via the pituitary gland (hypophysis).<br><br>The hypothalamus is located below the thalamus, just above the brain stem. |
| Thalamus | The thalamus is a midline symmetrical structure within the brains of vertebrates including humans, situated between the cerebral cortex and midbrain. Its function includes relaying sensory and motor signals to the cerebral cortex, along with the regulation of consciousness, sleep, and alertness. The thalamus surrounds the third ventricle. |
| James-Lange theory | The James-Lange theory refers to a hypothesis on the origin and nature of emotions and is one of the earliest theories of emotion, developed independently by two 19th-century scholars, William James and Carl Lange. |

The theory states that within human beings, as a response to experiences in the world, the autonomic nervous system creates physiological events such as muscular tension, a rise in heart rate, perspiration, and dryness of the mouth. Emotions, then, are feelings which come about as a result of these physiological changes, rather than being their cause. James and Lange arrived at the theory independently. Lange specifically stated that vasomotor changes are emotions.

**Endocrine system**

In physiology, the endocrine system is a system of glands, each of which secretes a type of hormone into the bloodstream to regulate the body. The endocrine system is an information signal system like the nervous system. Hormones are substances (chemical mediators) released from endocrine tissue into the bloodstream that attach to target tissue and allow communication among cells.

**Hormone**

A hormone is a chemical released by a cell or a gland in one part of the body that sends out messages that affect cells in other parts of the organism. Only a small amount of hormone is required to alter cell metabolism. In essence, it is a chemical messenger that transports a signal from one cell to another. All multicellular organisms produce hormones; plant hormones are also called phytohormones. Hormones in animals are often transported in the blood. Cells respond to a hormone when they express a specific receptor for that hormone. The hormone binds to the receptor protein, resulting in the activation of a signal transduction mechanism that ultimately leads to cell type-specific responses.

**Limbic system**

The limbic system is a set of brain structures including the hippocampus, amygdala, anterior thalamic nuclei, septum, limbic cortex and fornix, which seemingly support a variety of functions including emotion, behavior, long term memory, and olfaction. The term 'limbic' comes from the Latin limbus, for 'border' or 'edge'. Some scientists have suggested that the concept of the limbic system should be abandoned as obsolete, as it is grounded more in transient tradition than in facts.

**Olfactory bulb**

The olfactory bulb is a structure of the vertebrate forebrain involved in olfaction, the perception of odors.

In most vertebrates, the olfactory bulb is the most rostral (forward) part of the brain. In humans, however, the olfactory bulb is on the inferior (bottom) side of the brain.

**Pleasure center**

Pleasure center is the general term used for the brain regions involved in pleasure. Discoveries made in the 1950s initially suggested that rodents could not stop electrically stimulating parts of their brain, mainly the nucleus accumbens, which was theorized to produce great pleasure.

# Chapter 3. The Biological Bases of Behavior

| | |
|---|---|
| Cerebral hemisphere | A cerebral hemisphere is one of the two regions of the eutherian brain that are delineated by the median plane, (medial longitudinal fissure). The brain can thus be described as being divided into left and right cerebral hemispheres. Each of these hemispheres has an outer layer of grey matter called the cerebral cortex that is supported by an inner layer of white matter. |
| Medial forebrain bundle | The Medial forebrain bundle is a complex bundle of axons coming from the basal olfactory regions, the periamygdaloid region, and the septal nuclei.<br><br>Anatomy<br><br>It passes to the lateral hypothalamus, with some carrying on into the tegmentum. It contains both ascending and descending fibers. |
| Occipital lobe | The occipital lobe is the visual processing center of the mammalian brain containing most of the anatomical region of the visual cortex. The primary visual cortex is Brodmann area 17, commonly called V1 (visual one). Human V1 is located on the medial side of the occipital lobe within the calcarine sulcus; the full extent of V1 often continues onto the posterior pole of the occipital lobe. |
| Parietal lobe | The parietal lobe is a part of the brain positioned above (superior to) the occipital lobe and behind (posterior to) the frontal lobe.<br><br>The parietal lobe integrates sensory information from different modalities, particularly determining spatial sense and navigation. For example, it comprises somatosensory cortex and the dorsal stream of the visual system. |
| Temporal lobe | The temporal lobe is a region of the cerebral cortex that is located beneath the Sylvian fissure on both cerebral hemispheres of the mammalian brain.<br><br>The temporal lobe is involved in auditory perception and is home to the primary auditory cortex. It is also important for the processing of semantics in both speech and vision. The temporal lobe contains the hippocampus and plays a key role in the formation of long-term memory. |
| Visual cortex | The visual cortex of the brain is the part of the cerebral cortex responsible for processing visual information. It is located in the occipital lobe, in the back of the brain.<br><br>The term visual cortex refers to the primary visual cortex and extrastriate visual cortical areas such as V2, V3, V4, and V5. The primary visual cortex is anatomically equivalent to Brodmann area 17, or BA17. The extrastriate cortical areas consist of Brodmann area 18 and Brodmann area 19. |

| | |
|---|---|
| Visual processing | Visual processing is the sequence of steps that information takes as it flows from visual sensors to cognitive processing. The sensors may be zoological eyes or they may be cameras or sensor arrays that sense various portions of the electromagnetic spectrum. |
| Prefrontal cortex | The prefrontal cortex. is the anterior part of the frontal lobes of the brain, lying in front of the motor and premotor areas.<br><br>This brain region has been implicated in planning complex cognitive behavior, personality expression, decision making and moderating social behavior. |
| Mirror neuron | A mirror neuron is a neuron that fires both when an animal acts and when the animal observes the same action performed by another. Thus, the neuron 'mirrors' the behavior of the other, as though the observer were itself acting. Such neurons have been directly observed in primate and other species including birds. |
| Motor cortex | Motor cortex is a term that describes regions of the cerebral cortex involved in the planning, control, and execution of voluntary movements.<br><br>The motor cortex can be divided into several main parts:•the primary motor cortex is the main contributor to generating neural impulses that pass down to the spinal cord and control the execution of movement. However, some of the other motor cortical fields also play a role in this function.•the premotor cortex is responsible for some aspects of motor control, possibly including the preparation for movement, the sensory guidance of movement, the spatial guidance of reaching, or the direct control of some movements with an emphasis on control of proximal and trunk muscles of the body.•the supplementary motor area (or SMA), has many proposed functions including the internally generated planning of movement, the planning of sequences of movement, and the coordination of the two sides of the body such as in bi-manual coordination.•The posterior parietal cortex is sometimes also considered to be part of the group of motor cortical areas. |
| Motor skill | A motor skill is a learned sequence of movements that combine to produce a smooth, efficient action in order to master a particular task. The development of motor skill occurs in the motor cortex, the region of the cerebral cortex that controls voluntary muscle groups.<br><br>Development of motor skills<br><br>Due to the immaturity of the human nervous system at the time of birth, children grow continually throughout their childhood years. |
| Primary auditory cortex | The primary auditory cortex is a region of the brain that processes sound and thereby contributes to our ability to hear. It is the first cortical region of the auditory pathway. |

# Chapter 3. The Biological Bases of Behavior

| | |
|---|---|
| Social class | Social class is a set of concepts in the social sciences and political theory centered on models of social stratification in which people are grouped into a set of hierarchical social categories. |
| | Class is an essential object of analysis for sociologists, political scientists, anthropologists and social historians. However, there is not a consensus on the best definition of the term 'class', and the term has different contextual meanings. |
| Dentate gyrus | The dentate gyrus is part of the hippocampal formation. It is thought to contribute to the formation of new memories, as well as possessing other functional roles. It is notable as being one of a select few brain structures currently known to have high rates of neurogenesis in adult rats (other sites include the olfactory bulb and cerebellum). |
| Neurogenesis | Neurogenesis is the process by which neurons are generated from neural stem and progenitor cells. Most active during pre-natal development, neurogenesis is responsible for populating the growing brain with neurons. Recently neurogenesis was shown to continue in several small parts of the brain of mammals: the hippocampus and the subventricular zone. |
| Visual field | The term visual field is sometimes used as a synonym to field of view, though they do not designate the same thing. The visual field is the 'spatial array of visual sensations available to observation in introspectionist psychological experiments', while 'field of view' 'refers to the physical objects and light sources in the external world that impinge the retina'. In other words, field of view is everything that (at a given time) causes light to fall onto the retina. |
| Verbal Behavior | Verbal Behavior is a 1957 book by psychologist B. F. Skinner, in which he analyzes human behavior, encompassing what is traditionally called language, linguistics, or speech. For Skinner, verbal behavior is simply behavior subject to the same controlling variables as any other operant behavior, although Skinner differentiates between verbal behavior which is mediated by other people, and that which is mediated by the natural world. The book Verbal Behavior is almost entirely theoretical, involving little experimental research in the work itself. |
| Gonadotropin | Glycoprotein hormone |
| | Gonadotropins are protein hormones secreted by gonadotrope cells of the pituitary gland of vertebrates. This is a family of proteins, which include the mammalian hormones follitropin (FSH), lutropin (LH), placental chorionic gonadotropins hCG and eCG and chorionic gonadotropin as well as at least two forms of fish gonadotropins. These hormones are central to the complex endocrine system that regulates normal growth, sexual development, and reproductive function. |
| Gonad | The gonad is the organ that makes gametes. The gonads in males are the testicles and the gonads in females are the ovaries. |

| | |
|---|---|
| Insulin | Insulin is a hormone that is central to regulating carbohydrate and fat metabolism in the body. Insulin causes cells in the liver, muscle, and fat tissue to take up glucose from the blood, storing it as glycogen in the liver and muscle.<br><br>Insulin stops the use of fat as an energy source by inhibiting the release of glucagon. When insulin is absent, glucose is not taken up by body cells and the body begins to use fat as an energy source or gluconeogenesis; for example, by transfer of lipids from adipose tissue to the liver for mobilization as an energy source. As its level is a central metabolic control mechanism, its status is also used as a control signal to other body systems (such as amino acid uptake by body cells). In addition, it has several other anabolic effects throughout the body. |
| Oxytocin | Oxytocin ( ) is a mammalian hormone that acts primarily as a neuromodulator in the brain.<br><br>Oxytocin is best known for its roles in sexual reproduction, in particular during and after childbirth. It is released in large amounts after distension of the cervix and uterus during labor, facilitating birth, and after stimulation of the nipples, facilitating breastfeeding. |
| Social behavior | In physics, physiology and sociology, social behavior is behavior directed towards society, or taking place between, members of the same species. Behavior such as predation which involves members of different species is not social. While many social behaviors are communication (provoke a response, or change in behavior, without acting directly on the receiver) communication between members of different species is not social behavior. |
| Stress hormone | Stress hormones such as cortisol, GH and norepinephrine are released at periods of high stress. The hormone regulating system is known as the endocrine system. Cortisol is believed to affect the metabolic system and norepinephrine is believed to play a role in ADHD as well as depression and hypertension. |
| Puberty | Puberty is the process of physical changes by which a child's body becomes an adult body capable of reproduction. Puberty is initiated by hormone signals from the brain to the gonads (the ovaries and testes). In response, the gonads produce a variety of hormones that stimulate the growth, function, or transformation of brain, bones, muscle, blood, skin, hair, breasts, and sex organs. |
| Chromosomal crossover | Chromosomal crossover is an exchange of genetic material between homologous chromosomes. It is one of the final phases of genetic recombination, which occurs during prophase I of meiosis (pachytene) in a process called synapsis. Synapsis begins before the synaptonemal complex develops, and is not completed until near the end of prophase I. Crossover usually occurs when matching regions on matching chromosomes break and then reconnect to the other chromosome. |

# Chapter 3. The Biological Bases of Behavior

| | |
|---|---|
| Mutation | In molecular biology and genetics, mutations are changes in a genomic sequence: the DNA sequence of a cell's genome or the DNA or RNA sequence of a virus. These random sequences can be defined as sudden and spontaneous changes in the cell. Mutations are caused by radiation, viruses, transposons and mutagenic chemicals, as well as errors that occur during meiosis or DNA replication. |
| Zygote | A zygote is the initial cell formed when a new organism is produced by means of sexual reproduction. A zygote is synthesized from the union of two gametes, and constitutes the first stage in a unique organism's development. Zygotes are usually produced by a fertilization event between two haploid cells--an ovum from a female and a sperm cell from a male--which combine to form the single diploid cell. |
| Phenotype | A phenotype is any observable characteristic or trait of an organism: such as its morphology, development, biochemical or physiological properties, behavior, and products of behavior (such as a bird's nest). Phenotypes result from the expression of an organism's genes as well as the influence of environmental factors and the interactions between the two. |
| Dizygotic twins | Dizygotic twins usually occur when two fertilized eggs are implanted in the uterus wall at the same time. When two eggs are independently fertilized by two different sperm cells, fraternal twins result. The two eggs, or ova, form two zygotes, hence the terms dizygotic and biovular. |
| Heredity | Heredity is the passing of traits to offspring (from its parent or ancestors). This is the process by which an offspring cell or organism acquires or becomes predisposed to the characteristics of its parent cell or organism. Through heredity, variations exhibited by individuals can accumulate and cause some species to evolve. |
| Psychoanalytic theory | Psychoanalytic theory refers to the definition and dynamics of personality development which underlie and guide psychoanalytic and psychodynamic psychotherapy. First laid out by Sigmund Freud, psychoanalytic theory has undergone many refinements since his work . Psychoanalytic theory came to full prominence as a critical force in the last third of the twentieth century as part of 'the flow of critical discourse after the 1960's. |
| Cystic fibrosis | Cystic fibrosis is an autosomal recessive genetic disorder affecting most critically the lungs, and also the pancreas, liver, and intestine. It is characterized by abnormal transport of chloride and sodium across an epithelium, leading to thick, viscous secretions.<br><br>The name cystic fibrosis refers to the characteristic scarring (fibrosis) and cyst formation within the pancreas, first recognized in the 1930s. |

| Epigenetics | In biology, and specifically genetics, epigenetics is the study of heritable changes in phenotype (appearance) or gene expression caused by mechanisms other than changes in the underlying DNA sequence, hence the name epigenetics. These changes may remain through cell divisions for the remainder of the cell's life and may also last for multiple generations. However, there is no change in the underlying DNA sequence of the organism; instead, non-genetic factors cause the organism's genes to behave (or 'express themselves') differently. |
|---|---|
| Muscular dystrophy | Muscular dystrophy refers to a group of hereditary muscle diseases that weaken the muscles that move the human body. Muscular dystrophies are characterized by progressive skeletal muscle weakness, defects in muscle proteins, and the death of muscle cells and tissue. Nine diseases including Duchenne, Becker, limb girdle, congenital, facioscapulohumeral, myotonic, oculopharyngeal, distal, and Emery-Dreifuss are always classified as muscular dystrophy but there are more than 100 diseases in total with similarities to muscular dystrophy. |
| Natural selection | Natural selection is the process by which traits become more or less common in a population due to consistent effects upon the survival or reproduction of their bearers. It is a key mechanism of evolution. The natural genetic variation within a population of organisms may cause some individuals to survive and reproduce more successfully than others in their current environment. |
| Gene pool | In population genetics, a gene pool is the complete set of unique alleles in a species or population.<br><br>A large gene pool indicates extensive genetic diversity, which is associated with robust populations that can survive bouts of intense selection. Meanwhile, low genetic diversity can cause reduced biological fitness and an increased chance of extinction, although as explained by genetic drift new genetic variants, that may cause an increase in the fitness of organisms, are more likely to fix in the population if it is rather small. |
| Reproductive success | Reproductive success is defined as the passing of genes onto the next generation in a way that they too can pass those genes on. In practice, this is often a tally of the number of offspring produced by an individual. A more correct definition, which incorporates inclusive fitness, is the relative production of fertile offspring by a genotype. |
| Metaphor | A metaphor is a literary figure of speech that describes a subject by asserting that it is, on some point of comparison, the same as another otherwise unrelated object. Metaphor is a type of analogy and is closely related to other rhetorical figures of speech that achieve their effects via association, comparison or resemblance including allegory, hyperbole, and simile.<br><br>One of the most prominent examples of a metaphor in English literature is the All the world's a stage monologue from As You Like It:All the world's a stage,And all the men and women merely players;They have their exits and their entrances; -- William Shakespeare, As You Like It, 2/7 |

# Chapter 3. The Biological Bases of Behavior

| | |
|---|---|
| Empiricism | Empiricism is a theory of knowledge that asserts that knowledge comes only or primarily from sensory experience. One of several views of epistemology, the study of human knowledge, along with rationalism, idealism and historicism, empiricism emphasizes the role of experience and evidence, especially sensory perception, in the formation of ideas, over the notion of innate ideas or traditions.<br><br>Empiricism in the philosophy of science emphasizes evidence, especially as discovered in experiments. |
| Rating scale | A rating scale is a set of categories designed to elicit information about a quantitative or a qualitative attribute. In the social sciences, common examples are the Likert scale and 1-10 rating scales in which a person selects the number which is considered to reflect the perceived quality of a product.<br><br>A rating scale is a method that requires the rater to assign a value, sometimes numeric, to the rated object, as a measure of some rated attribute. |
| Cognitive style | Cognitive style is a term used in cognitive psychology to describe the way individuals think, perceive and remember information. Cognitive style differs from cognitive ability , the latter being measured by aptitude tests or so-called intelligence tests. Controversy exists over the exact meaning of the term cognitive style and also as to whether it is a single or multiple dimension of human personality. |
| Handedness | Handedness is an attribute of humans defined by their unequal distribution of fine motor skill between the left and right hands. An individual who is more dexterous with the right hand is called right-handed, and one who is more skilled with the left is said to be left-handed. A minority of people are equally skilled with both hands, and are termed ambidextrous. |
| Critical period | In general, a critical period is a limited time in which an event can occur, usually to result in some kind of transformation. In developmental psychology and developmental biology, a critical period is a phase in the life span during which an organism has heightened sensitivity to exogenous stimuli that are compulsory for the development of a particular skill. If the organism does not receive the appropriate stimulus during this 'critical period', it may be difficult, ultimately less successful, or even impossible, to develop some functions later in life. |
| Neural development | Neural development comprises the processes that generate, shape, and reshape the nervous system, from the earliest stages of embryogenesis to the final years of life. The study of neural development aims to describe the cellular basis of brain development and to address the underlying mechanisms. |

| Mozart effect | The Mozart effect can refer to:•A set of research results that indicate that listening to Mozart's music may induce a short-term improvement on the performance of certain kinds of mental tasks known as 'spatial-temporal reasoning;'•Popularized versions of the theory, which suggest that 'listening to Mozart makes you smarter,' or that early childhood exposure to classical music has a beneficial effect on mental development;•A US trademark for a set of commercial recordings and related materials, which are claimed to harness the effect for a variety of purposes. The trademark owner, Don Campbell, Inc., claims benefits far beyond improving spatio-temporal reasoning or raising intelligence, defining the mark as 'an inclusive term signifying the transformational powers of music in health, education, and well-being.'<br><br>The term was first coined by Alfred A. Tomatis who used Mozart's music as the listening stimulus in his work attempting to cure a variety of disorders. The approach has been popularized in a book by Don Campbell, and is based on an experiment published in Nature suggesting that listening to Mozart temporarily boosted scores on one portion of the IQ test. |
|---|---|

CHAPTER QUIZ: KEY TERMS, PEOPLE, PLACES, CONCEPTS

1. The _____ e are almond-shaped groups of nuclei located deep within the medial temporal lobes of the brain in complex vertebrates, including humans. Shown in research to perform a primary role in the processing and memory of emotional reactions, the _____ e are considered part of the limbic system.

   The regions described as _____ nuclei encompass several structures with distinct functional traits.

   a. Archicortex
   b. Amygdala
   c. Islands of Calleja
   d. Olfactory bulb

2. The _____ is the principle that the strength by which a nerve or muscle fiber responds to a stimulus is not dependent on the strength of the stimulus. If the stimulus is any strength above threshold, the nerve or muscle fiber will give a complete response or otherwise no response at all.

   It was first established by the American physiologist Henry Pickering Bowditch in 1871 for the contraction of heart muscle.

   a. Amygdalohippocampal area
   b. Antennal lobe
   c. All-or-none law
   d. Anterolateral corticospinal tract

# Chapter 3. The Biological Bases of Behavior

3.  In physics, physiology and sociology, _____ is behavior directed towards society, or taking place between, members of the same species. Behavior such as predation which involves members of different species is not social. While many _____s are communication (provoke a response, or change in behavior, without acting directly on the receiver) communication between members of different species is not _____.

    a. Social proof
    b. Spoiled child
    c. Superficial charm
    d. Social behavior

4.  _____s ('endogenous morphine') are endogenous opioid peptides that function as neurotransmitters. They are produced by the pituitary gland and the hypothalamus in vertebrates during exercise, excitement, pain, consumption of spicy food, love and orgasm, and they resemble the opiates in their abilities to produce analgesia and a feeling of well-being.

    The term implies a pharmacological activity (analogous to the activity of the corticosteroid category of biochemicals) as opposed to a specific chemical formulation.

    a. Etazocine
    b. Endorphin
    c. Trace
    d. Transparallel processing

5.  The _____ is the bulbous end of a neuron, containing the cell nucleus. There are many different specialized types of neurons, and their sizes vary from as small as about 30 micrometres to over 10 millimetre for some of the largest neurons of invertebrates. The _____ contains many organelles, including granules called Nissl granules, which are composed largely of rough endoplasmic reticulum and free polyribosomes. The cell nucleus is a key feature of the _____. The nucleus is the source of most of the RNA that is produced in neurons.

    a. Soma
    b. Stromal cell
    c. Green children of Woolpit
    d. Revised NEO Personality Inventory

**1.** b
**2.** c
**3.** d
**4.** b
**5.** a

---

## You can take the complete Chapter Practice Test

**for Chapter 3. The Biological Bases of Behavior**
on all key terms, persons, places, and concepts.

## Online 99 Cents

## *http://www.epub3.2.20111.3.cram101.com/*

**Use www.Cram101.com for all your study needs**

**including Cram101's online interactive problem solving labs in**

**chemistry, statistics, mathematics, and more.**

# Chapter 4. Sensation and Perception

CHAPTER OUTLINE: KEY TERMS, PEOPLE, PLACES, CONCEPTS

Psychophysics

Absolute threshold

Case study

Stimulus

Poggendorff illusion

Color vision

Visual system

Lens

PRiSM

Retina

Elaboration likelihood model

Optic nerve

Amacrine cells

Bipolar cell

Classical conditioning

Gamma-Aminobutyric acid

Operant conditioning

Peripheral Vision

Visual acuity

Optic chiasm

Lateral geniculate nucleus

Occipital lobe

Superior colliculus

Visual cortex

Visual field

Personality Assessment Inventory

Parallel processing

Receptive field

Greeble

Hippocampus

On Colors

Temporal lobe

Color mixing

Color solid

Mental disorder

Afterimage

Color wheel

Complementary color

CHAPTER OUTLINE: KEY TERMS, PEOPLE, PLACES, CONCEPTS

Opponent process

Primary color

Process theory

Reversible figure

Subjectivity

Inattentional blindness

Functional selectivity

Gestalt psychology

Popular psychology

Illusion

Phi phenomenon

Necker Cube

Depth perception

Conspicuous consumption

Ames room

Ponzo illusion

Moon illusion

Size constancy

Auditory system

Basilar membrane

Cochlea

Eardrum

Inner ear

Gustatory system

Taste bud

Wine tasting

Flynn effect

Umami

Supertaster

Olfactory bulb

Olfactory system

Brainstem

Meissner's corpuscle

Lamellar corpuscle

Parietal lobe

Mesencephalon

Acupuncture

Glial cell

| | Morphine |
| --- | --- |
| | Periaqueductal gray |
| | Serotonin |
| | Spinal cord |
| | Sensory integration |
| | Futurism |
| | Contrast effect |
| | Door-in-the-face technique |

CHAPTER HIGHLIGHTS & NOTES: KEY TERMS, PEOPLE, PLACES, CONCEPTS

| Psychophysics | Psychophysics quantitatively investigates the relationship between physical stimuli and the sensations and perceptions they affect. Psychophysics has been described as 'the scientific study of the relation between stimulus and sensation' or, more completely, as 'the analysis of perceptual processes by studying the effect on a subject's experience or behaviour of systematically varying the properties of a stimulus along one or more physical dimensions'.

Psychophysics also refers to a general class of methods that can be applied to study a perceptual system. |
| --- | --- |
| Absolute threshold | In neuroscience and psychophysics, an absolute threshold is the smallest detectable level of a stimulus. However, at this low level, subjects will sometimes detect the stimulus and at other times not. Therefore, an alternative definition of absolute threshold is the lowest intensity at which a stimulus can be detected 50% of the time. |
| Case study | A case study is a research method common in social science. It is based on an in-depth investigation of a single individual, group, or event. |

# Chapter 4. Sensation and Perception

| | |
|---|---|
| Stimulus | In physiology, a stimulus (pl. stimuli) is a detectable change in the internal or external environment. The ability of an organism or organ to respond to external stimuli is called sensitivity. |
| Poggendorff illusion | The Poggendorff Illusion is a geometrical-optical illusion that involves the misperception of the position of one segment of a transverse line that has been interrupted by the contour of an intervening structure (here a rectangle). It is named after Poggendorff, the editor of the journal, who discovered it in the figures Johann Karl Friedrich Zöllner submitted when first reporting on what is now known as the Zöllner illusion, in 1860. <br><br> In the picture to the right, a straight black and red line is obscured by a grey rectangle. |
| Color vision | Color vision is the capacity of an organism or machine to distinguish objects based on the wavelengths (or frequencies) of the light they reflect, emit, or transmit. The nervous system derives color by comparing the responses to light from the several types of cone photoreceptors in the eye. These cone photoreceptors are sensitive to different portions of the visible spectrum. |
| Visual system | The visual system is the part of the central nervous system which enables organisms to process visual detail, as well as enabling several non-image forming photoresponse functions. It interprets information from visible light to build a representation of the surrounding world. The visual system accomplishes a number of complex tasks, including the reception of light and the formation of monocular representations; the construction of a binocular perception from a pair of two dimensional projections; the identification and categorization of visual objects; assessing distances to and between objects; and guiding body movements in relation to visual objects. |
| Lens | The crystalline lens is a transparent, biconvex structure in the eye that, along with the cornea, helps to refract light to be focused on the retina. The lens, by changing shape, functions to change the focal distance of the eye so that it can focus on objects at various distances, thus allowing a sharp real image of the object of interest to be formed on the retina. This adjustment of the lens is known as accommodation . |
| PRiSM | Projects integrating Sustainable Methods (PRiSM) is a structured project management method developed to align organizational sustainability initiatives with project delivery. By Design, PRiSM is a repeatable, practical and proactive methodology that ensures project success while decreasing an organization's negative environmental impact. The methodology encompasses the management, control and organization of a project with consideration and emphasis beyond the project life-cycle and on the five aspects of sustainability. |
| Retina | The vertebrate retina is a light-sensitive tissue lining the inner surface of the eye. The optics of the eye create an image of the visual world on the retina, which serves much the same function as the film in a camera. |

| Elaboration likelihood model | The elaboration likelihood model of persuasion is a model of how attitudes are formed and changed that was developed by R. E. Petty and J. T. Cacioppo in the early 1980s . Central to this model is the 'elaboration continuum', which ranges from low elaboration (low thought) to high elaboration (high thought). The ELM distinguishes between two routes to persuasion: the 'central route,' where a subject considers an idea logically, and the 'peripheral route,' in which the audience uses preexisting ideas and superficial qualities to be persuaded. |
|---|---|
| Optic nerve | The optic nerve, transmits visual information from the retina to the brain. Derived from the embryonic retinal ganglion cell, a diverticulum located in the diencephalon, the optic nerve does not regenerate after transection. <br><br> The optic nerve is the second of twelve paired cranial nerves but is considered to be part of the central nervous system, as it is derived from an outpouching of the diencephalon during embryonic development. |
| Amacrine cells | Amacrine cells are interneurons in the retina. Amacrine cells are responsible for 70% of input to retinal ganglion cells. Bipolar cells, which are responsible for the other 30% of input to retinal ganglia, are regulated by amacrine cells. |
| Bipolar cell | A bipolar cell is a type of neuron which has two extensions. Bipolar cells are specialized sensory neurons for the transmission of special senses. As such, they are part of the sensory pathways for smell, sight, taste, hearing and vestibular functions. |
| Classical conditioning | Introduction <br><br> Classical conditioning is a form of learning in which one stimulus comes to signal the occurrence of a second stimulus. This is often brought about by pairing the two stimuli, as in Pavlov's classic experiments. Pavlov presented dogs with a ringing bell followed by food. |
| Gamma-Aminobutyric acid | γ-Aminobutyric acid is the chief inhibitory neurotransmitter in the mammalian central nervous system. It plays a role in regulating neuronal excitability throughout the nervous system. In humans, GABA is also directly responsible for the regulation of muscle tone. <br><br> Although chemically it is an amino acid, GABA is rarely referred to as such in the scientific or medical communities, because the term 'amino acid,' used without a qualifier, conventionally refers to the alpha amino acids, which GABA is not, nor is it ever incorporated into a protein. <br><br> In spastic diplegia in humans, GABA absorption becomes impaired by nerves damaged from the condition's upper motor neuron lesion, which leads to hypertonia of the muscles signaled by those nerves that can no longer absorb GABA.Function Neurotransmitter |

# Chapter 4. Sensation and Perception

In vertebrates, GABA acts at inhibitory synapses in the brain by binding to specific transmembrane receptors in the plasma membrane of both pre- and postsynaptic neuronal processes. This binding causes the opening of ion channels to allow the flow of either negatively charged chloride ions into the cell or positively charged potassium ions out of the cell. Depending on which ion channels open, the membrane potential is either hyperpolarized or depolarized. This action results in a negative change in the transmembrane potential, usually causing hyperpolarization. Two general classes of GABA receptor are known: $GABA_A$ in which the receptor is part of a ligand-gated ion channel complex, and $GABA_B$ metabotropic receptors, which are G protein-coupled receptors that open or close ion channels via intermediaries (G proteins).

Neurons that produce GABA as their output are called GABAergic neurons, and have chiefly inhibitory action at receptors in the adult vertebrate. Medium Spiny Cells are a typical example of inhibitory CNS GABAergic cells. In contrast, GABA exhibits both excitatory and inhibitory actions in insects, mediating muscle activation at synapses between nerves and muscle cells, and also the stimulation of certain glands. In mammals, some GABAergic neurons, such as chandelier cells, are also able to excite their glutamatergic counterparts.

$GABA_A$ receptors are ligand-activated chloride channels; that is, when activated by GABA, they allow the flow of chloride ions across the membrane of the cell. Whether this chloride flow is excitatory/depolarizing (makes the voltage across the cell's membrane less negative), shunting (has no effect on the cell's membrane) or inhibitory/hyperpolarizing (makes the cell's membrane more negative) depends on the direction of the flow of chloride. When net chloride flows out of the cell, GABA is excitatory or depolarizing; when the net chloride flows into the cell, GABA is inhibitory or hyperpolarizing. When the net flow of chloride is close to zero, the action of GABA is shunting. Shunting inhibition has no direct effect on the membrane potential of the cell; however, it minimises the effect of any coincident synaptic input essentially by reducing the electrical resistance of the cell's membrane (in essence, equivalent to Ohm's law). A developmental switch in the molecular machinery controlling concentration of chloride inside the cell - and, hence, the direction of this ion flow - is responsible for the changes in the functional role of GABA between the neonatal and adult stages. That is to say, GABA's role changes from excitatory to inhibitory as the brain develops into adulthood. Brain development

For the past two decades, the theory of excitatory action of GABA early in development was unquestioned based on experiments in vitro, on brain slices. The main observation was that in the hippocampus and neocortex of the mammalian brain, GABA has primarily excitatory effects, and is in fact the major excitatory neurotransmitter in many regions of the brain before the maturation of glutamateergic synapses.

However, this theory has been questioned based on results showing that in brain slices of immature mice incubated in artificial cerebrospinal fluid (ACSF) (modified in a way that takes into account the normal composition of the neuronal milieu in sucklings by adding an energy substrate alternative to glucose, beta-hydroxybutyrate) GABA action shifts from excitatory to inhibitory mode. This effect has been later repeated when other energy substrates, pyruvate and lactate, supplemented glucose in the slices' media. The effects of beta-hydroxybutyrate were later confirmed for pyruvate and for lactate. However it was argued that the concentrations of the alternative energy substrates used in these experiments were non-physiological and the GABA-shift was instead caused by changes in pH resulting from the substrates acting as 'weak acids'. These arguments were later rebutted by further findings showing that changes in pH even greater than that caused by energy substrates do not affect the GABA-shift described in the presence of energy substrate-fortified ACSF and that the mode of action of beta-hydroxybutyrate, pyruvate and lactate (assessed by measurement NAD(P)H and oxygen utilization) was energy metabolism-related.

In the developmental stages preceding the formation of synaptic contacts, GABA is synthesized by neurons and acts both as an autocrine (acting on the same cell) and paracrine (acting on nearby cells) signalling mediator.

GABA regulates the proliferation of neural progenitor cells the migration and differentiation the elongation of neurites and the formation of synapses.

GABA also regulates the growth of embryonic and neural stem cells. GABA can in?uence the development of neural progenitor cells via brain-derived neurotrophic factor (BDNF) expression. GABA activates the GABA$_A$ receptor, causing cell cycle arrest in the S-phase, limiting growth. Beyond the nervous system

GABAergic mechanisms have been demonstrated in various peripheral tissues and organs including, but not restricted to the intestine, stomach, pancreas, Fallopian tube, uterus, ovary, testis, kidney, urinary bladder, lung, and liver.

In 2007, an excitatory GABAergic system was described in the airway epithelium. The system activates following exposure to allergens and may participate in the mechanisms of asthma. GABAergic systems have also been found in the testis and in the eye lens. Structure and conformation

GABA is found mostly as a zwitterion, that is, with the carboxy group deprotonated and the amino group protonated. Its conformation depends on its environment. In the gas phase, a highly folded conformation is strongly favored because of the electrostatic attraction between the two functional groups.

The stabilization is about 50 kcal/mol, according to quantum chemistry calculations. In the solid state, a more extended conformation is found, with a trans conformation at the amino end and a gauche conformation at the carboxyl end. This is due to the packing interactions with the neighboring molecules. In solution, five different conformations, some folded and some extended, are found as a result of solvation effects. The conformational flexibility of GABA is important for its biological function, as it has been found to bind to different receptors with different conformations. Many GABA analogues with pharmaceutical applications have more rigid structures in order to control the binding better. History

Gamma-aminobutyric acid was first synthesized in 1883, and was first known only as a plant and microbe metabolic product.

| Operant conditioning | Operant conditioning is the use of a behavior's antecedent and/or its consequence to influence the occurrence and form of behavior. Operant conditioning is distinguished from classical conditioning (also called respondent conditioning) in that operant conditioning deals with the modification of 'voluntary behavior' or operant behavior. Operant behavior 'operates' on the environment and is maintained by its consequences, while classical conditioning deals with the conditioning of reflexive (reflex) behaviors which are elicited by antecedent conditions. |
|---|---|
| Peripheral Vision | Peripheral Vision (2007) was the name of a collaboration and exhibition between the Edinburgh artists Martin Smith, Reuben Paris and Colin Usher. The show, conceived and executed within a 48-hour time period, was shot in the Leith area of Edinburgh. It featured a style of photography that mixed crime scene incidents with associated visual narratives and occasionally texts that were both found and devised. |
| Visual acuity | Visual acuity is acuteness or clearness of vision, which is dependent on the sharpness of the retinal focus within the eye and the sensitivity of the interpretative faculty of the brain.<br><br>Visual acuity is a measure of the spatial resolution of the visual processing system. VA is tested by requiring the person whose vision is being tested to identify characters (like letters and numbers) on a chart from a set distance. |
| Optic chiasm | The optic chiasm is the part of the brain where the optic nerves (CN II) partially cross. The optic chiasm is located at the bottom of the brain immediately below the hypothalamus.<br><br>The images on the nasal sides of each retina cross over to the opposite side of the brain via the optic nerve at the optic chiasm. |
| Lateral geniculate nucleus | The lateral geniculate nucleus is the primary relay center for visual information received from the retina of the eye. The LGN is found inside the thalamus of the brain. |

| | |
|---|---|
| Occipital lobe | The occipital lobe is the visual processing center of the mammalian brain containing most of the anatomical region of the visual cortex. The primary visual cortex is Brodmann area 17, commonly called V1 (visual one). Human V1 is located on the medial side of the occipital lobe within the calcarine sulcus; the full extent of V1 often continues onto the posterior pole of the occipital lobe. |
| Superior colliculus | The optic tectum or simply tectum is a paired structure that forms a major component of the vertebrate midbrain. In mammals, this structure is more commonly called the superior colliculus, but, even in mammals, the adjective tectal is commonly used. The tectum is a layered structure, with a number of layers that vary by species. |
| Visual cortex | The visual cortex of the brain is the part of the cerebral cortex responsible for processing visual information. It is located in the occipital lobe, in the back of the brain.<br><br>The term visual cortex refers to the primary visual cortex and extrastriate visual cortical areas such as V2, V3, V4, and V5. The primary visual cortex is anatomically equivalent to Brodmann area 17, or BA17. The extrastriate cortical areas consist of Brodmann area 18 and Brodmann area 19. |
| Visual field | The term visual field is sometimes used as a synonym to field of view, though they do not designate the same thing. The visual field is the 'spatial array of visual sensations available to observation in introspectionist psychological experiments', while 'field of view' 'refers to the physical objects and light sources in the external world that impinge the retina'. In other words, field of view is everything that (at a given time) causes light to fall onto the retina. |
| Personality Assessment Inventory | Personality Assessment Inventory PhD, is a multi-scale test of psychological functioning that assesses constructs relevant to personality and psychopathology evaluation (e.g., depression, anxiety, aggression) in various contexts including psychotherapy, crisis/evaluation, forensic, personnel selection, pain/medical, and child custody assessment. The PAI has 22 non-overlapping scales, providing a comprehensive overview of psychopathology in adults. The PAI contains four kinds of scales: 1) validity scales, which measure the respondent's approach to the test, including faking good or bad, exaggeration, or defensiveness; 2) clinical scales, which correspond to psychiatric diagnostic categories; 3) treatment consideration scales, which assess factors that may relate to treatment of clinical disorders or other risk factors but which are not captured in psychiatric diagnoses (e.g., suicidal ideation); and 4) interpersonal scales, which provide indicators of interpersonal dimensions of personality functioning. |
| Parallel processing | Parallel processing is the ability to carry out multiple operations or tasks simultaneously. The term is used in the contexts of both human cognition, particularly in the ability of the brain to simultaneously process incoming stimuli, and in parallel computing by machines. |

# Chapter 4. Sensation and Perception

| | |
|---|---|
| Receptive field | The receptive field of a sensory neuron is a region of space in which the presence of a stimulus will alter the firing of that neuron. Receptive fields have been identified for neurons of the auditory system, the somatosensory system, and the visual system. |
| | The concept of receptive fields can be extended to further up the neural system; if many sensory receptors all form synapses with a single cell further up, they collectively form the receptive field of that cell. |
| Greeble | A greeble is a fine detailing added to the surface of a larger object that makes it appear more complex, and therefore more visually interesting. It usually gives the audience an impression of increased scale. The detail can be made from simple geometric primitives (such as cylinders, cubes, and rectangles), or more complex shapes, such as pieces of machinery (sprockets, cables, tanks). |
| Hippocampus | The hippocampus is a major component of the brains of humans and other mammals. It belongs to the limbic system and plays important roles in long-term memory and spatial navigation. Like the cerebral cortex, with which it is closely associated, it is a paired structure, with mirror-image halves in the left and right sides of the brain. In humans and other primates, the hippocampus is located inside the medial temporal lobe, beneath the cortical surface. It contains two main interlocking parts: Ammon's horn and the dentate gyrus. |
| On Colors | On Colors is a treatise attributed to Aristotle but sometimes ascribed to Theophrastus or Strato. The work outlines the theory that all colors (yellow, red, purple, green, and blue) are derived from mixtures of black and white. |
| Temporal lobe | The temporal lobe is a region of the cerebral cortex that is located beneath the Sylvian fissure on both cerebral hemispheres of the mammalian brain. |
| | The temporal lobe is involved in auditory perception and is home to the primary auditory cortex. It is also important for the processing of semantics in both speech and vision. The temporal lobe contains the hippocampus and plays a key role in the formation of long-term memory. |
| Color mixing | There are two types of color mixing: Additive and Subtractive. In both cases there are three primary colors, three secondary colors (colors made from 2 of the three primary colors in equal amounts), and one tertiary color made from all three primary colors. |
| | Additive Mixing |
| | Additive mixing of colors generally involves mixing colors of light. |

| Color solid | A color solid is the three-dimensional representation of a color model, an analog of the two-dimensional color wheel. The added spatial dimension allows a color solid to depict an added dimension of color variation. Whereas a two-dimensional color wheel typically depicts the variables of hue (red, green, blue, etc). |
|---|---|
| Mental disorder | A mental disorder is a psychological or behavioral pattern generally associated with subjective distress or disability that occurs in an individual, and which is not a part of normal development or culture. The recognition and understanding of mental health conditions has changed over time and across cultures, and there are still variations in the definition, assessment, and classification of mental disorders, although standard guideline criteria are widely accepted. A few mental disorders are diagnosed based on the harm to others, regardless of the subject's perception of distress. |
| Afterimage | An afterimage is an optical illusion that refers to an image continuing to appear in one's vision after the exposure to the original image has ceased. One of the most common afterimages is the bright glow that seems to float before one's eyes after looking into a light source for a few seconds.<br><br>Closing the eye can help achieve a better sense of the color in its own aspect. |
| Color wheel | A color wheel is either:•An abstract illustrative organization of color hues around a circle, that shows relationships between primary colors, secondary colors, complementary colors, etc.•A mechanical device that rotates an array of colors arranged as petals or gradients around an axis, such as one used in DLP TV technology.<br><br>Some sources use the terms color wheel and color circle interchangeably; however, one term or the other may be more prevalent in certain fields or certain versions as mentioned above. For instance, some reserve the term color wheel for mechanical rotating devices, such as color tops or filter wheels. Others classify various color wheels as color disc, color chart, and color scale varieties. |
| Complementary color | Complementary colors are pairs of colors that are of 'opposite' hue in some color model. The exact hue 'complementary' to a given hue depends on the model in question, and perceptually uniform, additive, and subtractive color models, for example, have differing complements for any given color.<br><br>Color theory<br><br>In color theory, two colors are called complementary if, when mixed in the proper proportion, they produce a neutral color (grey, white, or black). |

# Chapter 4. Sensation and Perception

| | |
|---|---|
| Opponent process | The color opponent process is a color theory that states that the human visual system interprets information about color by processing signals from cones and rods in an antagonistic manner. The three types of cones (L for long, M for medium and S for short) have some overlap in the wavelengths of light to which they respond, so it is more efficient for the visual system to record differences between the responses of cones, rather than each type of cone's individual response. The opponent color theory suggests that there are three opponent channels: red versus green, blue versus yellow, and black versus white (the latter type is achromatic and detects light-dark variation, or luminance). |
| Primary color | Primary colors are sets of colors that can be combined to make a useful range of colors. For human applications, three primary colors are usually used, since human color vision is trichromatic. |
| | For additive combination of colors, as in overlapping projected lights or in CRT displays, the primary colors normally used are red, green, and blue. |
| Process theory | Process theory is a commonly used form of scientific research study in which events or occurrences are said to be the result of certain input states leading to a certain outcome (output) state, following a set process. |
| | Process theory holds that if an outcome is to be duplicated, so too must the process which originally created it, and that there are certain constant necessary conditions for the outcome to be reached. When the phrase is used in connection with human motivation, process theory attempts to explain the mechanism by which human needs changes. |
| Reversible figure | A reversible figure is an optical illusion that is designed to create an unstable visual perception, one which leads the beholder to vacillate between two or more different interpretations. |
| | Examples include Necker cubes, the rhombille tiling (viewed as an isometric drawing of cubes), face/vase drawings, the Rabbit-Duck Illusion and impossible objects. |
| Subjectivity | Subjectivity refers to the subject and his or her perspective, feelings, beliefs, and desires. In philosophy, the term is usually contrasted with objectivity. |
| | Subjectivity may refer to the specific discerning interpretations of any aspect of experiences. |
| Inattentional blindness | Inattentional blindness, is when a person fails to notice some stimulus that is in plain sight. This stimulus is usually unexpected but fully visible. This typically happens because humans are overloaded with inputs. |

| | |
|---|---|
| Functional selectivity | Functional selectivity is the ligand-dependent selectivity for certain signal transduction pathways in one and the same receptor. This can be present when a receptor has several possible signal transduction pathways. To which degree each pathway is activated thus depends on which ligand binds to the receptor . |
| Gestalt psychology | Gestalt psychology is holistic, parallel, and analog, with self-organizing tendencies. The principle maintains that the human eye sees objects in their entirety before perceiving their individual parts. Gestalt psychologists stipulate that perception is the product of complex interactions among various stimuli. |
| Popular psychology | The term popular psychology refers to concepts and theories about human mental life and behavior that are purportedly based on psychology and that attain popularity among the general population. The concept is closely related to the human potential movement of the 1950s and '60s.<br><br>The term 'pop psychologist' can be used to describe authors, consultants, lecturers and entertainers who are widely perceived as being psychologists, not because of their academic credentials, but because they have projected that image or have been perceived in that way in response to their work. |
| Illusion | An illusion is a distortion of the senses, revealing how the brain normally organizes and interprets sensory stimulation. While illusions distort reality, they are generally shared by most people. Illusions may occur with more of the human senses than vision, but visual illusions, optical illusions, are the most well known and understood. |
| Phi phenomenon | The phi phenomenon is an optical illusion defined by Max Wertheimer in the Gestalt psychology in 1912, in which the persistence of vision formed a part of the base of the theory of the cinema, applied by Hugo Münsterberg in 1916. This optical illusion is based in the principle that the human eye is capable of perceiving movement from pieces of information, for example, a succession of images. In other words, from a slideshow of a group of frozen images at a certain speed of images per second, we are going to observe constant movement.<br><br>The phi phenomenon is an optical illusion of our brains and eyes that allows us to perceive constant movement instead of a sequence of images. |
| Necker Cube | The Necker Cube is an optical illusion first published as a rhomboid in 1832 by Swiss crystallographer Louis Albert Necker.<br><br>Ambiguity<br><br>The Necker Cube is an ambiguous line drawing. |

# Chapter 4. Sensation and Perception

| | |
|---|---|
| Depth perception | Depth perception is the visual ability to perceive the world in three dimensions (3D) and the distance of an object. Depth sensation is the ability to move accurately, or to respond consistently, based on the distances of objects in an environment.<br><br>Depth perception arises from a variety of depth cues. |
| Conspicuous consumption | Conspicuous consumption is the spending of money on and the acquiring of luxury goods and services to publicly display economic power -- either the buyer's income or the buyer's accumulated wealth. Sociologically, to the conspicuous consumer, such a public display of discretionary economic power is a means either of attaining or of maintaining a given social status. Moreover, invidious consumption, a more specialized sociologic term, denotes the deliberate conspicuous consumption of goods and services intended to provoke the envy of other people, as a means of displaying the buyer's superior socio-economic status. |
| Ames room | An Ames room is a distorted room that is used to create an optical illusion. Probably influenced by the writings of Hermann Helmholtz, it was invented by American ophthalmologist Adelbert Ames, Jr. in 1934, and constructed in the following year. |
| Ponzo illusion | The Ponzo illusion is a geometrical-optical illusion that was first demonstrated by the Italian psychologist Mario Ponzo (1882-1960) in 1913. He suggested that the human mind judges an object's size based on its background. He showed this by drawing two identical lines across a pair of converging lines, similar to railway tracks. The upper line looks longer because we interpret the converging sides according to linear perspective as parallel lines receding into the distance. |
| Moon illusion | The Moon illusion is an optical illusion in which the Moon appears larger near the horizon than it does while higher up in the sky. This optical illusion also occurs with the sun and star constellations. It has been known since ancient times, and recorded by numerous different cultures. |
| Size constancy | Size constancy is one type of visual subjective constancy. Within a certain range, people's perception of one particular objects' size will not change completely as neither distance is changed, nor the video size changed on the retina. The perception of image is still based upon the actual size of the perceptual characteristics. |
| Auditory system | The auditory system is the sensory system for the sense of hearing.<br><br>Ear<br><br>Outer ear |

| | |
|---|---|
| | The folds of cartilage surrounding the ear canal are called the pinna. Sound waves are reflected and attenuated when they hit the pinna, and these changes provide additional information that will help the brain determine the direction from which the sounds came. |
| Basilar membrane | The basilar membrane within the cochlea of the inner ear is a stiff structural element that separates two liquid-filled tubes that run along the coil of the cochlea, the scala media and the scala tympani . Endolymph/perilymph separation <br><br> The fluids in these two tubes, the endolymph and the perilymph are very different chemically, biochemically, and electrically. Therefore they are kept strictly separated. |
| Cochlea | The cochlea is the auditory portion of the inner ear. It is a spiral-shaped cavity in the bony labyrinth, making 2.5 turns around its axis, the modiolus. A core component of the cochlea is the Organ of Corti, the sensory organ of hearing, which is distributed along the partition separating fluid chambers in the coiled tapered tube of the cochlea. |
| Eardrum | The eardrum, is a thin, cone-shaped membrane that separates the external ear from the middle ear in humans and other tetrapods. Its function is to transmit sound from the air to the ossicles inside the middle ear. The malleus bone bridges the gap between the eardrum and the other ossicles. |
| Inner ear | The inner ear is the innermost part of the vertebrate ear. In mammals, it consists of the bony labyrinth, a hollow cavity in the temporal bone of the skull with a system of passages comprising two main functional parts:•The cochlea, dedicating to hearing; converting sound pressure impulses from the outer ear into electrical impulses which are passed on to the brain via the auditory nerve.•The vestibular system, dedicated to balance <br><br> The inner ear is found in all vertebrates, with substantial variations in form and function. The inner ear is innervated by the eighth cranial nerve in all vertebrates. |
| Gustatory system | The gustatory system is the sensory system for the sense of taste. <br><br> The gustatory system allows humans to distinguish between safe and harmful food. Bitter and sour foods we find unpleasant, while salty, sweet, and meaty tasting foods generally provide a pleasurable sensation. |
| Taste bud | Taste buds contain the receptors for taste. They are located around the small structures on the upper surface of the tongue, soft palate, upper esophagus and epiglottis, which are called papillae. |

# Chapter 4. Sensation and Perception

| | |
|---|---|
| Wine tasting | Wine tasting is the sensory examination and evaluation of wine. While the practice of wine tasting is as ancient as its production, a more formalized methodology has slowly become established from the 14th century onwards. Modern, professional wine tasters (such as sommeliers or buyers for retailers) use a constantly-evolving formal terminology which is used to describe the range of perceived flavors, aromas and general characteristics of a wine. |
| Flynn effect | The Flynn effect is the name given to a substantial and long-sustained increase in intelligence test scores measured in many parts of the world. When intelligence quotient (IQ) tests are initially standardized using a sample of test-takers, by convention the average of the test results is set to 100 and their standard deviation is set to 15 or 16 IQ points. When IQ tests are revised, they are again standardized using a new sample of test-takers, usually born more recently than the first. |
| Umami | Umami is a savory taste which is one of the five basic tastes, together with sweet, sour, bitter, and salty. Umami is a loanword from the Japanese umami meaning 'pleasant savory taste'. This particular writing was chosen by Professor Kikunae Ikeda from umai 'delicious' and mi 'taste'. |
| Supertaster | A supertaster is a person who experiences the sense of taste with far greater intensity than average. Women are more likely to be supertasters, as are individuals of Asian, African and South American descent. The cause of this heightened response is currently unknown, although it is thought to be, at least in part, due to an increased number of fungiform papillae. |
| Olfactory bulb | The olfactory bulb is a structure of the vertebrate forebrain involved in olfaction, the perception of odors.<br><br>In most vertebrates, the olfactory bulb is the most rostral (forward) part of the brain. In humans, however, the olfactory bulb is on the inferior (bottom) side of the brain. |
| Olfactory system | The olfactory system is the sensory system used for olfaction, or the sense of smell. Most mammals and reptiles have two distinct parts to their olfactory system: a main olfactory system and an accessory olfactory system. The main olfactory system detects volatile, airborne substances, while the accessory olfactory system senses fluid-phase stimuli. |
| Brainstem | In vertebrate anatomy the brainstem is the posterior part of the brain, adjoining and structurally continuous with the spinal cord. The brain stem provides the main motor and sensory innervation to the face and neck via the cranial nerves. Though small, this is an extremely important part of the brain as the nerve connections of the motor and sensory systems from the main part of the brain to the rest of the body pass through the brain stem. |
| Meissner's corpuscle | Meissner's corpuscles (or tactile corpuscles) are a type of mechanoreceptor. |

|  |  |
|---|---|
|  | They are a type of nerve ending in the skin that is responsible for sensitivity to light touch. In particular, they have highest sensitivity (lowest threshold) when sensing vibrations lower than 50 Hertz. |
| Lamellar corpuscle | Lamellar corpuscles are one of the four major types of mechanoreceptor. They are nerve endings in the skin, responsible for sensitivity to vibration and pressure. Vibrational role may be used to detect surface e.g. rough vs. smooth. |
| Parietal lobe | The parietal lobe is a part of the brain positioned above (superior to) the occipital lobe and behind (posterior to) the frontal lobe.<br><br>The parietal lobe integrates sensory information from different modalities, particularly determining spatial sense and navigation. For example, it comprises somatosensory cortex and the dorsal stream of the visual system. |
| Mesencephalon | In biological anatomy, the mesencephalon (or midbrain) comprises the tectum (or corpora quadrigemina), tegmentum, the ventricular mesocoelia (or 'iter'), and the cerebral peduncles, as well as several nuclei and fasciculi. Caudally the mesencephalon adjoins the pons (metencephalon) and rostrally it adjoins the diencephalon (Thalamus, hypothalamus, et al)..<br><br>During development, the mesencephalon forms from the middle of three vesicles that arise from the neural tube to generate the brain. |
| Acupuncture | Acupuncture is an alternative medicine that treats patients by insertion and manipulation of needles in the body. Its proponents variously claim that it relieves pain, treats infertility, treats disease, prevents disease, promotes general health, or can be used for therapeutic purposes. Acupuncture typically incorporates traditional Chinese medicine (TCM) as an integral part of its practice and theory. |
| Glial cell | Glial cells are non-neuronal cells that maintain homeostasis, form myelin, and provide support and protection for the brain's neurons. In the human brain, there is roughly one glia for every neuron with a ratio of about two neurons for every three glia in the cerebral gray matter. |
| Morphine | Morphine ( ; MS Contin, MSIR, Avinza, Kadian, Oramorph, Roxanol, Kapanol) is a potent opiate analgesic drug that is used to relieve severe pain. It was first isolated in 1804 by Friedrich Sertürner, first distributed by him in 1817, and first commercially sold by Merck in 1827, which at the time was a single small chemists' shop. It was more widely used after the invention of the hypodermic needle in 1857. It took its name from the Greek god of dreams Morpheus . |
| Periaqueductal gray | Periaqueductal gray is the gray matter located around the cerebral aqueduct within the tegmentum of the midbrain. |

# Chapter 4. Sensation and Perception

| | |
|---|---|
| | It plays a role in the descending modulation of pain and in defensive behaviour. The ascending pain and temperature fibers of the spinothalamic tract also send information to the PAG via the spinomesencephalic tract . |
| Serotonin | Serotonin is a monoamine neurotransmitter. Biochemically derived from tryptophan, serotonin is primarily found in the gastrointestinal (GI) tract, platelets, and in the central nervous system (CNS) of animals including humans. It is a well-known contributor to feelings of well-being; therefore it is also known as a 'happiness hormone' despite not being a hormone. |
| Spinal cord | The spinal cord is a long, thin, tubular bundle of nervous tissue and support cells that extends from the brain (the medulla oblongata specifically). The brain and spinal cord together make up the central nervous system (CNS). The spinal cord begins at the occipital bone and extends down to the space between the first and second lumbar vertebrae; it does not extend the entire length of the vertebral column. |
| Sensory integration | Sensory integration is defined as the neurological process that organizes sensation from one's own body and the environment, thus making it possible to use the body effectively within the environment. Specifically, it deals with how the brain processes multiple sensory modality inputs into usable functional outputs. It has been believed for some time that inputs from different sensory organs are processed in different areas in the brain. |
| Futurism | Futurism was an artistic and social movement that originated in Italy in the early 20th century. It emphasized and glorified themes associated with contemporary concepts of the future, including speed, technology, youth and violence, and objects such as the car, the airplane and the industrial city. It was largely an Italian phenomenon, though there were parallel movements in Russia, England and elsewhere. |
| Contrast effect | A contrast effect is the enhancement or diminishment, relative to normal, of perception, cognition and related performance as a result of immediately previous or simultaneous exposure to a stimulus of lesser or greater value in the same dimension. (Here, normal perception or performance is that which would be obtained in the absence of the comparison stimulus--i.e., one based on all previous experience).<br><br>Contrast effects are ubiquitous throughout human and non-human animal perception, cognition, and resultant performance. |
| Door-in-the-face technique | The door-in-the-face (DITF) technique is a persuasion method. The persuader attempts to convince someone to comply with a request by first making an extremely large request that the respondent will obviously turn down, with a metaphorical slamming of a door in the persuader's face. The respondent is then more likely to accede to a second, more reasonable request than if this second request were made without the first, extreme request. |

Robert Cialdini suggests this as a form of reciprocity, i.e. the (induced) sharp negative response to the first request creates a sense of debt or guilt that the second request offers to clear, and the reduced second request is interpreted by the receiver as a concession which is reciprocated by compliance with the request. Alternately, a reference point (or framing) construal may explain this phenomenon, as the initial bad offer sets a reference point from which the second offer looks like an improvement.

In a classic experiment to test the door-in-the-face technique, Cialdini asked students to volunteer to counsel juvenile delinquents for two hours a week for two years.

1. The vertebrate _____ is a light-sensitive tissue lining the inner surface of the eye. The optics of the eye create an image of the visual world on the _____, which serves much the same function as the film in a camera. Light striking the _____ initiates a cascade of chemical and electrical events that ultimately trigger nerve impulses.

    a. Retina
    b. Retinotopy
    c. Saccadic masking
    d. Saccadic suppression of image displacement

2. There are two types of _____: Additive and Subtractive. In both cases there are three primary colors, three secondary colors (colors made from 2 of the three primary colors in equal amounts), and one tertiary color made from all three primary colors.

    Additive Mixing

    Additive mixing of colors generally involves mixing colors of light.

    a. Color of water
    b. Color photography
    c. Color mixing
    d. Color rendering index

3. . _____ PhD, is a multi-scale test of psychological functioning that assesses constructs relevant to personality and psychopathology evaluation (e.g., depression, anxiety, aggression) in various contexts including psychotherapy, crisis/evaluation, forensic, personnel selection, pain/medical, and child custody assessment. The PAI has 22 non-overlapping scales, providing a comprehensive overview of psychopathology in adults.

The PAI contains four kinds of scales: 1) validity scales, which measure the respondent's approach to the test, including faking good or bad, exaggeration, or defensiveness; 2) clinical scales, which correspond to psychiatric diagnostic categories; 3) treatment consideration scales, which assess factors that may relate to treatment of clinical disorders or other risk factors but which are not captured in psychiatric diagnoses (e.g., suicidal ideation); and 4) interpersonal scales, which provide indicators of interpersonal dimensions of personality functioning.

a. Personality quiz
b. Personality Assessment Inventory
c. Purity test
d. Revised NEO Personality Inventory

4. The _____ is a major component of the brains of humans and other mammals. It belongs to the limbic system and plays important roles in long-term memory and spatial navigation. Like the cerebral cortex, with which it is closely associated, it is a paired structure, with mirror-image halves in the left and right sides of the brain. In humans and other primates, the _____ is located inside the medial temporal lobe, beneath the cortical surface. It contains two main interlocking parts: Ammon's horn and the dentate gyrus.

a. Hippocampus
b. leukoaraiosis
c. superior longitudinal fasciculus
d. Cingulate sulcus

5. _____(2007) was the name of a collaboration and exhibition between the Edinburgh artists Martin Smith, Reuben Paris and Colin Usher. The show, conceived and executed within a 48-hour time period, was shot in the Leith area of Edinburgh. It featured a style of photography that mixed crime scene incidents with associated visual narratives and occasionally texts that were both found and devised.

a. Piictu
b. Peripheral Vision
c. Project Planet Bioia
d. Project-Open

**1.** a

**2.** c

**3.** b

**4.** a

**5.** b

*You can take the complete Chapter Practice Test*

**for Chapter 4. Sensation and Perception**
on all key terms, persons, places, and concepts.

*Online 99 Cents*

*http://www.epub3.2.20111.4.cram101.com/*

**Use www.Cram101.com for all your study needs**

**including Cram101's online interactive problem solving labs in**

**chemistry, statistics, mathematics, and more.**

CHAPTER OUTLINE: KEY TERMS, PEOPLE, PLACES, CONCEPTS

Anesthesia awareness

Beta wave

Delta wave

Electroconvulsive therapy

Circadian rhythm

Meissner's corpuscle

Alertness

Jet lag

Pineal gland

Suprachiasmatic nucleus

Hypnic jerk

Sleep spindle

Slow-wave sleep

Poggendorff illusion

Reticular activating system

Mesencephalon

Reticular formation

Sleep deprivation

Functional selectivity

Personality Assessment Inventory

Fatigue

Insomnia

Benzodiazepine

Sedative

Case study

Night terror

Nightmare

Sleep apnea

Snoring

Sleepwalking

Gamma-Aminobutyric acid

Wish fulfillment

Hypnosis

Hypnotic susceptibility

Hypnotic induction

Psychoanalytic theory

Suggestibility

Ames room

# Chapter 5. Variations in Consciousness

CHAPTER OUTLINE: KEY TERMS, PEOPLE, PLACES, CONCEPTS

Ponzo illusion

Amazing Kreskin

Highway hypnosis

Meditation

Transcendental Meditation

Cannon-Bard theory

Pethidine

Codeine

Heroin

Methadone

Morphine

Narcotic

Oxycodone

Psychoactive drug

Down syndrome

Amphetamine

Barbiturate

Cocaine

Crack cocaine

Hashish

Mescaline

Methamphetamine

Psilocybin

Side effect

Stimulant

MDMA

Subjectivity

Norepinephrine

Psychological dependence

Reuptake

Serotonin

Health effect

Medial forebrain bundle

Nucleus accumbens

Pleasure center

Prefrontal cortex

Testosterone

Autogenic training

CHAPTER OUTLINE: KEY TERMS, PEOPLE, PLACES, CONCEPTS

| | Systematics |
| --- | --- |
| | Lucid dream |
| | Circular reasoning |

CHAPTER HIGHLIGHTS & NOTES: KEY TERMS, PEOPLE, PLACES, CONCEPTS

| | |
| --- | --- |
| Anesthesia awareness | Anesthesia awareness, on the operating table, when the patient has not been given enough of the general anesthetic or analgesic to render the patient unconscious during general anesthesia (often when agents used to paralyze the patient have been administered). In brief, it is the post-operative recall of intra-operative events.<br><br>However, it can also occur in the post-anesthesia care unit (PACU) or in the intensive-care unit (ICU), where patients are kept sedated, tranquilized and sometimes paralyzed (and intubated) and are connected to life support systems, awaiting normalization of their physiology. |
| Beta wave | Beta wave is the term used to designate the frequency range of human brain activity between 12 and 30 Hz (12 to 30 transitions or cycles per second). Beta waves are split into three sections: High Beta Waves (19 Hz+); Beta Waves (15-18 Hz); and Low Beta Waves (12-15 Hz). Beta states are the states associated with normal waking consciousness. |
| Delta wave | A delta wave is a high amplitude brain wave with a frequency of oscillation between 0-4 hertz. Delta waves, like other brain waves, are recorded with an electroencephalogram (EEG) and are usually associated with the deepest stages of sleep (3 and 4 NREM), also known as slow-wave sleep (SWS), and aid in characterizing the depth of sleep. |
| Electroconvulsive therapy | Electroconvulsive therapy formerly known as electroshock, is a psychiatric treatment in which seizures are electrically induced in anesthetized patients for therapeutic effect. Its mode of action is unknown. Today, ECT is most often recommended for use as a treatment for severe depression that has not responded to other treatment, and is also used in the treatment of mania and catatonia. |

# Chapter 5. Variations in Consciousness

| | |
|---|---|
| Circadian rhythm | A circadian rhythm is an endogenously driven roughly 24-hour cycle in biochemical, physiological, or behavioural processes. Circadian rhythms have been widely observed, in plants, animals, fungi and cyanobacteria . The term 'circadian' comes from the Latin circa, meaning 'around', and diem or dies, meaning 'day'. |
| Meissner's corpuscle | Meissner's corpuscles (or tactile corpuscles) are a type of mechanoreceptor. They are a type of nerve ending in the skin that is responsible for sensitivity to light touch. In particular, they have highest sensitivity (lowest threshold) when sensing vibrations lower than 50 Hertz. |
| Alertness | Alertness is the state of paying close and continuous attention, being watchful and prompt to meet danger or emergency, or being quick to perceive and act. It is related to psychology as well as to physiology. A lack of alertness is a symptom of a number of conditions, including narcolepsy, attention deficit disorder, chronic fatigue syndrome, depression, Addison's disease, or sleep deprivation. |
| Jet lag | Jet lag, medically referred to as desynchronosis, is a physiological condition which results from alterations to the body's circadian rhythms; it is classified as one of the circadian rhythm sleep disorders. Jet lag results from rapid long-distance transmeridian (east-west or west-east) travel, as on a jet plane. <br><br> The condition of jet lag may last several days, and a recovery rate of one day per time zone crossed is a fair guideline. |
| Pineal gland | The pineal gland is a small endocrine gland in the vertebrate brain. It produces the serotonin derivative melatonin, a hormone that affects the modulation of wake/sleep patterns and seasonal functions. Its shape resembles a tiny pine cone (hence its name), and it is located near the center of the brain, between the two hemispheres, tucked in a groove where the two rounded thalamic bodies join. |
| Suprachiasmatic nucleus | The suprachiasmatic nucleus, abbreviated SCN, is a tiny region on the brain's midline, situated directly above the optic chiasm. It is responsible for controlling circadian rhythms. The neuronal and hormonal activities it generates regulate many different body functions in a 24-hour cycle, using around 20,000 neurons. |
| Hypnic jerk | A hypnic jerk, hypnagogic jerk, sleep start, or night start, is an involuntary myoclonic twitch which occurs during hypnagogia, just as a person is beginning to fall asleep, often causing them to awaken suddenly for a moment. Physically, hypnic jerks resemble the 'jump' experienced by a person when startled, often accompanied by a falling sensation. A higher occurrence in people with irregular sleep schedules is reported. |

| | |
|---|---|
| Sleep spindle | A sleep spindle is a burst of oscillatory brain activity visible on an EEG that occurs during stage 2 sleep. It consists of 12-14 Hz waves that occur for at least 0.5 seconds.

Sleep spindles (sometimes referred to as 'sigma bands' or 'sigma waves') may represent periods where the brain is inhibiting processing to keep the sleeper in a tranquil state. |
| Slow-wave sleep | Slow-wave sleep often referred to as deep sleep, consists of stages 3 and 4 of non-rapid eye movement sleep, according to the Rechtschaffen & Kales (R & K) standard of 1968. As of 2008, the American Academy of Sleep Medicine (AASM) has discontinued the use of stage 4, such that the previous stages 3 and 4 now are combined as stage 3. An epoch (30 seconds of sleep) which consists of 20% or more slow wave (delta) sleep, now is considered to be stage 3.

The highest arousal thresholds (i.e. difficulty of awakening, such as by a sound of a particular volume) are observed in deep sleep. A person will typically feel more groggy when awoken from slow-wave sleep, and indeed, cognitive tests administered after awakening then indicate that mental performance is somewhat impaired for periods of up to 30 minutes or so, relative to awakenings from other stages. |
| Poggendorff illusion | The Poggendorff Illusion is a geometrical-optical illusion that involves the misperception of the position of one segment of a transverse line that has been interrupted by the contour of an intervening structure (here a rectangle). It is named after Poggendorff, the editor of the journal, who discovered it in the figures Johann Karl Friedrich Zöllner submitted when first reporting on what is now known as the Zöllner illusion, in 1860.

In the picture to the right, a straight black and red line is obscured by a grey rectangle. |
| Reticular activating system | The reticular activating system is an area of the brain (including the reticular formation and its connections) responsible for regulating arousal and sleep-wake transitions. |
| Mesencephalon | In biological anatomy, the mesencephalon (or midbrain) comprises the tectum (or corpora quadrigemina), tegmentum, the ventricular mesocoelia (or 'iter'), and the cerebral peduncles, as well as several nuclei and fasciculi. Caudally the mesencephalon adjoins the pons (metencephalon) and rostrally it adjoins the diencephalon (Thalamus, hypothalamus, et al)..

During development, the mesencephalon forms from the middle of three vesicles that arise from the neural tube to generate the brain. |
| Reticular formation | The reticular formation is a region in the pons that is involved in regulating the sleep-wake cycle and filtering incoming stimuli to discriminate irrelevant background stimuli. It is essential for governing some of the basic functions of higher organisms, and is one of the phylogenetically oldest portions of the brain. |

The reticular formation consists of more than 100 small neural networks, with varied functions including the following:

1. Somatic motor control - Some motor neurons send their axons to the reticular formation nuclei, giving rise to the reticulospinal tracts of the spinal cord.

| | |
|---|---|
| Sleep deprivation | Sleep deprivation is the condition of not having enough sleep; it can be either chronic or acute. A chronic sleep-restricted state can cause fatigue, daytime sleepiness, clumsiness and weight loss or weight gain. It adversely affects the brain and cognitive function. |
| Functional selectivity | Functional selectivity is the ligand-dependent selectivity for certain signal transduction pathways in one and the same receptor. This can be present when a receptor has several possible signal transduction pathways. To which degree each pathway is activated thus depends on which ligand binds to the receptor . |
| Personality Assessment Inventory | Personality Assessment Inventory PhD, is a multi-scale test of psychological functioning that assesses constructs relevant to personality and psychopathology evaluation (e.g., depression, anxiety, aggression) in various contexts including psychotherapy, crisis/evaluation, forensic, personnel selection, pain/medical, and child custody assessment. The PAI has 22 non-overlapping scales, providing a comprehensive overview of psychopathology in adults. The PAI contains four kinds of scales: 1) validity scales, which measure the respondent's approach to the test, including faking good or bad, exaggeration, or defensiveness; 2) clinical scales, which correspond to psychiatric diagnostic categories; 3) treatment consideration scales, which assess factors that may relate to treatment of clinical disorders or other risk factors but which are not captured in psychiatric diagnoses (e.g., suicidal ideation); and 4) interpersonal scales, which provide indicators of interpersonal dimensions of personality functioning. |
| Fatigue | Fatigue (also called exhaustion, lethargy, languidness, languor, lassitude, and listlessness) is a state of awareness describing a range of afflictions, usually associated with physical and/or mental weakness, though varying from a general state of lethargy to a specific work-induced burning sensation within one's muscles. Physical fatigue is the inability to continue functioning at the level of one's normal abilities. It is widespread in everyday life, but usually becomes particularly noticeable during heavy exercise. |
| Insomnia | Insomnia is most often defined by an individual's report of sleeping difficulties. While the term is sometimes used in sleep literature to describe a disorder demonstrated by polysomnographic evidence of disturbed sleep, insomnia is often defined as a positive response to either of two questions: 'Do you experience difficulty sleeping?' or 'Do you have difficulty falling or staying asleep?' |

Thus, insomnia is most often thought of as both a sign and a symptom that can accompany several sleep, medical, and psychiatric disorders, characterized by persistent difficulty falling asleep and/or staying asleep or sleep of poor quality. Insomnia is typically followed by functional impairment while awake.

| | |
|---|---|
| Benzodiazepine | A benzodiazepine is a psychoactive drug whose core chemical structure is the fusion of a benzene ring and a diazepine ring. The first benzodiazepine, chlordiazepoxide (Librium), was discovered accidentally by Leo Sternbach in 1955, and made available in 1960 by Hoffmann-La Roche, which has also marketed diazepam (Valium) since 1963.<br><br>Benzodiazepines enhance the effect of the neurotransmitter gamma-aminobutyric acid (GABA), which results in sedative, hypnotic (sleep-inducing), anxiolytic (anti-anxiety), anticonvulsant, muscle relaxant and amnesic action. |
| Sedative | A sedative is a substance that induces sedation by reducing irritability or excitement.<br><br>At higher doses it may result in slurred speech, staggering gait, poor judgment, and slow, uncertain reflexes. Doses of sedatives such as benzodiazepines, when used as a hypnotic to induce sleep, tend to be higher than amounts used to relieve anxiety, whereas only low doses are needed to provide a peaceful and calming sedative effect. |
| Case study | A case study is a research method common in social science. It is based on an in-depth investigation of a single individual, group, or event. Case studies may be descriptive or explanatory. |
| Night terror | A night terror, incubus attack, or pavor nocturnus, is a parasomnia disorder, causing feelings of terror or dread, and typically occurring in the first few hours of sleep during stage 3 or 4 non-rapid eye movement NREM sleep. However, they can also occur during daytime naps. Night terrors should not be confused with nightmares, which are bad dreams that cause feelings of horror or fear. |
| Nightmare | A nightmare is a dream that can cause a strong negative emotional response from the sleeper, typically fear and/or horror. The dream may contain situations of danger, discomfort, psychological or physical terror. Sufferers usually awaken in a state of distress and may be unable to return to sleep for a prolonged period of time. |
| Sleep apnea | Sleep apnea is a sleep disorder characterized by abnormal pauses in breathing or instances of abnormally low breathing, during sleep. Each pause in breathing, called an apnea, can last from a few seconds to minutes, and may occur 5 to 30 times or more an hour. |

# Chapter 5. Variations in Consciousness

| | |
|---|---|
| Snoring | Snoring is the vibration of respiratory structures and the resulting sound, due to obstructed air movement during breathing while sleeping. In some cases the sound may be soft, but in other cases, it can be loud and unpleasant.<br><br>Generally speaking, the structures involved are the uvula and soft palate. |
| Sleepwalking | Sleepwalking, is a sleep disorder belonging to the parasomnia family. Sleepwalkers arise from the slow wave sleep stage in a state of low consciousness and perform activities that are usually performed during a state of full consciousness. These activities can be as benign as sitting up in bed, walking to the bathroom, and cleaning, or as hazardous as cooking, driving, having sex, violent gestures, grabbing at hallucinated objects, or even homicide. |
| Gamma-Aminobutyric acid | γ-Aminobutyric acid is the chief inhibitory neurotransmitter in the mammalian central nervous system. It plays a role in regulating neuronal excitability throughout the nervous system. In humans, GABA is also directly responsible for the regulation of muscle tone.<br><br>Although chemically it is an amino acid, GABA is rarely referred to as such in the scientific or medical communities, because the term 'amino acid,' used without a qualifier, conventionally refers to the alpha amino acids, which GABA is not, nor is it ever incorporated into a protein.<br><br>In spastic diplegia in humans, GABA absorption becomes impaired by nerves damaged from the condition's upper motor neuron lesion, which leads to hypertonia of the muscles signaled by those nerves that can no longer absorb GABA.Function Neurotransmitter<br><br>In vertebrates, GABA acts at inhibitory synapses in the brain by binding to specific transmembrane receptors in the plasma membrane of both pre- and postsynaptic neuronal processes. This binding causes the opening of ion channels to allow the flow of either negatively charged chloride ions into the cell or positively charged potassium ions out of the cell. Depending on which ion channels open, the membrane potential is either hyperpolarized or depolarized. This action results in a negative change in the transmembrane potential, usually causing hyperpolarization. Two general classes of GABA receptor are known: $GABA_A$ in which the receptor is part of a ligand-gated ion channel complex, and $GABA_B$ metabotropic receptors, which are G protein-coupled receptors that open or close ion channels via intermediaries (G proteins).<br><br>Neurons that produce GABA as their output are called GABAergic neurons, and have chiefly inhibitory action at receptors in the adult vertebrate. Medium Spiny Cells are a typical example of inhibitory CNS GABAergic cells. In contrast, GABA exhibits both excitatory and inhibitory actions in insects, mediating muscle activation at synapses between nerves and muscle cells, and also the stimulation of certain glands. In mammals, some GABAergic neurons, such as chandelier cells, are also able to excite their glutamatergic counterparts. |

GABA$_A$ receptors are ligand-activated chloride channels; that is, when activated by GABA, they allow the flow of chloride ions across the membrane of the cell. Whether this chloride flow is excitatory/depolarizing (makes the voltage across the cell's membrane less negative), shunting (has no effect on the cell's membrane) or inhibitory/hyperpolarizing (makes the cell's membrane more negative) depends on the direction of the flow of chloride. When net chloride flows out of the cell, GABA is excitatory or depolarizing; when the net chloride flows into the cell, GABA is inhibitory or hyperpolarizing. When the net flow of chloride is close to zero, the action of GABA is shunting. Shunting inhibition has no direct effect on the membrane potential of the cell; however, it minimises the effect of any coincident synaptic input essentially by reducing the electrical resistance of the cell's membrane (in essence, equivalent to Ohm's law). A developmental switch in the molecular machinery controlling concentration of chloride inside the cell - and, hence, the direction of this ion flow - is responsible for the changes in the functional role of GABA between the neonatal and adult stages. That is to say, GABA's role changes from excitatory to inhibitory as the brain develops into adulthood. Brain development

For the past two decades, the theory of excitatory action of GABA early in development was unquestioned based on experiments in vitro, on brain slices. The main observation was that in the hippocampus and neocortex of the mammalian brain, GABA has primarily excitatory effects, and is in fact the major excitatory neurotransmitter in many regions of the brain before the maturation of glutamateergic synapses.

However, this theory has been questioned based on results showing that in brain slices of immature mice incubated in artificial cerebrospinal fluid (ACSF) (modified in a way that takes into account the normal composition of the neuronal milieu in sucklings by adding an energy substrate alternative to glucose, beta-hydroxybutyrate) GABA action shifts from excitatory to inhibitory mode. This effect has been later repeated when other energy substrates, pyruvate and lactate, supplemented glucose in the slices' media. The effects of beta-hydroxybutyrate were later confirmed for pyruvate and for lactate. However it was argued that the concentrations of the alternative energy substrates used in these experiments were non-physiological and the GABA-shift was instead caused by changes in pH resulting from the substrates acting as 'weak acids'. These arguments were later rebutted by further findings showing that changes in pH even greater than that caused by energy substrates do not affect the GABA-shift described in the presence of energy substrate-fortified ACSF and that the mode of action of beta-hydroxybutyrate, pyruvate and lactate (assessed by measurement NAD(P)H and oxygen utilization) was energy metabolism-related.

In the developmental stages preceding the formation of synaptic contacts, GABA is synthesized by neurons and acts both as an autocrine (acting on the same cell) and paracrine (acting on nearby cells) signalling mediator.

# Chapter 5. Variations in Consciousness

GABA regulates the proliferation of neural progenitor cells the migration and differentiation the elongation of neurites and the formation of synapses.

GABA also regulates the growth of embryonic and neural stem cells. GABA can in?uence the development of neural progenitor cells via brain-derived neurotrophic factor (BDNF) expression. GABA activates the $GABA_A$ receptor, causing cell cycle arrest in the S-phase, limiting growth. Beyond the nervous system

GABAergic mechanisms have been demonstrated in various peripheral tissues and organs including, but not restricted to the intestine, stomach, pancreas, Fallopian tube, uterus, ovary, testis, kidney, urinary bladder, lung, and liver.

In 2007, an excitatory GABAergic system was described in the airway epithelium. The system activates following exposure to allergens and may participate in the mechanisms of asthma. GABAergic systems have also been found in the testis and in the eye lens. Structure and conformation

GABA is found mostly as a zwitterion, that is, with the carboxy group deprotonated and the amino group protonated. Its conformation depends on its environment. In the gas phase, a highly folded conformation is strongly favored because of the electrostatic attraction between the two functional groups. The stabilization is about 50 kcal/mol, according to quantum chemistry calculations. In the solid state, a more extended conformation is found, with a trans conformation at the amino end and a gauche conformation at the carboxyl end. This is due to the packing interactions with the neighboring molecules. In solution, five different conformations, some folded and some extended, are found as a result of solvation effects. The conformational flexibility of GABA is important for its biological function, as it has been found to bind to different receptors with different conformations. Many GABA analogues with pharmaceutical applications have more rigid structures in order to control the binding better. History

Gamma-aminobutyric acid was first synthesized in 1883, and was first known only as a plant and microbe metabolic product.

| | |
|---|---|
| Wish fulfillment | Wish fulfillment in psychology is the satisfaction of a desire through such involuntary thought processes such as dreams, daydreams, and neurotic symptoms. In Freudian psychoanalysis, it is when desires of the unconscious are unacceptable to the ego and superego because of feeling of guilt or societal or cultural restrictions such as taboos, giving rise to dreams. For Sigmund Freud, dreams result from attempts by the unconscious to resolve a conflict of some sort, whether something recent or something from the recesses of the past. |

| Hypnosis | Hypnosis is a mental state (according to 'state theory') or imaginative role-enactment (according to 'non-state theory'). It is usually induced by a procedure known as a hypnotic induction, which is commonly composed of a long series of preliminary instructions and suggestions. Hypnotic suggestions may be delivered by a hypnotist in the presence of the subject, or may be self-administered ('self-suggestion' or 'autosuggestion'). The use of hypnotism for therapeutic purposes is referred to as 'hypnotherapy', while its use as a form of entertainment for an audience is known as 'stage hypnosis'. |
|---|---|
| Hypnotic susceptibility | Hypnotic susceptibility measures how easily a person can be hypnotized. Several types of scales are used; however, the most common are the Harvard Group Scale of Hypnotic Susceptibility and the Stanford Hypnotic Susceptibility Scales.<br><br>The Harvard Group Scale (HGSS), as the name implies, is administered predominantly to large groups of people while the Stanford Hypnotic Susceptibility Scale (SHSS) is administered to individuals. |
| Hypnotic induction | Hypnotic induction is the process undertaken by a hypnotist to establish the state or conditions required for hypnosis to occur. Self-hypnosis is possible, in which a subject listens to a taped induction or plays the roles of both hypnotist and subject.<br><br>It is contended that hypnotic induction is a necessary process designed to cause the subject to enter a state of increased suggestibility, during which their critical faculties are reduced and they are more prone to accept the commands and suggestions of the hypnotist. |
| Psychoanalytic theory | Psychoanalytic theory refers to the definition and dynamics of personality development which underlie and guide psychoanalytic and psychodynamic psychotherapy. First laid out by Sigmund Freud, psychoanalytic theory has undergone many refinements since his work . Psychoanalytic theory came to full prominence as a critical force in the last third of the twentieth century as part of 'the flow of critical discourse after the 1960's. |
| Suggestibility | Suggestibility is the quality of being inclined to accept and act on the suggestions of others.<br><br>A person experiencing intense emotions tends to be more receptive to ideas and therefore more suggestible. Generally, suggestibility decreases as age increases. |
| Ames room | An Ames room is a distorted room that is used to create an optical illusion. Probably influenced by the writings of Hermann Helmholtz, it was invented by American ophthalmologist Adelbert Ames, Jr. in 1934, and constructed in the following year. |
| Ponzo illusion | The Ponzo illusion is a geometrical-optical illusion that was first demonstrated by the Italian psychologist Mario Ponzo (1882-1960) in 1913. |

He suggested that the human mind judges an object's size based on its background. He showed this by drawing two identical lines across a pair of converging lines, similar to railway tracks. The upper line looks longer because we interpret the converging sides according to linear perspective as parallel lines receding into the distance.

| | |
|---|---|
| Amazing Kreskin | George Joseph Kresge, who had his name legally changed to The Amazing Kreskin, is a mentalist who became popular on North American television in the 1970s. He was inspired to become a mentalist by Lee Falk's famous comic strip Mandrake the Magician, which features a crime-fighting stage magician. |
| Highway hypnosis | Highway hypnosis, also popularly known as driving without attention mode (DWAM) or white line fever, is a mental state in which a person can drive a truck or automobile great distances, responding to external events in the expected manner with no recollection of having consciously done so. In this state the driver's conscious mind is apparently fully focused elsewhere, with seemingly direct processing of the masses of information needed to drive safely. Highway hypnosis is just one manifestation of a relatively commonplace experience, where the conscious and subconscious minds appear to concentrate on different things. |
| Meditation | Meditation is any form of a family of practices in which practitioners train their minds or self-induce a mode of consciousness to realize some benefit. |
| | Meditation is generally an inwardly oriented, personal practice, which individuals do by themselves. Prayer beads or other ritual objects are commonly used during meditation. |
| Transcendental Meditation | Transcendental Meditation refers to the Transcendental Meditation technique, a specific form of mantra meditation, and to the Transcendental Meditation movement, a spiritual movement. The Transcendental Meditation technique and Transcendental Meditation movement were introduced in India in the mid-1950s by Maharishi Mahesh Yogi (1914-2008) and had reached global proportions by the 1960s. |
| | The Transcendental Meditation technique came out of and is based on Indian philosophy and the teachings of Krishna, the Buddha, and Shankara, as well as the Yoga Sutras of Patanjali, and is a version of a technique passed down from the Maharishi's teacher, Brahmananda Saraswati (Guru Dev). |
| Cannon-Bard theory | The Cannon-Bard theory, is a theory of emotion developed by physiologists Walter Cannon and Philip Bard, suggesting that individuals experience emotions and physiologically react simultaneously. These actions include changes in muscular tension, perspiration, etc. This theory challenges the James-Lange theory of emotion introduced in the late 19th century, which suggests that emotion results from one's 'bodily change,' rather than the other way around. |

| Pethidine | Pethidine is a fast-acting opioid analgesic drug. In the United States and Canada, it is more commonly known as meperidine or by its brand name Demerol.

Pethidine was the first synthetic opioid synthesized in 1932 as a potential anti-spasmodic agent by the chemist Otto Eislib. Its analgesic properties were first recognized by Otto Schaumann working for IG Farben, Germany. |
|---|---|
| Codeine | Codeine, the other being the semi-synthetic 6-methylmorphine) is an opiate used for its analgesic, antitussive, and antidiarrheal properties. Codeine is the second-most predominant alkaloid in opium, at up to three percent; it is much more prevalent in the Iranian poppy (Papaver bractreatum), and codeine is extracted from this species in some places although the below-mentioned morphine methylation process is still much more common. It is considered the prototype of the weak to midrange opioids (tramadol, dextropropoxyphene, dihydrocodeine, hydrocodone). |
| Heroin | Heroin (diacetylmorphine or morphine diacetate (INN)), also known as diamorphine (BAN), is an opiate analgesic synthesized by C.R Alder Wright in 1874 by adding two acetyl groups to the molecule morphine, a derivative of the opium poppy. When used in medicine it is typically used to treat severe pain, such as that resulting from a heart attack. It is the 3,6-diacetyl ester of morphine, and functions as a morphine prodrug (meaning that it is metabolically converted to morphine inside the body in order for it to work). |
| Methadone | Methadone is a synthetic opioid, used medically as an analgesic and a maintenance anti-addictive for use in patients with opioid dependency. It was developed in Germany in 1937. Although chemically unlike morphine or heroin, methadone acts on the same opioid receptors as these drugs, and thus has many of the same effects. Methadone is also used in managing severe chronic pain, owing to its long duration of action, extremely powerful effects, and very low cost. |
| Morphine | Morphine ( ; MS Contin, MSIR, Avinza, Kadian, Oramorph, Roxanol, Kapanol) is a potent opiate analgesic drug that is used to relieve severe pain. It was first isolated in 1804 by Friedrich Sertürner, first distributed by him in 1817, and first commercially sold by Merck in 1827, which at the time was a single small chemists' shop. It was more widely used after the invention of the hypodermic needle in 1857. It took its name from the Greek god of dreams Morpheus . |
| Narcotic | The term narcotic originally referred medically to any psychoactive compound with sleep-inducing properties. In the United States of America it has since become associated with opioids, commonly morphine and heroin. The term is, today, imprecisely defined and typically has negative connotations. |
| Oxycodone | Oxycodone is an analgesic medication synthesized from poppy-derived thebaine. |

It was developed in 1916 in Germany, as one of several new semi-synthetic opioids in an attempt to improve on the existing opioids: morphine, diacetylmorphine (heroin), and codeine.

Oxycodone oral medications are generally prescribed for the relief of moderate to severe pain.

| | |
|---|---|
| Psychoactive drug | A psychoactive drug, psychopharmaceutical, or psychotropic is a chemical substance that crosses the blood-brain barrier and acts primarily upon the central nervous system where it affects brain function, resulting in changes in perception, mood, consciousness, cognition, and behavior. These substances may be used recreationally, to purposefully alter one's consciousness, as entheogens, for ritual, spiritual, and/or shamanic purposes, as a tool for studying or augmenting the mind, or therapeutically as medication.<br><br>Because psychoactive substances bring about subjective changes in consciousness and mood that the user may find pleasant (e.g. euphoria) or advantageous (e.g. increased alertness), many psychoactive substances are abused, that is, used excessively, despite the health risks or negative consequences. |
| Down syndrome | Down syndrome is a chromosomal condition caused by the presence of all or part of an extra 21st chromosome. It is named after John Langdon Down, the British physician who described the syndrome in 1866. The condition was identified as a chromosome 21 trisomy by Jérôme Lejeune in 1959. Down syndrome in a fetus can be identified with amniocentesis (with risks of fetal injury and/or miscarriage) during pregnancy, or in a baby at birth. |
| Amphetamine | Amphetamine or amfetamine (INN) is a psychostimulant drug of the phenethylamine class that produces increased wakefulness and focus in association with decreased fatigue and appetite.<br><br>Brand names of medications that contain, or metabolize into, amphetamine include Adderall, Dexedrine, Dextrostat, Desoxyn, ProCentra, and Vyvanse, as well as Benzedrine in the past.<br><br>The drug is also used recreationally and as a performance enhancer. |
| Barbiturate | Barbiturates are drugs that act as central nervous system depressants, and, by virtue of this, they produce a wide spectrum of effects, from mild sedation to total anesthesia. They are also effective as anxiolytics, as hypnotics, and as anticonvulsants. They have addiction potential, both physical and psychological. Barbiturates have now largely been replaced by benzodiazepines in routine medical practice - for example, in the treatment of anxiety and insomnia - mainly because benzodiazepines are significantly less dangerous in overdose. However, barbiturates are still used in general anesthesia, as well as for epilepsy. Barbiturates are derivatives of barbituric acid. |

| | |
|---|---|
| Cocaine | Cocaine benzoylmethylecgonine (INN) is a crystalline tropane alkaloid that is obtained from the leaves of the coca plant. The name comes from 'coca' in addition to the alkaloid suffix -ine, forming cocaine. It is a stimulant of the central nervous system, an appetite suppressant, and a topical anesthetic. Specifically, it is a serotonin-norepinephrine-dopamine reuptake inhibitor, which mediates functionality of these neurotransmitters as an exogenous catecholamine transporter ligand. Because of the way it affects the mesolimbic reward pathway, cocaine is addictive. |
| Crack cocaine | Crack cocaine is the freebase form of cocaine that can be smoked. It may also be termed rock, hard, iron, cavvy, base, or just crack.<br><br>Appearance and characteristics<br><br>In purer forms, crack rocks appear as off-white nuggets with jagged edges, with a slightly higher density than candle wax. |
| Hashish | Hashish, often known as 'hash', is a cannabis preparation composed of compressed and/or purified preparations of stalked resin glands, called trichomes, collected from the unfertilized buds of the cannabis plant. It contains the same active ingredients - such as THC and other cannabinoids - but in higher concentrations than unsifted buds or leaves. Hashish may be solid or resinous depending on the preparation; pressed hashish is usually solid, whereas water-purified hashish - often called 'bubble melt hash' - is often a paste-like substance with varying hardness and pliability, its color most commonly light to dark brown but varying toward green, yellow, black or red. |
| Mescaline | Mescaline is a naturally-occurring psychedelic alkaloid of the phenethylamine class used mainly as an entheogen.<br><br>It occurs naturally in the peyote cactus (Lophophora williamsii), the San Pedro cactus (Echinopsis pachanoi) and the Peruvian Torch cactus (Echinopsis peruviana), and in a number of other members of the Cactaceae plant family. It is also found in small amounts in certain members of the Fabaceae (bean) family, including Acacia berlandieri. |
| Methamphetamine | Methamphetamine ( ), also known as methamfetamine (INN), meth, N-methylamphetamine, methylamphetamine, and desoxyephedrine, is a psychostimulant of the phenethylamine and amphetamine class of psychoactive drugs.<br><br>Methamphetamine increases alertness, concentration, energy, and in high doses, can induce euphoria, enhance self-esteem and increase libido. |

# Chapter 5. Variations in Consciousness

| | |
|---|---|
| Psilocybin | Psilocybin is a prodrug for the classical hallucinogen compound psilocin, or 4-HO-DMT (4-hydroxyl-dimethyltryptamine), the active metabolite of psilocybin, responsible the psychoactive effects of the drug. Both drugs are members of the indole and tryptamine classes. Psilocybin-containing mushrooms are used both recreationally, and traditionally, for spiritual purposes, as entheogens, with a history of use spanning millennia. |
| Side effect | In medicine, a side effect is an effect, whether therapeutic or adverse, that is secondary to the one intended; although the term is predominantly employed to describe adverse effects, it can also apply to beneficial, but unintended, consequences of the use of a drug. |
| | Occasionally, drugs are prescribed or procedures performed specifically for their side effects; in that case, said side effect ceases to be a side effect, and is now an intended effect. For instance, X-rays were historically (and are currently) used as an imaging technique; the discovery of their oncolytic capability led to their employ in radiotherapy (ablation of malignant tumours. |
| Stimulant | Stimulants (also referred to as psychostimulants) are psychoactive drugs which induce temporary improvements in either mental or physical function or both. Examples of these kinds of effects may include enhanced alertness, wakefulness, and locomotion, among others. Due to their effects typically having an 'up' quality to them, stimulants are also occasionally referred to as 'uppers'. |
| MDMA | MDMA - colloquially known as ecstasy, often abbreviated 'E' or 'X' - is an entactogenic drug of the phenethylamine and amphetamine class of drugs. |
| | MDMA can induce euphoria, a sense of intimacy with others, and diminished anxiety and depression. Many, particularly in the fields of psychology and cognitive therapy, have suggested MDMA might have therapeutic benefits and facilitate therapy sessions in certain individuals, a practice which it had formally been used for in the past. |
| Subjectivity | Subjectivity refers to the subject and his or her perspective, feelings, beliefs, and desires. In philosophy, the term is usually contrasted with objectivity. |
| | Subjectivity may refer to the specific discerning interpretations of any aspect of experiences. |
| Norepinephrine | Norepinephrine is a catecholamine with multiple roles including as a hormone and a neurotransmitter. |
| | As a stress hormone, norepinephrine affects parts of the brain, such as the amygdala, where attention and responses are controlled. Along with epinephrine, norepinephrine also underlies the fight-or-flight response, directly increasing heart rate, triggering the release of glucose from energy stores, and increasing blood flow to skeletal muscle. |

|  |  |
|---|---|
|  | It increases the brain's oxygen supply. Norepinephrine can also suppress neuroinflammation when released diffusely in the brain from the locus ceruleus. |
| Psychological dependence | In the APA Dictionary of Psychology, psychological dependence is defined as 'dependence on a psychoactive substance for the reinforcement it provides.' Most times psychological dependence is classified under addiction. They are similar in that addiction is a physiological 'craving' for something and psychological dependence is a 'need' for a particular substance because it causes enjoyable mental affects.<br><br>A person becomes dependent on something to help alleviate specific emotions. |
| Reuptake | Reuptake, is the reabsorption of a neurotransmitter by a neurotransmitter transporter of a pre-synaptic neuron after it has performed its function of transmitting a neural impulse.<br><br>Reuptake is necessary for normal synaptic physiology because it allows for the recycling of neurotransmitters and regulates the level of neurotransmitter present in the synapse and controls how long a signal resulting from neurotransmitter release lasts. Because neurotransmitters are too large and hydrophilic to diffuse through the membrane, specific transport proteins are necessary for the reabsorption of neurotransmitters. |
| Serotonin | Serotonin is a monoamine neurotransmitter. Biochemically derived from tryptophan, serotonin is primarily found in the gastrointestinal (GI) tract, platelets, and in the central nervous system (CNS) of animals including humans. It is a well-known contributor to feelings of well-being; therefore it is also known as a 'happiness hormone' despite not being a hormone. |
| Health effect | Health effects are changes in health resulting from exposure to a source. Health effects are an important consideration in many areas, such as hygiene, pollution studies, workplace safety, nutrition and health sciences in general. Some of the major environmental sources of health effects are air pollution, water pollution, soil contamination, noise pollution and over-illumination. |
| Medial forebrain bundle | The Medial forebrain bundle is a complex bundle of axons coming from the basal olfactory regions, the periamygdaloid region, and the septal nuclei.<br><br>Anatomy<br><br>It passes to the lateral hypothalamus, with some carrying on into the tegmentum. It contains both ascending and descending fibers. |
| Nucleus accumbens | The nucleus accumbens also known as the accumbens nucleus or as the nucleus accumbens septi, is a collection of neurons and forms the main part of the ventral striatum. |

# Chapter 5. Variations in Consciousness

|  | It is thought to play an important role in reward, pleasure, laughter, addiction, aggression, fear, and the placebo effect. |
|---|---|
|  | Each half of the brain has one nucleus accumbens. |
| Pleasure center | Pleasure center is the general term used for the brain regions involved in pleasure. Discoveries made in the 1950s initially suggested that rodents could not stop electrically stimulating parts of their brain, mainly the nucleus accumbens, which was theorized to produce great pleasure. Further investigations revealed that the septum pellucidium and the hypothalamus can also be targets for self-stimulation. |
| Prefrontal cortex | The prefrontal cortex. is the anterior part of the frontal lobes of the brain, lying in front of the motor and premotor areas. |
|  | This brain region has been implicated in planning complex cognitive behavior, personality expression, decision making and moderating social behavior. |
| Testosterone | Testosterone is a steroid hormone from the androgen group and is found in mammals, reptiles, birds, and other vertebrates. In mammals, testosterone is primarily secreted in the testes of males and the ovaries of females, although small amounts are also secreted by the adrenal glands. It is the principal male sex hormone and an anabolic steroid. |
| Autogenic training | Autogenic training is a relaxation technique developed by the German psychiatrist Johannes Heinrich Schultz and first published in 1932. The technique involves the daily practice of sessions that last around 15 minutes, usually in the morning, at lunch time, and in the evening. During each session, the practitioner will repeat a set of visualisations that induce a state of relaxation. Each session can be practiced in a position chosen amongst a set of recommended postures (for example, lying down, sitting meditation, sitting like a rag doll). |
| Systematics | Biological systematics is the study of the diversification of life on the planet Earth, both past and present, and the relationships among living things through time. Relationships are visualized as evolutionary trees . Phylogenies have two components, branching order (showing group relationships) and branch length (showing amount of evolution). |
| Lucid dream | A lucid dream, in simplest terms, is a dream in which one is aware that one is dreaming. The term was coined by the Dutch psychiatrist and writer Frederik van Eeden (1860-1932). |
|  | A lucid dream can begin in one of two ways. |
| Circular reasoning | Circular reasoning is a formal logical fallacy in which the proposition to be proved is assumed implicitly or explicitly in one of the premises. For example: |

'Only an untrustworthy person would run for office. The fact that politicians are untrustworthy is proof of this.'

Such an argument is fallacious, because it relies upon its own proposition -- 'politicians are untrustworthy' -- in order to support its central premise.

1. _____ is the freebase form of cocaine that can be smoked. It may also be termed rock, hard, iron, cavvy, base, or just crack.

Appearance and characteristics

In purer forms, crack rocks appear as off-white nuggets with jagged edges, with a slightly higher density than candle wax.

a. Crack epidemic
b. Paolo Mantegazza
c. Prenatal cocaine exposure
d. Crack cocaine

2. _____ or amfetamine (INN) is a psychostimulant drug of the phenethylamine class that produces increased wakefulness and focus in association with decreased fatigue and appetite.

Brand names of medications that contain, or metabolize into, _____ include Adderall, Dexedrine, Dextrostat, Desoxyn, ProCentra, and Vyvanse, as well as Benzedrine in the past.

The drug is also used recreationally and as a performance enhancer.

a. Amphetamine
b. Armodafinil
c. Atromentin
d. ECA stack

3. . _____ is any form of a family of practices in which practitioners train their minds or self-induce a mode of consciousness to realize some benefit.

_____ is generally an inwardly oriented, personal practice, which individuals do by themselves. Prayer beads or other ritual objects are commonly used during _____.

    a. Meditation
    b. Metamorphic Technique
    c. Feldenkrais Method
    d. Min Zin

4. _____ is a relaxation technique developed by the German psychiatrist Johannes Heinrich Schultz and first published in 1932. The technique involves the daily practice of sessions that last around 15 minutes, usually in the morning, at lunch time, and in the evening. During each session, the practitioner will repeat a set of visualisations that induce a state of relaxation. Each session can be practiced in a position chosen amongst a set of recommended postures (for example, lying down, sitting meditation, sitting like a rag doll).

    a. Autosuggestion
    b. Eidetic Imagery
    c. Embodied imagination
    d. Autogenic training

5. _____ is a monoamine neurotransmitter. Biochemically derived from tryptophan, _____ is primarily found in the gastrointestinal (GI) tract, platelets, and in the central nervous system (CNS) of animals including humans. It is a well-known contributor to feelings of well-being; therefore it is also known as a 'happiness hormone' despite not being a hormone.

    a. Serotonin
    b. Trace amine
    c. Vasopressin
    d. 2-Arachidonoylglycerol

**1.** d

**2.** a

**3.** a

**4.** d

**5.** a

*You can take the complete Chapter Practice Test*

**for Chapter 5. Variations in Consciousness**
on all key terms, persons, places, and concepts.

*Online 99 Cents*

*http://www.epub3.2.20111.5.cram101.com/*

**Use www.Cram101.com for all your study needs**

**including Cram101's online interactive problem solving labs in**

**chemistry, statistics, mathematics, and more.**

CHAPTER OUTLINE: KEY TERMS, PEOPLE, PLACES, CONCEPTS

_____ Superstition

_____ Classical conditioning

_____ Phobia

_____ Cannon-Bard theory

_____ Electroconvulsive therapy

_____ Antibody

_____ Evaluative conditioning

_____ Generalization

_____ Gamma-Aminobutyric acid

_____ Panic disorder

_____ Discrimination

_____ Operant conditioning

_____ Reinforcement

_____ Response rate

_____ Secondary reference

_____ Animal mind

_____ Resistance

_____ Stimulus control

_____ Avoidance learning

| | Corporal punishment |
|---|---|
| | Spanking |
| | Biological constraints |
| | Taste aversion |
| | Latent learning |
| | Cognitive map |
| | Observational learning |
| | Role model |
| | Desensitization |
| | Case study |
| | Learning |
| | Behavior modification |
| | James-Lange theory |
| | Poggendorff illusion |
| | Politics |
| | Propaganda |

| Superstition | Superstition is a belief in supernatural causality: that one event leads to the cause of another without any process in the physical world linking the two events.

Opposition to superstition was a central concern of the intellectuals during the 18th century Age of Enlightenment. The philosophes at that time ridiculed any belief in miracles, revelation, magic, or the supernatural, as 'superstition,' and typically included as well much of Christian doctrine. |
| --- | --- |
| Classical conditioning | Introduction

Classical conditioning is a form of learning in which one stimulus comes to signal the occurrence of a second stimulus. This is often brought about by pairing the two stimuli, as in Pavlov's classic experiments. Pavlov presented dogs with a ringing bell followed by food. |
| Phobia | A phobia is defined as a persistent fear of an object or situation in which the sufferer commits to great lengths in avoiding despite the fear, typically disproportional to the actual danger posed, often being recognized as irrational. In the event the phobia cannot be avoided entirely, the sufferer will endure the situation or object with marked distress and significant interference in social or occupational activities. The terms distress and impairment as defined by the Diagnostic and Statistical Manual of Mental Disorders, Fourth Edition (DSM-IV-TR) should also take into account the context of the sufferer's environment if attempting a diagnosis. |
| Cannon-Bard theory | The Cannon-Bard theory, is a theory of emotion developed by physiologists Walter Cannon and Philip Bard, suggesting that individuals experience emotions and physiologically react simultaneously. These actions include changes in muscular tension, perspiration, etc. This theory challenges the James-Lange theory of emotion introduced in the late 19th century, which suggests that emotion results from one's 'bodily change,' rather than the other way around. |
| Electroconvulsive therapy | Electroconvulsive therapy formerly known as electroshock, is a psychiatric treatment in which seizures are electrically induced in anesthetized patients for therapeutic effect. Its mode of action is unknown. Today, ECT is most often recommended for use as a treatment for severe depression that has not responded to other treatment, and is also used in the treatment of mania and catatonia. |
| Antibody | An antibody is a large Y-shaped protein used by the immune system to identify and neutralize foreign objects like bacteria and viruses. The antibody recognizes a unique part of the foreign target, termed an antigen. Each tip of the 'Y' of an antibody contains a paratope (a structure analogous to a lock) that is specific for one particular epitope (that is equivelent to a key) on an antigen, allowing these two structures to bind together with precision. |

# Chapter 6. Learning

Using this binding mechanism, an antibody can tag a microbe or an infected cell for attack by other parts of the immune system, or can neutralize its target directly (for example, by blocking a part of a microbe that is essential for its invasion and survival). The production of antibodies is the main function of the humoral immune system.

| | |
|---|---|
| Evaluative conditioning | Evaluative conditioning concerns how we can come to like or dislike something through an association (association of ideas).<br><br>If something that we have no strong feelings towards (such as an unfamiliar person, object, or picture, and so on) appears to us with something that we strongly dislike (such as a very unpleasant odour) then our feelings to that once innocuous item can change--we can come to dislike that thing too. The same can happen when something is paired with something else that we strongly like--we can come to like that item more. |
| Generalization | A generalization of a concept is an extension of the concept to less-specific criteria. It is a foundational element of logic and human reasoning. Generalizations posit the existence of a domain or set of elements, as well as one or more common characteristics shared by those elements. |
| Gamma-Aminobutyric acid | γ-Aminobutyric acid is the chief inhibitory neurotransmitter in the mammalian central nervous system. It plays a role in regulating neuronal excitability throughout the nervous system. In humans, GABA is also directly responsible for the regulation of muscle tone.<br><br>Although chemically it is an amino acid, GABA is rarely referred to as such in the scientific or medical communities, because the term 'amino acid,' used without a qualifier, conventionally refers to the alpha amino acids, which GABA is not, nor is it ever incorporated into a protein.<br><br>In spastic diplegia in humans, GABA absorption becomes impaired by nerves damaged from the condition's upper motor neuron lesion, which leads to hypertonia of the muscles signaled by those nerves that can no longer absorb GABA.Function Neurotransmitter<br><br>In vertebrates, GABA acts at inhibitory synapses in the brain by binding to specific transmembrane receptors in the plasma membrane of both pre- and postsynaptic neuronal processes. This binding causes the opening of ion channels to allow the flow of either negatively charged chloride ions into the cell or positively charged potassium ions out of the cell. Depending on which ion channels open, the membrane potential is either hyperpolarized or depolarized. This action results in a negative change in the transmembrane potential, usually causing hyperpolarization. Two general classes of GABA receptor are known: $GABA_A$ in which the receptor is part of a ligand-gated ion channel complex, and $GABA_B$ metabotropic receptors, which are G protein-coupled receptors that open or close ion channels via intermediaries (G proteins). |

Neurons that produce GABA as their output are called GABAergic neurons, and have chiefly inhibitory action at receptors in the adult vertebrate. Medium Spiny Cells are a typical example of inhibitory CNS GABAergic cells. In contrast, GABA exhibits both excitatory and inhibitory actions in insects, mediating muscle activation at synapses between nerves and muscle cells, and also the stimulation of certain glands. In mammals, some GABAergic neurons, such as chandelier cells, are also able to excite their glutamatergic counterparts.

$GABA_A$ receptors are ligand-activated chloride channels; that is, when activated by GABA, they allow the flow of chloride ions across the membrane of the cell. Whether this chloride flow is excitatory/depolarizing (makes the voltage across the cell's membrane less negative), shunting (has no effect on the cell's membrane) or inhibitory/hyperpolarizing (makes the cell's membrane more negative) depends on the direction of the flow of chloride. When net chloride flows out of the cell, GABA is excitatory or depolarizing; when the net chloride flows into the cell, GABA is inhibitory or hyperpolarizing. When the net flow of chloride is close to zero, the action of GABA is shunting. Shunting inhibition has no direct effect on the membrane potential of the cell; however, it minimises the effect of any coincident synaptic input essentially by reducing the electrical resistance of the cell's membrane (in essence, equivalent to Ohm's law). A developmental switch in the molecular machinery controlling concentration of chloride inside the cell - and, hence, the direction of this ion flow - is responsible for the changes in the functional role of GABA between the neonatal and adult stages. That is to say, GABA's role changes from excitatory to inhibitory as the brain develops into adulthood. Brain development

For the past two decades, the theory of excitatory action of GABA early in development was unquestioned based on experiments in vitro, on brain slices. The main observation was that in the hippocampus and neocortex of the mammalian brain, GABA has primarily excitatory effects, and is in fact the major excitatory neurotransmitter in many regions of the brain before the maturation of glutamateergic synapses.

However, this theory has been questioned based on results showing that in brain slices of immature mice incubated in artificial cerebrospinal fluid (ACSF) (modified in a way that takes into account the normal composition of the neuronal milieu in sucklings by adding an energy substrate alternative to glucose, beta-hydroxybutyrate) GABA action shifts from excitatory to inhibitory mode. This effect has been later repeated when other energy substrates, pyruvate and lactate, supplemented glucose in the slices' media. The effects of beta-hydroxybutyrate were later confirmed for pyruvate and for lactate. However it was argued that the concentrations of the alternative energy substrates used in these experiments were non-physiological and the GABA-shift was instead caused by changes in pH resulting from the substrates acting as 'weak acids'.

# Chapter 6. Learning

These arguments were later rebutted by further findings showing that changes in pH even greater than that caused by energy substrates do not affect the GABA-shift described in the presence of energy substrate-fortified ACSF and that the mode of action of beta-hydroxybutyrate, pyruvate and lactate (assessed by measurement NAD(P)H and oxygen utilization) was energy metabolism-related.

In the developmental stages preceding the formation of synaptic contacts, GABA is synthesized by neurons and acts both as an autocrine (acting on the same cell) and paracrine (acting on nearby cells) signalling mediator.

GABA regulates the proliferation of neural progenitor cells the migration and differentiation the elongation of neurites and the formation of synapses.

GABA also regulates the growth of embryonic and neural stem cells. GABA can in?uence the development of neural progenitor cells via brain-derived neurotrophic factor (BDNF) expression. GABA activates the $GABA_A$ receptor, causing cell cycle arrest in the S-phase, limiting growth. Beyond the nervous system

GABAergic mechanisms have been demonstrated in various peripheral tissues and organs including, but not restricted to the intestine, stomach, pancreas, Fallopian tube, uterus, ovary, testis, kidney, urinary bladder, lung, and liver.

In 2007, an excitatory GABAergic system was described in the airway epithelium. The system activates following exposure to allergens and may participate in the mechanisms of asthma. GABAergic systems have also been found in the testis and in the eye lens. Structure and conformation

GABA is found mostly as a zwitterion, that is, with the carboxy group deprotonated and the amino group protonated. Its conformation depends on its environment. In the gas phase, a highly folded conformation is strongly favored because of the electrostatic attraction between the two functional groups. The stabilization is about 50 kcal/mol, according to quantum chemistry calculations. In the solid state, a more extended conformation is found, with a trans conformation at the amino end and a gauche conformation at the carboxyl end. This is due to the packing interactions with the neighboring molecules. In solution, five different conformations, some folded and some extended, are found as a result of solvation effects. The conformational flexibility of GABA is important for its biological function, as it has been found to bind to different receptors with different conformations. Many GABA analogues with pharmaceutical applications have more rigid structures in order to control the binding better. History

| | |
|---|---|
| Panic disorder | Panic disorder is an anxiety disorder characterized by recurring severe panic attacks. It may also include significant behavioral changes lasting at least a month and of ongoing worry about the implications or concern about having other attacks. The latter are called anticipatory attacks (DSM-IVR). |
| Discrimination | Discrimination is the cognitive and sensory capacity or ability to see fine distinctions and perceive differences between objects, subjects, concepts and patterns, or possess exceptional development of the senses. Used in this way to identify exceptional discernment since the 17th century, the term began to be used as an expression of derogatory racial prejudice in the 1830s from Thomas D. Rice's performances as 'Jim Crow'. |
| Operant conditioning | Operant conditioning is the use of a behavior's antecedent and/or its consequence to influence the occurrence and form of behavior. Operant conditioning is distinguished from classical conditioning (also called respondent conditioning) in that operant conditioning deals with the modification of 'voluntary behavior' or operant behavior. Operant behavior 'operates' on the environment and is maintained by its consequences, while classical conditioning deals with the conditioning of reflexive (reflex) behaviors which are elicited by antecedent conditions. |
| Reinforcement | Reinforcement is a term in operant conditioning and behavior analysis for a process of strengthening a directly measurable dimension of behavior--such as rate (e.g., pulling a lever more frequently), duration (e.g., pulling a lever for longer periods of time), magnitude (e.g., pulling a lever with greater force), or latency (e.g., pulling a lever more quickly following the onset of an environmental event)--as a function of the delivery of a 'valued' stimulus (e.g. money from a slot machine) immediately or shortly after the occurrence of the behavior.<br><br>A reinforcer is a temporally contiguous environmental event, or an effect directly produced by a response (e.g., a musician playing a melody), that functions to strengthen or maintain the response that preceded the event. A reinforcer is demonstrated only if the strengthening or maintenance effect occurs. |
| Response rate | Response rate in survey research refers to the number of people who answered the survey divided by the number of people in the sample. It is usually expressed in the form of a percentage.<br><br>Example: if 1,000 surveys were sent by mail, and 257 were successfully completed and returned, then the response rate would be 25.7%. |
| Secondary reference | Secondary reference points to the representation as a necessary part in granting a meaning to a (part of a) sentence. In this approach, words that don't contribute to the representation are void; they can only provide a figurative expression. |

# Chapter 6. Learning

| | |
|---|---|
| Animal mind | The question of animal minds asks whether it is meaningful to describe a non-human animal as having a mind. |
| | Discussion of this subject is frequently confused by the fact that some schools of philosophy and psychology (e.g. radical behaviorism) would question whether one should ascribe mind to anyone else (or even to oneself). Such an approach would naturally deny the existence of animal minds. |
| Resistance | 'Resistance' as initially used by Sigmund Freud, referred to patients blocking memories from conscious memory. This was a key concept, since the primary treatment method of Freud's talk therapy required making these memories available to the patient's consciousness. |
| | 'Resistance' expanded |
| | Later, Freud described five different forms of resistance. |
| Stimulus control | Stimulus control is said to occur when an organism behaves in one way in the presence of a given stimulus and another way in its absence. For example, the presence of a stop sign increases the probability that 'braking' behavior will occur. Typically such behavior is brought about by reinforcing the behavior in the presence of one stimulus and omitting reinforcement in the presence of another stimulus. |
| Avoidance learning | Avoidance learning is a type of learning in which a certain behavior results in the cessation of an aversive stimulus. For example, performing the behavior of shielding one's eyes when in the sunlight (or going indoors) will help avoid the aversive stimulation of having light in one's eyes. |
| Corporal punishment | Corporal punishment is a kind of physical punishment that involves the deliberate infliction of pain as retribution for an offence, or for the purpose of disciplining or reforming a wrongdoer, or to deter attitudes or behaviour deemed unacceptable. The term usually refers to methodically striking the offender with an implement, whether in judicial, domestic, or educational settings. |
| | Corporal punishment may be divided into three main types:•parental or domestic corporal punishment: within the family--typically, children punished by parents or guardians;•school corporal punishment: within schools, when students are punished by teachers or school administrators;•judicial corporal punishment: as part of a criminal sentence ordered by a court of law. |
| Spanking | Spanking is a form of corporal punishment commonly used to discipline a toddler, child, or teenager. It generally involves an adult- typically a parent, guardian, or teacher--striking the offender's buttocks as a response to poor behavior, with either an open hand or an implement, to cause temporary pain without producing physical injury. |

| | |
|---|---|
| Biological constraints | Biological constraints are factors which make populations resistant to evolutionary change. Constraint has played an important role in the development of such ideas as homology and body plans. |
| | Any aspect of an organism that has not changed over a certain period of time could be considered to provide evidence for 'constraint' of some sort. |
| Taste aversion | Conditioned taste aversion, also known as Garcia effect (after Dr. John Garcia), and as 'Sauce-Bearnaise Syndrome', a term coined by Seligman and Hager, is an example of classical conditioning or Pavlovian conditioning. Conditioned taste aversion occurs when a subject associates the taste of a certain food with symptoms caused by a toxic, spoiled, or poisonous substance. Generally, taste aversion is caused after ingestion of the food causes nausea, sickness, or vomiting. |
| Latent learning | Latent learning is a form of learning that is not immediately expressed in an overt response; it occurs without obvious reinforcement to be applied later. |
| | Latent learning is when an organism learns a new concept in its life, however, the knowledge is not immediately expressed. Instead, it remains dormant, and may not be available to consciousness, until specific events/experiences might need this knowledge to be demonstrated. |
| Cognitive map | Cognitive maps (also known as mental maps, mind maps, cognitive models, or mental models) are a type of mental processing composed of a series of psychological transformations by which an individual can acquire, code, store, recall, and decode information about the relative locations and attributes of phenomena in their everyday or metaphorical spatial environment. |
| | The credit for the creation of this term is given to Edward Tolman. Cognitive maps have been studied in various fields, such as psychology, education, archaeology, planning, geography, cartography, architecture, landscape architecture, urban planning, management and conspiracy theories. |
| Observational learning | Observational learning is a type of learning that occurs as a function of observing, retaining and replicating novel behavior executed by others. It is argued that reinforcement has the effect of influencing which responses one will partake in, more than it influences the actual acquisition of the new response. |
| | Although observational learning can take place at any stage in life, it is thought to be of greater importance during childhood, particularly as authority becomes important. |

# Chapter 6. Learning

| | |
|---|---|
| Role model | The term role model generally means any 'person who serves as an example, whose behavior is emulated by others'.<br><br>The term first appeared in Robert K. Merton's socialization research of medical students. Merton hypothesized that individuals compare themselves with reference groups of people who occupy the social role to which the individual aspires. |
| Desensitization | In psychology, desensitization (also called inurement) is defined as the diminished emotional responsiveness to a negative or aversive stimulus after repeated exposure to it. It also occurs when an emotional response is repeatedly evoked in situations in which the action tendency that is associated with the emotion proves irrelevant or unnecessary. Desensitization is a process primarily used to assist individuals unlearn phobias and anxieties and was developed by psychologist Mary Cover Jones. |
| Case study | A case study is a research method common in social science. It is based on an in-depth investigation of a single individual, group, or event. Case studies may be descriptive or explanatory. |
| Learning | Learning is acquiring new or modifying existing knowledge, behaviors, skills, values, or preferences and may involve synthesizing different types of information. The ability to learn is possessed by humans, animals and some machines. Progress over time tends to follow learning curves. |
| Behavior modification | Behavior modification is the use of empirically demonstrated behavior change techniques to increase or decrease the frequency of behaviors, such as altering an individual's behaviors and reactions to stimuli through positive and negative reinforcement of adaptive behavior and/or the reduction of behavior through its extinction, punishment and/or satiation. Most behavior modification programs currently used are those based on Applied behavior analysis (ABA), formerly known as the experimental analysis of behavior which was pioneered by B. F. Skinner. |
| James-Lange theory | The James-Lange theory refers to a hypothesis on the origin and nature of emotions and is one of the earliest theories of emotion, developed independently by two 19th-century scholars, William James and Carl Lange.<br><br>The theory states that within human beings, as a response to experiences in the world, the autonomic nervous system creates physiological events such as muscular tension, a rise in heart rate, perspiration, and dryness of the mouth. Emotions, then, are feelings which come about as a result of these physiological changes, rather than being their cause. James and Lange arrived at the theory independently. Lange specifically stated that vasomotor changes are emotions. |

| Poggendorff illusion | The Poggendorff Illusion is a geometrical-optical illusion that involves the misperception of the position of one segment of a transverse line that has been interrupted by the contour of an intervening structure (here a rectangle). It is named after Poggendorff, the editor of the journal, who discovered it in the figures Johann Karl Friedrich Zöllner submitted when first reporting on what is now known as the Zöllner illusion, in 1860.

In the picture to the right, a straight black and red line is obscured by a grey rectangle. |
| --- | --- |
| Politics | Politics as a term is generally applied to the art or science of running governmental or state affairs, including behavior within civil governments, but also applies to institutions, fields, and special interest groups such as the corporate, academic, and religious segments of society. It consists of 'social relations involving authority or power' and to the methods and tactics used to formulate and apply policy.

Modern political discourse focuses on democracy and the relationship between people and politics. |
| Propaganda | Propaganda is a form of communication that is aimed at influencing the attitude of a community toward some cause or position. Propaganda is usually repeated and dispersed over a wide variety of media in order to create the desired result in audience attitudes.

As opposed to impartially providing information, propaganda, in its most basic sense, presents information primarily to influence an audience. |

# Chapter 6. Learning

1. _____ is the cognitive and sensory capacity or ability to see fine distinctions and perceive differences between objects, subjects, concepts and patterns, or possess exceptional development of the senses. Used in this way to identify exceptional discernment since the 17th century, the term began to be used as an expression of derogatory racial prejudice in the 1830s from Thomas D. Rice's performances as 'Jim Crow'.

   a. Benevolent prejudice
   b. Discrimination
   c. Communion and the developmentally disabled
   d. Dalit

2. A _____ is defined as a persistent fear of an object or situation in which the sufferer commits to great lengths in avoiding despite the fear, typically disproportional to the actual danger posed, often being recognized as irrational. In the event the _____ cannot be avoided entirely, the sufferer will endure the situation or object with marked distress and significant interference in social or occupational activities. The terms distress and impairment as defined by the Diagnostic and Statistical Manual of Mental Disorders, Fourth Edition (DSM-IV-TR) should also take into account the context of the sufferer's environment if attempting a diagnosis.

   a. clerk
   b. Phobia
   c. Thorax
   d. Chromium

3. _____s (also known as mental maps, mind maps, cognitive models, or mental models) are a type of mental processing composed of a series of psychological transformations by which an individual can acquire, code, store, recall, and decode information about the relative locations and attributes of phenomena in their everyday or metaphorical spatial environment.

   The credit for the creation of this term is given to Edward Tolman. _____s have been studied in various fields, such as psychology, education, archaeology, planning, geography, cartography, architecture, landscape architecture, urban planning, management and conspiracy theories.

   a. Four Fs
   b. Linkword
   c. Memory sport
   d. Cognitive map

4. . _____ is a form of communication that is aimed at influencing the attitude of a community toward some cause or position. _____ is usually repeated and dispersed over a wide variety of media in order to create the desired result in audience attitudes.

   As opposed to impartially providing information, _____, in its most basic sense, presents information primarily to influence an audience.

   a. Green children of Woolpit
   b. Crypto-politics

c. Youth politics

d. Propaganda

5. _____ are factors which make populations resistant to evolutionary change. Constraint has played an important role in the development of such ideas as homology and body plans.

Any aspect of an organism that has not changed over a certain period of time could be considered to provide evidence for 'constraint' of some sort.

a. Chemosynthesis

b. Megamonas

c. Biological constraints

d. Pharmacometabolomics

**1.** b
**2.** b
**3.** d
**4.** d
**5.** c

*You can take the complete Chapter Practice Test*

**for Chapter 6. Learning**
on all key terms, persons, places, and concepts.

**Online 99 Cents**

*http://www.epub3.2.20111.6.cram101.com/*

Use www.Cram101.com for all your study needs

including Cram101's online interactive problem solving labs in

chemistry, statistics, mathematics, and more.

# Chapter 7. Human Memory

Information processing

Cognitive load

Functional selectivity

Dual-coding theory

Aristotle

Afterimage

Long-term memory

Sensory memory

Short-term memory

Working memory

Temporal lobe

Clustering

Semantic network

Spreading activation

Personality Assessment Inventory

Misinformation effect

Source-monitoring error

Nonsense syllable

Encoding specificity principle

CHAPTER OUTLINE: KEY TERMS, PEOPLE, PLACES, CONCEPTS

Motivated forgetting

Transfer-appropriate processing

Child abuse

False memory syndrome

Sexual abuse

Deese-Roediger-McDermott paradigm

Neurogenesis

Hypnosis

Ames room

Amygdala

Anterograde amnesia

Cerebellum

Dentate gyrus

Long-term potentiation

Prefrontal cortex

Retrograde amnesia

Memory loss

Declarative memory

Procedural memory

Area studies

Episodic memory

Prospective memory

Retrospective memory

Semantic memory

Subjectivity

Learning power

Method of loci

Mnemonic

Overlearning

Testing effect

Memorization

Hindsight bias

| | |
|---|---|
| Information processing | Within the field of cognitive psychology, information processing is an approach to the goal of understanding human thinking. It arose in the 1940s and 1950s. The essence of the approach is to see cognition as being essentially computational in nature, with mind being the software and the brain being the hardware. The information processing approach in psychology is closely allied to the Computational theory of mind in philosophy ; it is also related, though not identical, to cognitivism in psychology and functionalism in philosophy. |
| Cognitive load | The term cognitive load is used in cognitive psychology to illustrate the load related to the executive control of working memory (WM). Theories contend that during complex learning activities the amount of information and interactions that must be processed simultaneously can either under-load, or overload the finite amount of working memory one possesses. All elements must be processed before meaningful learning can continue. |
| Functional selectivity | Functional selectivity is the ligand-dependent selectivity for certain signal transduction pathways in one and the same receptor. This can be present when a receptor has several possible signal transduction pathways. To which degree each pathway is activated thus depends on which ligand binds to the receptor . |
| Dual-coding theory | Dual-coding theory, a theory of cognition, was hypothesized by Allan Paivio of the University of Western Ontario in 1971. Paivio used the idea that the formation of mental images aids in learning when developing this theory (Reed, 2010). According to Paivio, there are two ways a person could expand on learned material: verbal associations and visual imagery. Dual-coding theory postulates that both visual and verbal information is used to represent information (Sternberg, 2003). |
| Aristotle | Aristotle was a Greek philosopher, a student of Plato and teacher of Alexander the Great. His writings cover many subjects, including physics, metaphysics, poetry, theater, music, logic, rhetoric, linguistics, politics, government, ethics, biology, and zoology. Together with Plato and Socrates (Plato's teacher), Aristotle is one of the most important founding figures in Western philosophy. |
| Afterimage | An afterimage is an optical illusion that refers to an image continuing to appear in one's vision after the exposure to the original image has ceased. One of the most common afterimages is the bright glow that seems to float before one's eyes after looking into a light source for a few seconds. Closing the eye can help achieve a better sense of the color in its own aspect. |
| Long-term memory | Long-term memory is memory in which associations among items are stored, as part of the theory of a dual-store memory model. |

# Chapter 7. Human Memory

According to the theory, long-term memory differs structurally and functionally from working memory or short-term memory, which ostensibly stores items for only around 20-30 seconds and can be recalled easily. This differs from the theory of the single-store retrieved context model that has no differentiation between short-term and long-term memory.

**Sensory memory**

During every moment of an organism's life, sensory information is being taken in by sensory receptors and processed by the nervous system. Humans have five main senses: sight, hearing, taste, smell, touch. Sensory memory allows individuals to retain impressions of sensory information after the original stimulus has ceased.

**Short-term memory**

Short-term memory is the capacity for holding a small amount of information in mind in an active, readily available state for a short period of time. The duration of short-term memory is believed to be in the order of seconds. A commonly-cited capacity is 7 ± 2 elements. In contrast, long-term memory indefinitely stores a seemingly unlimited amount of information.

**Working memory**

Working memory has been defined as the system which actively holds information in the mind to do verbal and nonverbal tasks such as reasoning and comprehension, and to make it available for further information processing. Working memory tasks are those that require the goal-oriented active monitoring or manipulation of information or behaviors in the face of interfering processes and distractions. Working memory can only retain a limited amount of information; however, its capacity can be increased by use of a method known as chunking.

**Temporal lobe**

The temporal lobe is a region of the cerebral cortex that is located beneath the Sylvian fissure on both cerebral hemispheres of the mammalian brain.

The temporal lobe is involved in auditory perception and is home to the primary auditory cortex. It is also important for the processing of semantics in both speech and vision. The temporal lobe contains the hippocampus and plays a key role in the formation of long-term memory.

**Clustering**

In demographics, clustering is the gathering of various populations based on ethnicity, economics, or religion.

In countries that hold equality as important, clustering occurs between groups because of polarizing factors such as religion, wealth or ethnocentrism. Clustering is often considered an enriching part of free cultures in which one can visit a Chinatown or a French quarter for restaurant choices.

**Semantic network**

A semantic network, is a network which represents semantic relations between concepts. This is often used as a form of knowledge representation. It is a directed or undirected graph consisting of vertices, which represent concepts, and edges.

| | |
|---|---|
| Spreading activation | Spreading activation is a method for searching associative networks, neural networks, or semantic networks. The search process is initiated by labeling a set of source nodes (e.g. concepts in a semantic network) with weights or 'activation' and then iteratively propagating or 'spreading' that activation out to other nodes linked to the source nodes. Most often these 'weights' are real values that decay as activation propagates through the network. |
| Personality Assessment Inventory | Personality Assessment Inventory PhD, is a multi-scale test of psychological functioning that assesses constructs relevant to personality and psychopathology evaluation (e.g., depression, anxiety, aggression) in various contexts including psychotherapy, crisis/evaluation, forensic, personnel selection, pain/medical, and child custody assessment. The PAI has 22 non-overlapping scales, providing a comprehensive overview of psychopathology in adults. The PAI contains four kinds of scales: 1) validity scales, which measure the respondent's approach to the test, including faking good or bad, exaggeration, or defensiveness; 2) clinical scales, which correspond to psychiatric diagnostic categories; 3) treatment consideration scales, which assess factors that may relate to treatment of clinical disorders or other risk factors but which are not captured in psychiatric diagnoses (e.g., suicidal ideation); and 4) interpersonal scales, which provide indicators of interpersonal dimensions of personality functioning. |
| Misinformation effect | The misinformation effect refers to the finding that exposure to misleading information presented between the encoding of an event and its subsequent recall causes impairment in memory. This effect occurs when participants' recall of an event they witnessed is altered by introducing misleading postevent information. It is a prime example of retroactive interference, which occurs when information presented later interferes with the ability to retain previously encoded information. |
| Source-monitoring error | A source monitoring error is a type of memory error where a specific recollected experience is incorrectly determined to be the source of a memory. This error occurs when normal perceptual and reflective processes are disrupted, either by limited encoding of source information or by disruption to the judgement processes used in source-monitoring. Depression, high stress levels and damage to relevant brain areas are examples of factors that can cause such disruption and hence source-monitoring errors. |
| Nonsense syllable | In cognitive psychology, a nonsense syllable is a word-like string of letters that is not intended to have any established meaning; it is a special case of a non-lexical vocable. Nonsense syllables have been extensively used in experimental psychology, especially the psychology of learning and memory.<br><br>Nonsense syllables were first introduced by Hermann Ebbinghaus in his experiments on the learning of lists. |

# Chapter 7. Human Memory

| | |
|---|---|
| Encoding specificity principle | The encoding specificity principle provides a framework for understanding how contextual information affects memory and recall. The principle, proposed by researchers Thompson and Tulving, states that memory is most effective when information available at encoding is also present at retrieval. The principle explains why a subject is able to recall a target word as part of an unrelated word pair at retrieval with much more accuracy when prompted with the unrelated word than if presented with a semantically related word that was not available during encoding. |
| Motivated forgetting | Motivated forgetting is a debated concept referring to a psychological defence mechanism in which people forget unwanted memories, either consciously or unconsciously. There are times when memories are reminders of unpleasant experiences that make people angry, sad, anxious, ashamed or afraid. Motivated forgetting is a method in which people protect themselves by blocking the recall of these anxiety-arousing memories. |
| Transfer-appropriate processing | Transfer-appropriate processing is a type of state-dependent memory specifically showing that memory performance is not only determined by the depth of processing , but by the relationship between how information is initially encoded and how it is later retrieved. Memory will be best when the processes engaged in during encoding match those engaged in during retrieval.<br><br>An example of this is how when a sound is associated with a memory, recall is enhanced. |
| Child abuse | Child abuse is the physical, sexual, emotional mistreatment, or neglect of children. In the United States, the Centers for Disease Control and Prevention (CDC) define child maltreatment as any act or series of acts of commission or omission by a parent or other caregiver that results in harm, potential for harm, or threat of harm to a child. Most child abuse occurs in a child's home, with a smaller amount occurring in the organizations, schools or communities the child interacts with. |
| False memory syndrome | False memory syndrome describes a condition in which a person's identity and relationships are affected by memories which are factually incorrect but are strongly believed. Peter J. Freyd originated the term, which the False Memory Syndrome Foundation (FMSF) subsequently popularized.<br><br>False memories may be the result of recovered memory therapy, a term also defined by the FMSF in the early 1990s, which describes a range of therapy methods that are prone to creating confabulations. |
| Sexual abuse | Sexual abuse, also referred to as molestation, is the forcing of undesired sexual behavior by one person upon another. When that force is immediate, of short duration, or infrequent, it is called sexual assault. The offender is referred to as a sexual abuser or (often pejoratively) molester. |

| | |
|---|---|
| Deese-Roediger-McDermott paradigm | The Deese-Roediger-McDermott (DRM) paradigm in cognitive psychology is an example of false memory. James Deese, an American psychologist and professor, first studied this paradigm in 1959. The DRM Paradigm refers to the tendency to falsely recall a target word from a set list of words centered around that target word. Henry L. Roediger III and Kathleen McDermott have done further research in more recent years to both confirm this phenomenon and find that it even extends into falsely recalling events, hence the name, the Deese-Roediger-McDermott paradigm. |
| Neurogenesis | Neurogenesis is the process by which neurons are generated from neural stem and progenitor cells. Most active during pre-natal development, neurogenesis is responsible for populating the growing brain with neurons. Recently neurogenesis was shown to continue in several small parts of the brain of mammals: the hippocampus and the subventricular zone. |
| Hypnosis | Hypnosis is a mental state (according to 'state theory') or imaginative role-enactment (according to 'non-state theory'). It is usually induced by a procedure known as a hypnotic induction, which is commonly composed of a long series of preliminary instructions and suggestions. Hypnotic suggestions may be delivered by a hypnotist in the presence of the subject, or may be self-administered ('self-suggestion' or 'autosuggestion'). The use of hypnotism for therapeutic purposes is referred to as 'hypnotherapy', while its use as a form of entertainment for an audience is known as 'stage hypnosis'. |
| Ames room | An Ames room is a distorted room that is used to create an optical illusion. Probably influenced by the writings of Hermann Helmholtz, it was invented by American ophthalmologist Adelbert Ames, Jr. in 1934, and constructed in the following year. |
| Amygdala | The amygdalae are almond-shaped groups of nuclei located deep within the medial temporal lobes of the brain in complex vertebrates, including humans. Shown in research to perform a primary role in the processing and memory of emotional reactions, the amygdalae are considered part of the limbic system.<br><br>The regions described as amygdala nuclei encompass several structures with distinct functional traits. |
| Anterograde amnesia | Anterograde amnesia is a loss of the ability to create new memories after the event that caused the amnesia, leading to a partial or complete inability to recall the recent past, while long-term memories from before the event remain intact. This is in contrast to retrograde amnesia, where memories created prior to the event are lost. Both can occur together in the same patient. |
| Cerebellum | The cerebellum is a region of the brain that plays an important role in motor control. It is also involved in some cognitive functions such as attention and language, and probably in some emotional functions such as regulating fear and pleasure responses. |

# Chapter 7. Human Memory

| | |
|---|---|
| Dentate gyrus | The dentate gyrus is part of the hippocampal formation. It is thought to contribute to the formation of new memories, as well as possessing other functional roles. It is notable as being one of a select few brain structures currently known to have high rates of neurogenesis in adult rats (other sites include the olfactory bulb and cerebellum). |
| Long-term potentiation | In neuroscience, long-term potentiation is a long-lasting enhancement in signal transmission between two neurons that results from stimulating them synchronously. It is one of several phenomena underlying synaptic plasticity, the ability of chemical synapses to change their strength. As memories are thought to be encoded by modification of synaptic strength, LTP is widely considered one of the major cellular mechanisms that underlies learning and memory. |
| Prefrontal cortex | The prefrontal cortex. is the anterior part of the frontal lobes of the brain, lying in front of the motor and premotor areas. <br><br> This brain region has been implicated in planning complex cognitive behavior, personality expression, decision making and moderating social behavior. |
| Retrograde amnesia | Retrograde amnesia is a loss of access to events that occurred, or information that was learned, before an injury or the onset of a disease. RA is often temporally graded, consistent with Ribot's Law: more recent memories closer to the traumatic incident are more likely to be forgotten than more remote memories. <br><br> The most commonly affected areas are associated with episodic and declarative memory such as the hippocampus, the diencephalon, and the temporal lobes. |
| Memory loss | Memory loss can be partial or total and it is normal when it comes with aging. Sudden memory loss is usually a result of brain trauma and it may be permanent or temporary. When it is caused by medical conditions such as Alzheimer's disease, the memory loss is gradual and tends to be permanent. |
| Declarative memory | Declarative memory is one of two types of long term human memory. It refers to memories which can be consciously recalled such as facts and knowledge. Its counterpart is known as non-declarative or Procedural memory, which refers to unconscious memories such as skills (e.g. learning to ride a bicycle). |
| Procedural memory | Procedural memory is memory for how to do things. Procedural memory guides the processes we perform and most frequently resides below the level of conscious awareness. When needed, procedural memories are automatically retrieved and utilized for the execution of the integrated procedures involved in both cognitive and motor skills; from tying shoes to flying an airplane to reading. |

| Area studies | Area studies are interdisciplinary fields of research and scholarship pertaining to particular geographical, national/federal, or cultural regions. The term exists primarily as a general description for what are, in the practice of scholarship, many heterogeneous fields of research, encompassing both the social sciences and the humanities. Typical area studies programs involve history, political science, sociology, cultural studies, languages, geography, literature, and related disciplines. |
|---|---|
| Episodic memory | Episodic memory is the memory of autobiographical events (times, places, associated emotions, and other contextual knowledge) that can be explicitly stated. Semantic and episodic memory together make up the category of declarative memory, which is one of the two major divisions in memory. The counterpart to declarative, or explicit memory, is procedural memory, or implicit memory. |
| Prospective memory | Prospective memory is a form of memory that involves remembering to perform a planned action or intention at the appropriate time. Prospective memory tasks are highly prevalent in daily life and range from relatively simple tasks to extreme life-or-death situations. Examples of simple tasks include remembering to put the toothpaste cap back on, remembering to reply to an email or remembering to return a rented movie. |
| Retrospective memory | Retrospective memory refers to memory for people, words, and events encountered or experienced in the past. It includes all other types of memory including episodic, semantic and non-declarative. It can be either implicit or explicit. |
| Semantic memory | Semantic memory refers to the memory of meanings, understandings, and other concept-based knowledge unrelated to specific experiences. The conscious recollection of factual information and general knowledge about the world is generally thought to be independent of context and personal relevance. Semantic and episodic memory together make up the category of declarative memory, which is one of the two major divisions in memory. |
| Subjectivity | Subjectivity refers to the subject and his or her perspective, feelings, beliefs, and desires. In philosophy, the term is usually contrasted with objectivity. Subjectivity may refer to the specific discerning interpretations of any aspect of experiences. |
| Learning power | Learning power refers to the collection of psychological traits and skills that enable a person to engage effectively with a variety of learning challenges. The concept emerged during the 1980s and 90s, for example in the writings of the cognitive scientist Guy Claxton, as a way of describing the form of intelligence possessed by someone who, to quote Jean Piaget's phrase,'...knows what to do when they don't know what to do.' The forms of learning envisaged are typically broader than those encountered in formal educational settings, for example those that are of most use in learning sports or musical instruments, or in mastering complex social situations. |

# Chapter 7. Human Memory

| Method of loci | The method of loci, is a mnemonic device introduced in ancient Roman rhetorical treatises (in the anonymous Rhetorica ad Herennium, Cicero's De Oratore, and Quintilian's Institutio oratoria). It relies on memorized spatial relationships to establish, order and recollect memorial content. The term is most often found in specialised works on psychology, neurobiology and memory, though it was used in the same general way at least as early as the first half of the nineteenth century in works on rhetoric, logic and philosophy. |
|---|---|
| Mnemonic | A mnemonic, is any learning technique that aids memory. Commonly met mnemonics are often verbal, something such as a very short poem or a special word used to help a person remember something, particularly lists, but may be visual, kinesthetic or auditory. Mnemonics rely on associations between easy-to-remember constructs which can be related back to the data that is to be remembered. |
| Overlearning | Overlearning is a pedagogical concept according to which newly acquired skills should be practiced well beyond the point of initial mastery, leading to automaticity. Once one has overlearned a task, one's skill level is higher than the challenge level for that task . The Yerkes-Dodson law predicts that overlearning can improve performance in states of high arousal. |
| Testing effect | The testing effect refers to the higher probability of recalling an item resulting from the act of retrieving the item from memory (testing) versus additional study trials of the item. However, in order for this effect to be demonstrated the test trials must have a medium to high retrieval success. Logically if the test trials are so difficult that no items are recalled or if the correct answers to the non-recalled items are not given to the test subject, then minimal or no learning will occur. |
| Memorization | Memorization is the process of committing something to memory. The act of memorization is often a deliberate mental process undertaken in order to store in memory for later recall items such as experiences, names, appointments, addresses, telephone numbers, lists, stories, poems, pictures, maps, diagrams, facts, music or other visual, auditory, or tactical information. Memorization may also refer to the process of storing particular data into the memory of a device. |
| Hindsight bias | Hindsight bias, is the inclination to see events that have already occurred as being more predictable than they were before they took place. It is a multifaceted phenomenon that can affect different stages of designs, processes, contexts, and situations. Hindsight bias may cause memory distortion, where the recollection and reconstruction of content can lead to false theoretical outcomes. |

1. An _____ is a distorted room that is used to create an optical illusion. Probably influenced by the writings of Hermann Helmholtz, it was invented by American ophthalmologist Adelbert Ames, Jr. in 1934, and constructed in the following year.

   a. Ames trapezoid
   b. ASCII stereogram
   c. Autostereogram
   d. Ames room

2. _____, is the inclination to see events that have already occurred as being more predictable than they were before they took place. It is a multifaceted phenomenon that can affect different stages of designs, processes, contexts, and situations. _____ may cause memory distortion, where the recollection and reconstruction of content can lead to false theoretical outcomes.

   a. Hindsight bias
   b. Functional fixedness
   c. Green children of Woolpit
   d. Memory rehearsal

3. _____ is the capacity for holding a small amount of information in mind in an active, readily available state for a short period of time. The duration of _____ is believed to be in the order of seconds. A commonly-cited capacity is 7 ± 2 elements. In contrast, long-term memory indefinitely stores a seemingly unlimited amount of information.

   a. decay theory
   b. long-term memory
   c. Short-term memory
   d. sensory memory

4. _____ is the memory of autobiographical events (times, places, associated emotions, and other contextual knowledge) that can be explicitly stated. Semantic and _____ together make up the category of declarative memory, which is one of the two major divisions in memory. The counterpart to declarative, or explicit memory, is procedural memory, or implicit memory.

   a. Episodic-like memory
   b. Episodic memory
   c. Iconic memory
   d. Interference theory

5. . During every moment of an organism's life, sensory information is being taken in by sensory receptors and processed by the nervous system. Humans have five main senses: sight, hearing, taste, smell, touch. _____ allows individuals to retain impressions of sensory information after the original stimulus has ceased.

   a. Serial memory processing
   b. Sensory memory
   c. Spike-timing-dependent plasticity

**1.** d
**2.** a
**3.** c
**4.** b
**5.** b

---

*You can take the complete Chapter Practice Test*

**for Chapter 7. Human Memory**
on all key terms, persons, places, and concepts.

*Online 99 Cents*

*http://www.epub3.2.20111.7.cram101.com/*

**Use www.Cram101.com for all your study needs**

**including Cram101's online interactive problem solving labs in**

**chemistry, statistics, mathematics, and more.**

# Chapter 8. Language and Thought

CHAPTER OUTLINE: KEY TERMS, PEOPLE, PLACES, CONCEPTS

Cognition

Cognitive revolution

Introspection

Language

Verbal Behavior

Consonant

Babbling

Language development

Fast mapping

Telegraphic speech

Multilingualism

Bilingual education

Grammars

Irony

Metalinguistic awareness

Overregularization

Dementia

American sign language

Animal mind

_____ Language acquisition

_____ Electroconvulsive therapy

_____ Linguistic relativity

_____ Problem solving

_____ Mendelian inheritance

_____ Insight

_____ Heuristic

_____ Trial and error

_____ Candle problem

_____ Cognitive style

_____ Hindsight bias

_____ Decision making

_____ Cannon-Bard theory

_____ Gamma-Aminobutyric acid

_____ Uncertainty

_____ Availability heuristic

_____ Representativeness heuristic

_____ Conjunction fallacy

_____ Recognition heuristic

CHAPTER OUTLINE: KEY TERMS, PEOPLE, PLACES, CONCEPTS

| | Confirmation bias |
| --- | --- |
| | Mortality rate |
| | James-Lange theory |
| | Loss aversion |
| | Sexism |
| | Name calling |

---

CHAPTER HIGHLIGHTS & NOTES: KEY TERMS, PEOPLE, PLACES, CONCEPTS

| | |
| --- | --- |
| Cognition | Cognition is the scientific term for 'the process of thought'. Usage of the term varies in different disciplines; for example in psychology and cognitive science, it usually refers to an information processing view of an individual's psychological functions. Other interpretations of the meaning of cognition link it to the development of concepts; individual minds, groups, and organizations. |
| Cognitive revolution | The cognitive revolution is the name for an intellectual movement in the 1950s that began what are known collectively as the cognitive sciences. It began in the modern context of greater interdisciplinary communication and research. The relevant areas of interchange were the combination of psychology, anthropology, and linguistics with approaches developed within the then-nascent fields of artificial intelligence, computer science, and neuroscience. |
| Introspection | Introspection is the self-examination of one's conscious thoughts and feelings. In psychology, the process of introspection relies exclusively on the purposeful and rational self-observation of one's mental state; however, introspection is sometimes referenced in a spiritual context as the examination of one's soul. Introspection is closely related to the philosophical concept of human self-reflection, and is contrasted with external observation. |
| Language | Language may refer either to the specifically human capacity for acquiring and using complex systems of communication, or to a specific instance of such a system of complex communication. The scientific study of language in any of its senses is called linguistics. |

# Chapter 8. Language and Thought

| | |
|---|---|
| Verbal Behavior | Verbal Behavior is a 1957 book by psychologist B. F. Skinner, in which he analyzes human behavior, encompassing what is traditionally called language, linguistics, or speech. For Skinner, verbal behavior is simply behavior subject to the same controlling variables as any other operant behavior, although Skinner differentiates between verbal behavior which is mediated by other people, and that which is mediated by the natural world. The book Verbal Behavior is almost entirely theoretical, involving little experimental research in the work itself. |
| Consonant | In articulatory phonetics, a consonant is a speech sound that is articulated with complete or partial closure of the vocal tract. Contrasting with consonants are vowels.<br><br>Since the number of possible sounds in all of the world's languages is much greater than the number of letters in any one alphabet, linguists have devised systems such as the International Phonetic Alphabet to assign a unique and unambiguous symbol to each attested consonant. |
| Babbling | Babbling is a stage in child development and a state in language acquisition, during which an infant appears to be experimenting with uttering sounds of language, but not yet producing any recognizable words. (Crucially, the larynx or voicebox, originally high in the throat to let the baby breathe while swallowing, descends during the first year of life, allowing a pharynx to develop and all the sounds of human speech to be formed). Babbling begins at approximately 5 to 7 months of age, when a baby's noises begin to sound like phonemes. |
| Language development | Language development is a process starting early in human life, when a person begins to acquire language by learning it as it is spoken and by mimicry. Children's language development moves from simple to complex. Infants start without language. |
| Fast mapping | In cognitive psychology, fast mapping is a hypothesized mental process whereby a new concept can be learned (or a new hypothesis formed) based only on a single exposure to a given unit of information. Fast mapping is thought by some researchers to be particularly important during language acquisition in young children, and may serve (at least in part) to explain the prodigious rate at which children gain vocabulary. The process was first formally articulated, and the term 'fast mapping' coined, by Harvard researchers Susan Carey and Elsa Bartlett in 1978. |
| Telegraphic speech | Telegraphic speech, according to linguistics and psychology, is speech during the two-word stage of language acquisition in children, which is laconic and efficient.<br><br>The name derives from the fact that someone sending a telegram was generally charged by the word. To save money, people typically wrote their telegrams in a very compressed style, without conjunctions or articles. |
| Multilingualism | Multilingualism is the act of using, or promoting the use of, multiple languages, either by an individual speaker or by a community of speakers. |

Multilingual speakers outnumber monolingual speakers in the world's population. The generic term for a multilingual person is polyglot.

| | |
|---|---|
| Bilingual education | Bilingual education involves teaching academic content in two languages, in a native and secondary language with varying amounts of each language used in accordance with the program model.<br><br>The following are several different types of bilingual education program models:•Transitional Bilingual Education. This involves education in a child's native language, typically for no more than three years, to ensure that students do not fall behind in content areas like mathematics, science, and social studies while they are learning English. |
| Grammars | Grammars: A Journal of Mathematical Research on Formal and Natural Languages is an academic journal devoted to the mathematical linguistics of formal and natural languages, published by Springer-Verlag. |
| Irony | Irony is a rhetorical device, literary technique, or situation in which there is a sharp incongruity or discordance that goes beyond the simple and evident intention of words or actions. There is presently no accepted method for textually indicating irony, though an irony mark has been proposed.<br><br>Ironic statements (verbal irony) are statements that imply a meaning in opposition to their literal meaning. |
| Metalinguistic awareness | Metalinguistic Awareness refers to the ability to objectify language as a process as well as a thing. The concept of Metalinguistic Awareness is helpful to explaining the execution and transfer of linguistic knowledge across languages Meta-linguistics can be classified as the ability to consciously reflect on the nature of language, by using the following skills:•an awareness that language has a potential greater than that of simple symbols (it goes beyond the meaning)•an awareness that words are separable from their referents (meaning resides in the mind, not in the name ie. Sonia is Sonia, and I will be the same person even if somebody calls me another name)•an awareness that language has a structure that can be manipulated (realizing that language is malleable: you can change and write things in many different ways (for example, if something is written in a grammatically incorrect way, you can change it).<br><br>Metalinguistic Awareness is also known as 'metalinguistic ability,' which can be defined similarly as Metacognition ('knowing about knowing') Meta-linguistic awareness can also be defined as the ability to reflect on the use of language. |

# Chapter 8. Language and Thought

| | |
|---|---|
| Overregularization | Overregularization is a language-learning process in which the regular ways of modifying or connecting words are mistakenly applied to words that require irregular modifications or connections. It is a normal effect observed in the language of beginner and intermediate language-learners, whether native-speaker children or foreign-speaker adults. Because most natural languages have some irregular forms, moving beyond overregularization is a part of mastering them. |
| Dementia | Dementia is a serious loss of global cognitive ability in a previously unimpaired person, beyond what might be expected from normal aging. It may be static, the result of a unique global brain injury, or progressive, resulting in long-term decline due to damage or disease in the body. Although dementia is far more common in the geriatric population, it can occur before the age of 65, in which case it is termed 'early onset dementia'. |
| American sign language | American Sign Language is the dominant sign language of Deaf Americans . It is the third most used language in the United States next to English and Spanish. Although the United Kingdom and the United States share English as a spoken and written language, British Sign Language (BSL) is quite different from American Sign Language, and the two sign languages are not mutually intelligible. American Sign Language, however, derived from French Sign Language. |
| Animal mind | The question of animal minds asks whether it is meaningful to describe a non-human animal as having a mind. |
| | Discussion of this subject is frequently confused by the fact that some schools of philosophy and psychology (e.g. radical behaviorism) would question whether one should ascribe mind to anyone else (or even to oneself). Such an approach would naturally deny the existence of animal minds. |
| Language acquisition | Language acquisition is the process by which humans acquire the capacity to perceive and comprehend language, as well as to produce and use words to communicate. The capacity to successfully use language requires one to acquire a range of tools including syntax, phonetics, and an extensive vocabulary. This language might be vocalized as with speech or manual as in sign. |
| Electroconvulsive therapy | Electroconvulsive therapy formerly known as electroshock, is a psychiatric treatment in which seizures are electrically induced in anesthetized patients for therapeutic effect. Its mode of action is unknown. Today, ECT is most often recommended for use as a treatment for severe depression that has not responded to other treatment, and is also used in the treatment of mania and catatonia. |
| Linguistic relativity | The principle of linguistic relativity holds that the structure of a language affects the ways in which its speakers conceptualize their world, i.e. |

their world view, or otherwise influence their cognitive processes. Popularly known as the Sapir-Whorf hypothesis, or Whorfianism, the principle is often defined as having two versions: (i) the strong version that language determines thought and that linguistic categories limit and determine cognitive categories and (ii) the weak version that linguistic categories and usage influence thought and certain kinds of non-linguistic behaviour. The term 'Sapir-Whorf Hypothesis' is a misnomer as the men never co-authored anything and never stated their ideas in terms of a hypothesis.

| | |
|---|---|
| Problem solving | Problem solving is a mental process and is part of the larger problem process that includes problem finding and problem shaping. Considered the most complex of all intellectual functions, problem solving has been defined as higher-order cognitive process that requires the modulation and control of more routine or fundamental skills. Problem solving occurs when an organism or an artificial intelligence system needs to move from a given state to a desired goal state. |
| Mendelian inheritance | Mendelian inheritance, hereditary characteristics from parent organisms to their offspring; it underlies much of genetics. They were initially derived from the work of Gregor Johann Mendel published in 1865 and 1866 which was 're-discovered' in 1900, and were initially very controversial. When they were integrated with the chromosome theory of inheritance by Thomas Hunt Morgan in 1915, they became the core of classical genetics. |
| Insight | Insight is the understanding of a specific cause and effect in a specific context. Insight can be used with several related meanings:•a piece of information•the act or result of understanding the inner nature of things or of seeing intuitively in Greek called noesis•an introspection•the power of acute observation and deduction, penetration, discernment, perception called intellection or noesis•an understanding of cause and effect based on identification of relationships and behaviors within a model, context, or scenario<br><br>An insight that manifests itself suddenly, such as understanding how to solve a difficult problem, is sometimes called by the German word Aha-Erlebnis. The term was coined by the German psychologist and theoretical linguist Karl Bühler. |
| Heuristic | Heuristic refers to experience-based techniques for problem solving, learning, and discovery. Where an exhaustive search is impractical, heuristic methods are used to speed up the process of finding a satisfactory solution. Examples of this method include using a rule of thumb, an educated guess, an intuitive judgment, or common sense. |
| Trial and error | Trial and error, is an experimental method of problem solving, repair, tuning, or obtaining knowledge. 'Learning doesn't happen from failure itself but rather from analyzing the failure, making a change, and then trying again.' |

# Chapter 8. Language and Thought

| | |
|---|---|
| | In the field of computer science, the method is called generate and test. In elementary algebra, when solving equations, it is 'guess and check'. |
| Candle problem | The candle problem, also known as Duncker's candle problem, is a cognitive performance test, measuring the influence of functional fixedness on a participant's problem solving capabilities. The test was created by Gestalt psychologist Karl Duncker and published posthumously in 1945. |
| Cognitive style | Cognitive style is a term used in cognitive psychology to describe the way individuals think, perceive and remember information. Cognitive style differs from cognitive ability , the latter being measured by aptitude tests or so-called intelligence tests. Controversy exists over the exact meaning of the term cognitive style and also as to whether it is a single or multiple dimension of human personality. |
| Hindsight bias | Hindsight bias, is the inclination to see events that have already occurred as being more predictable than they were before they took place. It is a multifaceted phenomenon that can affect different stages of designs, processes, contexts, and situations. Hindsight bias may cause memory distortion, where the recollection and reconstruction of content can lead to false theoretical outcomes. |
| Decision making | Decision making can be regarded as the mental processes (cognitive process) resulting in the selection of a course of action among several alternatives. Every decision making process produces a final choice. The output can be an action or an opinion of choice. |
| Cannon-Bard theory | The Cannon-Bard theory, is a theory of emotion developed by physiologists Walter Cannon and Philip Bard, suggesting that individuals experience emotions and physiologically react simultaneously. These actions include changes in muscular tension, perspiration, etc. This theory challenges the James-Lange theory of emotion introduced in the late 19th century, which suggests that emotion results from one's 'bodily change,' rather than the other way around. |
| Gamma-Aminobutyric acid | γ-Aminobutyric acid is the chief inhibitory neurotransmitter in the mammalian central nervous system. It plays a role in regulating neuronal excitability throughout the nervous system. In humans, GABA is also directly responsible for the regulation of muscle tone. Although chemically it is an amino acid, GABA is rarely referred to as such in the scientific or medical communities, because the term 'amino acid,' used without a qualifier, conventionally refers to the alpha amino acids, which GABA is not, nor is it ever incorporated into a protein. |

In spastic diplegia in humans, GABA absorption becomes impaired by nerves damaged from the condition's upper motor neuron lesion, which leads to hypertonia of the muscles signaled by those nerves that can no longer absorb GABA.Function Neurotransmitter

In vertebrates, GABA acts at inhibitory synapses in the brain by binding to specific transmembrane receptors in the plasma membrane of both pre- and postsynaptic neuronal processes. This binding causes the opening of ion channels to allow the flow of either negatively charged chloride ions into the cell or positively charged potassium ions out of the cell. Depending on which ion channels open, the membrane potential is either hyperpolarized or depolarized. This action results in a negative change in the transmembrane potential, usually causing hyperpolarization. Two general classes of GABA receptor are known: $GABA_A$ in which the receptor is part of a ligand-gated ion channel complex, and $GABA_B$ metabotropic receptors, which are G protein-coupled receptors that open or close ion channels via intermediaries (G proteins).

Neurons that produce GABA as their output are called GABAergic neurons, and have chiefly inhibitory action at receptors in the adult vertebrate. Medium Spiny Cells are a typical example of inhibitory CNS GABAergic cells. In contrast, GABA exhibits both excitatory and inhibitory actions in insects, mediating muscle activation at synapses between nerves and muscle cells, and also the stimulation of certain glands. In mammals, some GABAergic neurons, such as chandelier cells, are also able to excite their glutamatergic counterparts.

$GABA_A$ receptors are ligand-activated chloride channels; that is, when activated by GABA, they allow the flow of chloride ions across the membrane of the cell. Whether this chloride flow is excitatory/depolarizing (makes the voltage across the cell's membrane less negative), shunting (has no effect on the cell's membrane) or inhibitory/hyperpolarizing (makes the cell's membrane more negative) depends on the direction of the flow of chloride. When net chloride flows out of the cell, GABA is excitatory or depolarizing; when the net chloride flows into the cell, GABA is inhibitory or hyperpolarizing. When the net flow of chloride is close to zero, the action of GABA is shunting. Shunting inhibition has no direct effect on the membrane potential of the cell; however, it minimises the effect of any coincident synaptic input essentially by reducing the electrical resistance of the cell's membrane (in essence, equivalent to Ohm's law). A developmental switch in the molecular machinery controlling concentration of chloride inside the cell - and, hence, the direction of this ion flow - is responsible for the changes in the functional role of GABA between the neonatal and adult stages. That is to say, GABA's role changes from excitatory to inhibitory as the brain develops into adulthood. Brain development

For the past two decades, the theory of excitatory action of GABA early in development was unquestioned based on experiments in vitro, on brain slices.

# Chapter 8. Language and Thought

The main observation was that in the hippocampus and neocortex of the mammalian brain, GABA has primarily excitatory effects, and is in fact the major excitatory neurotransmitter in many regions of the brain before the maturation of glutamateergic synapses.

However, this theory has been questioned based on results showing that in brain slices of immature mice incubated in artificial cerebrospinal fluid (ACSF) (modified in a way that takes into account the normal composition of the neuronal milieu in sucklings by adding an energy substrate alternative to glucose, beta-hydroxybutyrate) GABA action shifts from excitatory to inhibitory mode. This effect has been later repeated when other energy substrates, pyruvate and lactate, supplemented glucose in the slices' media. The effects of beta-hydroxybutyrate were later confirmed for pyruvate and for lactate. However it was argued that the concentrations of the alternative energy substrates used in these experiments were non-physiological and the GABA-shift was instead caused by changes in pH resulting from the substrates acting as 'weak acids'. These arguments were later rebutted by further findings showing that changes in pH even greater than that caused by energy substrates do not affect the GABA-shift described in the presence of energy substrate-fortified ACSF and that the mode of action of beta-hydroxybutyrate, pyruvate and lactate (assessed by measurement NAD(P)H and oxygen utilization) was energy metabolism-related.

In the developmental stages preceding the formation of synaptic contacts, GABA is synthesized by neurons and acts both as an autocrine (acting on the same cell) and paracrine (acting on nearby cells) signalling mediator.

GABA regulates the proliferation of neural progenitor cells the migration and differentiation the elongation of neurites and the formation of synapses.

GABA also regulates the growth of embryonic and neural stem cells. GABA can in?uence the development of neural progenitor cells via brain-derived neurotrophic factor (BDNF) expression. GABA activates the GABA$_A$ receptor, causing cell cycle arrest in the S-phase, limiting growth. Beyond the nervous system

GABAergic mechanisms have been demonstrated in various peripheral tissues and organs including, but not restricted to the intestine, stomach, pancreas, Fallopian tube, uterus, ovary, testis, kidney, urinary bladder, lung, and liver.

In 2007, an excitatory GABAergic system was described in the airway epithelium. The system activates following exposure to allergens and may participate in the mechanisms of asthma. GABAergic systems have also been found in the testis and in the eye lens. Structure and conformation

GABA is found mostly as a zwitterion, that is, with the carboxy group deprotonated and the amino group protonated. Its conformation depends on its environment. In the gas phase, a highly folded conformation is strongly favored because of the electrostatic attraction between the two functional groups. The stabilization is about 50 kcal/mol, according to quantum chemistry calculations. In the solid state, a more extended conformation is found, with a trans conformation at the amino end and a gauche conformation at the carboxyl end. This is due to the packing interactions with the neighboring molecules. In solution, five different conformations, some folded and some extended, are found as a result of solvation effects. The conformational flexibility of GABA is important for its biological function, as it has been found to bind to different receptors with different conformations. Many GABA analogues with pharmaceutical applications have more rigid structures in order to control the binding better. History

Gamma-aminobutyric acid was first synthesized in 1883, and was first known only as a plant and microbe metabolic product.

**Uncertainty**

Uncertainty is a term used in subtly different ways in a number of fields, including physics, philosophy, statistics, economics, finance, insurance, psychology, sociology, engineering, and information science. It applies to predictions of future events, to physical measurements already made, or to the unknown.

Although the terms are used in various ways among the general public, many specialists in decision theory, statistics and other quantitative fields have defined uncertainty, risk, and their measurement as:•Uncertainty: The lack of certainty, A state of having limited knowledge where it is impossible to exactly describe the existing state, a future outcome, or more than one possible outcome.•Measurement of Uncertainty: A set of possible states or outcomes where probabilities are assigned to each possible state or outcome - this also includes the application of a probability density function to continuous variables•Risk: A state of uncertainty where some possible outcomes have an undesired effect or significant loss.•Measurement of Risk: A set of measured uncertainties where some possible outcomes are losses, and the magnitudes of those losses - this also includes loss functions over continuous variables.

Knightian uncertainty.

**Availability heuristic**

The availability heuristic is a mental shortcut that uses the ease with which examples come to mind to make judgements about the probability of events. The availability heuristic operates on the notion that 'if you can think of it, it must be important.' The availability of consequences associated with an action is positively related to perceptions of the magnitude of the consequences of that action. In other words, the easier it is to recall the consequences of something, the bigger we perceive these consequences to be.

# Chapter 8. Language and Thought

| | |
|---|---|
| Representativeness heuristic | The representativeness heuristic is used when making judgments about the probability of an event under uncertainty (Kahneman & Tversky, 1972). It was first proposed by Amos Tversky and Daniel Kahneman who defined representativeness as 'the degree to which [an event] (i) is similar in essential characteristics to its parent population and (ii) reflects the salient features of the process by which it is generated' (Kahneman & Tversky, 1982, p. 33). When people rely on representativeness to make judgements, they are likely to judge wrongly because the fact that something is more representative does not make it more likely (Tversky & Kahneman, 1982). |
| Conjunction fallacy | The conjunction fallacy is a logical fallacy that occurs when it is assumed that specific conditions are more probable than a single general one.

The most often-cited example of this fallacy originated with Amos Tversky and Daniel Kahneman:'

Linda is 31 years old, single, outspoken, and very bright. She majored in philosophy.' |
| Recognition heuristic | The recognition heuristic has been used as a model in the psychology of judgment and decision making and as a heuristic in artificial intelligence. It states: :

Daniel Goldstein and Gerd Gigerenzer quizzed students in Germany and the United States on the populations of both German and American cities. Each group scored slightly higher on the foreign cities despite only recognizing a fraction of them. |
| Confirmation bias | Confirmation bias is a tendency for people to favor information that confirms their preconceptions or hypotheses regardless of whether the information is true. As a result, people gather evidence and recall information from memory selectively, and interpret it in a biased way. The biases appear in particular for emotionally significant issues and for established beliefs. |
| Mortality rate | Mortality rate is a measure of the number of deaths (in general, or due to a specific cause) in some population, scaled to the size of that population, per unit time. Mortality rate is typically expressed in units of deaths per 1000 individuals per year; thus, a mortality rate of 9.5 in a population of 100,000 would mean 950 deaths per year in that entire population, or 0.95% out of the total. It is distinct from morbidity rate, which refers to the number of individuals in poor health during a given time period (the prevalence rate) or the number of newly appearing cases of the disease per unit of time (incidence rate). |
| James-Lange theory | The James-Lange theory refers to a hypothesis on the origin and nature of emotions and is one of the earliest theories of emotion, developed independently by two 19th-century scholars, William James and Carl Lange. |

|  | The theory states that within human beings, as a response to experiences in the world, the autonomic nervous system creates physiological events such as muscular tension, a rise in heart rate, perspiration, and dryness of the mouth. Emotions, then, are feelings which come about as a result of these physiological changes, rather than being their cause. James and Lange arrived at the theory independently. Lange specifically stated that vasomotor changes are emotions. |
|---|---|
| Loss aversion | In economics and decision theory, loss aversion refers to people's tendency to strongly prefer avoiding losses to acquiring gains. Some studies suggest that losses are twice as powerful, psychologically, as gains. Loss aversion was first convincingly demonstrated by Amos Tversky and Daniel Kahneman. |
| Sexism | Sexism, a term coined in the mid-20th century, is the belief or attitude that one sex is inherently superior to, more competent than, or more valuable than the other. It can also include this type of discrimination in regards to gender. Sexism primarily involves hatred of, or prejudice towards, either sex as a whole , or the application of stereotypes of masculinity in relation to men, or of femininity in relation to women. |
| Name calling | Name calling is abusive or insulting language referred to a person or group. This phenomenon is studied by a variety of academic disciplines from anthropology, to child psychology, to politics. It is also studied by rhetoricians, and a variety of other disciplines that study propaganda techniques and their causes and effects. |

CHAPTER QUIZ: KEY TERMS, PEOPLE, PLACES, CONCEPTS

1.  The _____ refers to a hypothesis on the origin and nature of emotions and is one of the earliest theories of emotion, developed independently by two 19th-century scholars, William James and Carl Lange.

The theory states that within human beings, as a response to experiences in the world, the autonomic nervous system creates physiological events such as muscular tension, a rise in heart rate, perspiration, and dryness of the mouth. Emotions, then, are feelings which come about as a result of these physiological changes, rather than being their cause. James and Lange arrived at the theory independently. Lange specifically stated that vasomotor changes are emotions.

  a. Bounded emotionality
  b. Butterflies in the stomach
  c. James-Lange theory
  d. Compassion fatigue

2. . _____, according to linguistics and psychology, is speech during the two-word stage of language acquisition in children, which is laconic and efficient.

The name derives from the fact that someone sending a telegram was generally charged by the word.

# Chapter 8. Language and Thought

To save money, people typically wrote their telegrams in a very compressed style, without conjunctions or articles.

    a. Telegraphic speech
    b. Garden path sentence
    c. Language and thought
    d. Language center

3. _____ is a language-learning process in which the regular ways of modifying or connecting words are mistakenly applied to words that require irregular modifications or connections. It is a normal effect observed in the language of beginner and intermediate language-learners, whether native-speaker children or foreign-speaker adults. Because most natural languages have some irregular forms, moving beyond _____ is a part of mastering them.

    a. Overregularization
    b. American Association of Teachers of French
    c. American Association of Teachers of German
    d. Euromobil

4. _____, hereditary characteristics from parent organisms to their offspring; it underlies much of genetics. They were initially derived from the work of Gregor Johann Mendel published in 1865 and 1866 which was 're-discovered' in 1900, and were initially very controversial. When they were integrated with the chromosome theory of inheritance by Thomas Hunt Morgan in 1915, they became the core of classical genetics.

    a. Genetically modified mouse
    b. Wastebasket taxon
    c. Mendelian inheritance
    d. West American Digest System

5. The _____ is the name for an intellectual movement in the 1950s that began what are known collectively as the cognitive sciences. It began in the modern context of greater interdisciplinary communication and research. The relevant areas of interchange were the combination of psychology, anthropology, and linguistics with approaches developed within the then-nascent fields of artificial intelligence, computer science, and neuroscience.

    a. Cognitive rhetoric
    b. Cognitive science of religion
    c. Cognitive specialization
    d. Cognitive revolution

**1.** c
**2.** a
**3.** a
**4.** c
**5.** d

## You can take the complete Chapter Practice Test

**for Chapter 8. Language and Thought**
on all key terms, persons, places, and concepts.

### Online 99 Cents

*http://www.epub3.2.20111.8.cram101.com/*

**Use www.Cram101.com for all your study needs**

**including Cram101's online interactive problem solving labs in**

**chemistry, statistics, mathematics, and more.**

CHAPTER OUTLINE: KEY TERMS, PEOPLE, PLACES, CONCEPTS

American Association on Intellectual and Developmental Disabilities

Mendelian inheritance

Aptitude

Personality test

Repeatability

Construct validity

Content validity

Hypothetical construct

Stanford-Binet Intelligence Scale

Gamma-Aminobutyric acid

Heredity

Inheritance

Intelligence quotient

Mental age

Wechsler Adult Intelligence Scale

Factor analysis

Normal distribution

Crystallized intelligence

Group intelligence

# Chapter 9. Intelligence and Psychological Testing
CHAPTER OUTLINE: KEY TERMS, PEOPLE, PLACES, CONCEPTS

Deviation

Standard deviation

Verbal Behavior

Case study

Social intelligence

Verbal intelligence

Personality Assessment Inventory

Job performance

Mental retardation

Intellectual disability

Down syndrome

Phenylketonuria

Electroconvulsive therapy

Talent development

Genius

Special education

Flynn effect

Malnutrition

Stereotype threat

CHAPTER OUTLINE: KEY TERMS, PEOPLE, PLACES, CONCEPTS

| | Test anxiety |
| --- | --- |
| | Brain size |
| | Longevity |
| | Prefrontal cortex |
| | Convergent thinking |
| | Divergent thinking |
| | Insight |
| | Acculturation |
| | Openness to experience |
| | Mental disorder |
| | Threshold hypothesis |
| | Cyberspace |

# Chapter 9. Intelligence and Psychological Testing

| | |
|---|---|
| American Association on Intellectual and Developmental Disabilities | The American Association on Intellectual and Developmental Disabilities (formerly the American Association on Mental Retardation (AAMR)) is an American non-profit professional organization that advocates on behalf of those with mental retardation. AAMR has members in the United States and 55 other countries. |
| Mendelian inheritance | Mendelian inheritance, hereditary characteristics from parent organisms to their offspring; it underlies much of genetics. They were initially derived from the work of Gregor Johann Mendel published in 1865 and 1866 which was 're-discovered' in 1900, and were initially very controversial. When they were integrated with the chromosome theory of inheritance by Thomas Hunt Morgan in 1915, they became the core of classical genetics. |
| Aptitude | An aptitude is an innate component of a competency (the others being knowledge, understanding, learned or acquired abilities (skills) and attitude) to do a certain kind of work at a certain level. Aptitudes may be physical or mental. The innate nature of aptitude is in contrast to achievement, which represents knowledge or ability that is gained. |
| Personality test | A personality test is a questionnaire or other standardized instrument designed to reveal aspects of an individual's character or psychological makeup. The first personality tests were developed in the early 20th century and were intended to ease the process of personnel selection, particularly in the armed forces. Since these early efforts of these test, a wide variety of personality tests have been developed, notably the Myers Briggs Type Indicator (MBTI), the MMPI, and a number of tests based on the Five Factor Model of personality. |
| Repeatability | Repeatability is the variation in measurements taken by a single person or instrument on the same item and under the same conditions. A measurement may be said to be repeatable when this variation is smaller than some agreed limit. According to the Guidelines for Evaluating and Expressing the Uncertainty of NIST Measurement Results, repeatability conditions include:•the same measurement procedure•the same observer•the same measuring instrument, used under the same conditions•the same location•repetition over a short period of time. Repeatability methods were developed by Bland and Altman (1986). |
| Construct validity | In science (e.g. social sciences and psychometrics), construct validity refers to whether a scale measures or correlates with the theorized psychological scientific construct (e.g., 'fluid intelligence') that it purports to measure. In other words, it is the extent to which what was to be measured was actually measured. It is related to the theoretical ideas behind the trait under consideration, i.e. the concepts that organize how aspects of personality, intelligence, etc. |
| Content validity | In psychometrics, content validity refers to the extent to which a measure represents all facets of a given social construct. |

| | For example, a depression scale may lack content validity if it only assesses the affective dimension of depression but fails to take into account the behavioral dimension. An element of subjectivity exists in relation to determining content validity, which requires a degree of agreement about what a particular personality trait such as extraversion represents. |
|---|---|
| Hypothetical construct | A construct in the philosophy of science is an ideal object, where the existence of the thing may be said to depend upon a subject's mind. This, as opposed to a 'real' object, where existence does not seem to depend on the existence of a mind. |
| | In a scientific theory, particularly within psychology, a hypothetical construct is an explanatory variable which is not directly observable. |
| Stanford-Binet Intelligence Scale | The development of the Stanford-Binet Intelligence Scales initiated the modern field of intelligence testing, originating in France, then revised in the U.S. The Stanford-Binet test started with the French psychologist Alfred Binet (1857-1911), whom the French government commissioned with developing a method of identifying intellectually deficient children for their placement in special-education programs. As Binet indicated, case studies might be more detailed and helpful, but the time required to test many people would be excessive. In 1916, at Stanford University, the psychologist Lewis Terman released a revised examination which became known as the 'Stanford-Binet test'. |
| Gamma-Aminobutyric acid | γ-Aminobutyric acid is the chief inhibitory neurotransmitter in the mammalian central nervous system. It plays a role in regulating neuronal excitability throughout the nervous system. In humans, GABA is also directly responsible for the regulation of muscle tone. |
| | Although chemically it is an amino acid, GABA is rarely referred to as such in the scientific or medical communities, because the term 'amino acid,' used without a qualifier, conventionally refers to the alpha amino acids, which GABA is not, nor is it ever incorporated into a protein. |
| | In spastic diplegia in humans, GABA absorption becomes impaired by nerves damaged from the condition's upper motor neuron lesion, which leads to hypertonia of the muscles signaled by those nerves that can no longer absorb GABA.Function Neurotransmitter |
| | In vertebrates, GABA acts at inhibitory synapses in the brain by binding to specific transmembrane receptors in the plasma membrane of both pre- and postsynaptic neuronal processes. This binding causes the opening of ion channels to allow the flow of either negatively charged chloride ions into the cell or positively charged potassium ions out of the cell. Depending on which ion channels open, the membrane potential is either hyperpolarized or depolarized. This action results in a negative change in the transmembrane potential, usually causing hyperpolarization. |

Two general classes of GABA receptor are known: $GABA_A$ in which the receptor is part of a ligand-gated ion channel complex, and $GABA_B$ metabotropic receptors, which are G protein-coupled receptors that open or close ion channels via intermediaries (G proteins).

Neurons that produce GABA as their output are called GABAergic neurons, and have chiefly inhibitory action at receptors in the adult vertebrate. Medium Spiny Cells are a typical example of inhibitory CNS GABAergic cells. In contrast, GABA exhibits both excitatory and inhibitory actions in insects, mediating muscle activation at synapses between nerves and muscle cells, and also the stimulation of certain glands. In mammals, some GABAergic neurons, such as chandelier cells, are also able to excite their glutamatergic counterparts.

$GABA_A$ receptors are ligand-activated chloride channels; that is, when activated by GABA, they allow the flow of chloride ions across the membrane of the cell. Whether this chloride flow is excitatory/depolarizing (makes the voltage across the cell's membrane less negative), shunting (has no effect on the cell's membrane) or inhibitory/hyperpolarizing (makes the cell's membrane more negative) depends on the direction of the flow of chloride. When net chloride flows out of the cell, GABA is excitatory or depolarizing; when the net chloride flows into the cell, GABA is inhibitory or hyperpolarizing. When the net flow of chloride is close to zero, the action of GABA is shunting. Shunting inhibition has no direct effect on the membrane potential of the cell; however, it minimises the effect of any coincident synaptic input essentially by reducing the electrical resistance of the cell's membrane (in essence, equivalent to Ohm's law). A developmental switch in the molecular machinery controlling concentration of chloride inside the cell - and, hence, the direction of this ion flow - is responsible for the changes in the functional role of GABA between the neonatal and adult stages. That is to say, GABA's role changes from excitatory to inhibitory as the brain develops into adulthood. Brain development

For the past two decades, the theory of excitatory action of GABA early in development was unquestioned based on experiments in vitro, on brain slices. The main observation was that in the hippocampus and neocortex of the mammalian brain, GABA has primarily excitatory effects, and is in fact the major excitatory neurotransmitter in many regions of the brain before the maturation of glutamateergic synapses.

However, this theory has been questioned based on results showing that in brain slices of immature mice incubated in artificial cerebrospinal fluid (ACSF) (modified in a way that takes into account the normal composition of the neuronal milieu in sucklings by adding an energy substrate alternative to glucose, beta-hydroxybutyrate) GABA action shifts from excitatory to inhibitory mode. This effect has been later repeated when other energy substrates, pyruvate and lactate, supplemented glucose in the slices' media. The effects of beta-hydroxybutyrate were later confirmed for pyruvate and for lactate. However it was argued that the concentrations of the alternative energy substrates used in these experiments were non-physiological and the GABA-shift was instead caused by changes in pH resulting from the substrates acting as 'weak acids'.

These arguments were later rebutted by further findings showing that changes in pH even greater than that caused by energy substrates do not affect the GABA-shift described in the presence of energy substrate-fortified ACSF and that the mode of action of beta-hydroxybutyrate, pyruvate and lactate (assessed by measurement NAD(P)H and oxygen utilization) was energy metabolism-related.

In the developmental stages preceding the formation of synaptic contacts, GABA is synthesized by neurons and acts both as an autocrine (acting on the same cell) and paracrine (acting on nearby cells) signalling mediator.

GABA regulates the proliferation of neural progenitor cells the migration and differentiation the elongation of neurites and the formation of synapses.

GABA also regulates the growth of embryonic and neural stem cells. GABA can in?uence the development of neural progenitor cells via brain-derived neurotrophic factor (BDNF) expression. GABA activates the $GABA_A$ receptor, causing cell cycle arrest in the S-phase, limiting growth. Beyond the nervous system

GABAergic mechanisms have been demonstrated in various peripheral tissues and organs including, but not restricted to the intestine, stomach, pancreas, Fallopian tube, uterus, ovary, testis, kidney, urinary bladder, lung, and liver.

In 2007, an excitatory GABAergic system was described in the airway epithelium. The system activates following exposure to allergens and may participate in the mechanisms of asthma. GABAergic systems have also been found in the testis and in the eye lens. Structure and conformation

GABA is found mostly as a zwitterion, that is, with the carboxy group deprotonated and the amino group protonated. Its conformation depends on its environment. In the gas phase, a highly folded conformation is strongly favored because of the electrostatic attraction between the two functional groups. The stabilization is about 50 kcal/mol, according to quantum chemistry calculations. In the solid state, a more extended conformation is found, with a trans conformation at the amino end and a gauche conformation at the carboxyl end. This is due to the packing interactions with the neighboring molecules. In solution, five different conformations, some folded and some extended, are found as a result of solvation effects. The conformational flexibility of GABA is important for its biological function, as it has been found to bind to different receptors with different conformations. Many GABA analogues with pharmaceutical applications have more rigid structures in order to control the binding better. History

# Chapter 9. Intelligence and Psychological Testing

| | |
|---|---|
| Heredity | Heredity is the passing of traits to offspring (from its parent or ancestors). This is the process by which an offspring cell or organism acquires or becomes predisposed to the characteristics of its parent cell or organism. Through heredity, variations exhibited by individuals can accumulate and cause some species to evolve. |
| Inheritance | Inheritance is the practice of passing on property, titles, debts, rights and obligations upon the death of an individual. It has long played an important role in human societies. The rules of inheritance differ between societies and have changed over time. |
| Intelligence quotient | An intelligence quotient, is a score derived from one of several standardized tests designed to assess intelligence. The abbreviation 'IQ' comes from the German term Intelligenz-Quotient, originally coined by psychologist William Stern. When modern IQ tests are devised, the mean (average) score within an age group is set to 100 and the standard deviation (SD) almost always to 15, although this was not always so historically. |
| Mental age | Mental age is a concept in relation to intelligence, expressed as the age at which a child is performing intellectually. The mental age of the child that is tested is the same as the average age at which normal children achieve a particular score.<br><br>However, a mental age result on an intelligence test does not mean that children function at their 'mental age level' in all aspects of life. |
| Wechsler Adult Intelligence Scale | The Wechsler Adult Intelligence Scale is a test designed to measure intelligence in adults and older adolescents. It is currently in its fourth edition (WAIS-IV). The original WAIS (Form I) was published in February 1955 by David Wechsler, as a revision of the Wechsler-Bellevue Intelligence Scale. |
| Factor analysis | Factor analysis is a statistical method used to describe variability among observed, correlated variables in terms of a potentially lower number of unobserved variables called factors. In other words, it is possible, for example, that variations in three or four observed variables mainly reflect the variations in fewer such unobserved variables. Factor analysis searches for such joint variations in response to unobserved latent variables. |
| Normal distribution | In probability theory, the normal distribution is a continuous probability distribution that has a bell-shaped probability density function, known as the Gaussian function or informally the bell curve:<br><br>$$f(x; \mu, \sigma^2) = \frac{1}{\sigma\sqrt{2\pi}} e^{-\frac{1}{2}\left(\frac{x-\mu}{\sigma}\right)^2}$$<br><br>The parameter μ is the mean or expectation (location of the peak) and $\sigma^2$ is the variance. σ is known as the standard deviation. The distribution with μ = 0 and |

CHAPTER HIGHLIGHTS & NOTES: KEY TERMS, PEOPLE, PLACES, CONCEPTS

| | |
|---|---|
| Crystallized intelligence | In psychology, fluid and crystallized intelligence are factors of general intelligence originally identified by Raymond Cattell.<br><br>Fluid intelligence or fluid reasoning is the capacity to think logically and solve problems in novel situations, independent of acquired knowledge. It is the ability to analyze novel problems, identify patterns and relationships that underpin these problems and the extrapolation of these using logic.Crystallized intelligence is the ability to use skills, knowledge, and experience. It should not be equated with memory or knowledge, but it does rely on accessing information from long-term memory. |
| Group intelligence | Group intelligence refers to a process by which large numbers of people simultaneously converge upon the same point(s) of knowledge.<br><br>Social psychologists study group intelligence and related topics such as decentralized decision making and group wisdom, using demographic information to study the ramifications for long-term social change. Marketing and behavioral finance experts use similar research to forecast consumer behavior (e.g. buying patterns) for corporate strategic purposes. |
| Deviation | In mathematics and statistics, deviation is a measure of difference between the observed value and the mean. The sign of deviation (positive or negative), reports the direction of that difference (it is larger when the sign is positive, and smaller if it is negative). The magnitude of the value indicates the size of the difference. |
| Standard deviation | Standard deviation is a widely used measurement of variability or diversity used in statistics and probability theory. It shows how much variation or 'dispersion' there is from the 'average' (mean, or expected/budgeted value). A low standard deviation indicates that the data points tend to be very close to the mean, whereas high standard deviation indicates that the data are spread out over a large range of values. |
| Verbal Behavior | Verbal Behavior is a 1957 book by psychologist B. F. Skinner, in which he analyzes human behavior, encompassing what is traditionally called language, linguistics, or speech. For Skinner, verbal behavior is simply behavior subject to the same controlling variables as any other operant behavior, although Skinner differentiates between verbal behavior which is mediated by other people, and that which is mediated by the natural world. The book Verbal Behavior is almost entirely theoretical, involving little experimental research in the work itself. |
| Case study | A case study is a research method common in social science. It is based on an in-depth investigation of a single individual, group, or event. Case studies may be descriptive or explanatory. |

# Chapter 9. Intelligence and Psychological Testing

| | |
|---|---|
| Social intelligence | Social intelligence describes the exclusively human capacity to effectively navigate and negotiate complex social relationships and environments. Psychologist and professor at the London School of Economics Nicholas Humphrey believes it is social intelligence or the richness of our qualitative life, rather than our quantitative intelligence, that truly makes humans what they are - for example what it's like to be a human being living at the centre of the conscious present, surrounded by smells and tastes and feels and the sense of being an extraordinary metaphysical entity with properties which hardly seem to belong to the physical world. Social scientist Ross Honeywill believes social intelligence is an aggregated measure of self and social awareness, evolved social beliefs and attitudes, and a capacity and appetite to manage complex social change. |
| Verbal intelligence | VERBAL INTELLIGENCE Definition Verbal Intelligence is the ability to 'juggle' with the alphabet of letters: to combine them into words and sentences. It is the ability to analyze information and solve problems using language-based reasoning.<br><br>Verbal task may involve concepts such as: •Concrete or abstract ideas •Internalized language-based reasoning<br><br>Skills involved with help of verbal intelligence:•The ability to listen and to recall spoken information•Understanding the meaning of written or spoken information•Solving language based problems a literacy, logical, or social type•The ability to perform complex language-based analysis. |
| Personality Assessment Inventory | Personality Assessment Inventory PhD, is a multi-scale test of psychological functioning that assesses constructs relevant to personality and psychopathology evaluation (e.g., depression, anxiety, aggression) in various contexts including psychotherapy, crisis/evaluation, forensic, personnel selection, pain/medical, and child custody assessment. The PAI has 22 non-overlapping scales, providing a comprehensive overview of psychopathology in adults. The PAI contains four kinds of scales: 1) validity scales, which measure the respondent's approach to the test, including faking good or bad, exaggeration, or defensiveness; 2) clinical scales, which correspond to psychiatric diagnostic categories; 3) treatment consideration scales, which assess factors that may relate to treatment of clinical disorders or other risk factors but which are not captured in psychiatric diagnoses (e.g., suicidal ideation); and 4) interpersonal scales, which provide indicators of interpersonal dimensions of personality functioning. |
| Job performance | Job performance is a commonly used, yet poorly defined concept in industrial and organizational psychology, the branch of psychology that deals with the workplace. It most commonly refers to whether a person performs their job well. Despite the confusion over how it should be exactly defined, performance is an extremely important criterion that relates to organizational outcomes and success. |

| | |
|---|---|
| Mental retardation | Mental retardation is a generalized disorder appearing before adulthood, characterized by significantly impaired cognitive functioning and deficits in two or more adaptive behaviors. It has historically been defined as an Intelligence Quotient score under 70. Once focused almost entirely on cognition, the definition now includes both a component relating to mental functioning and one relating to individuals' functional skills in their environment. As a result, a person with a below-average intelligence quotient (BAIQ) may not be considered mentally retarded. |
| Intellectual disability | Intellectual disability is a broad concept encompassing various intellectual deficits, including mental retardation (MR), deficits too mild to properly qualify as MR, various specific conditions (such as specific learning disability), and problems acquired later in life through acquired brain injuries or neurodegenerative diseases like dementia. Intellectual disabilities may appear at any age.<br><br>Intellectual disability is also increasingly being used as a synonym for the term mental retardation as used in standard medical references. |
| Down syndrome | Down syndrome is a chromosomal condition caused by the presence of all or part of an extra 21st chromosome. It is named after John Langdon Down, the British physician who described the syndrome in 1866. The condition was identified as a chromosome 21 trisomy by Jérôme Lejeune in 1959. Down syndrome in a fetus can be identified with amniocentesis (with risks of fetal injury and/or miscarriage) during pregnancy, or in a baby at birth. |
| Phenylketonuria | Phenylketonuria is an autosomal recessive metabolic genetic disorder characterized by a mutation in the gene for the hepatic enzyme phenylalanine hydroxylase (PAH), rendering it nonfunctional. This enzyme is necessary to metabolize the amino acid phenylalanine (Phe) to the amino acid tyrosine. When PAH activity is reduced, phenylalanine accumulates and is converted into phenylpyruvate (also known as phenylketone), which is detected in the urine. |
| Electroconvulsive therapy | Electroconvulsive therapy formerly known as electroshock, is a psychiatric treatment in which seizures are electrically induced in anesthetized patients for therapeutic effect. Its mode of action is unknown. Today, ECT is most often recommended for use as a treatment for severe depression that has not responded to other treatment, and is also used in the treatment of mania and catatonia. |
| Talent development | Talent development, part of human resource development, is the process of changing an organization, its employees, its stakeholders, and groups of people within it, using planned and unplanned learning, in order to achieve and maintain a competitive advantage for the organization. Rothwell notes that the name may well be a term in search of a meaning, like so much in management, and suggests that it be thought of as selective attention paid to the top 10% of employees, either by potential or performance. |

# Chapter 9. Intelligence and Psychological Testing

| | |
|---|---|
| Genius | A genius is something or someone embodying exceptional intellectual ability, creativity, or originality, typically to a degree that is associated with the achievement of unprecedented insight.<br><br>There is no scientifically precise definition of genius, and indeed the question of whether the notion itself has any real meaning is a subject of current debate. The term is used in various ways: to refer to a particular aspect of an individual, or the individual in their entirety; to a scholar in many subjects (e.g. Leonardo DaVinci) or a scholar in a single subject (e.g. Albert Einstein). |
| Special education | Special education is the education of students with special needs in a way that addresses the students' individual differences and needs. Ideally, this process involves the individually planned and systematically monitored arrangement of teaching procedures, adapted equipment and materials, accessible settings, and other interventions designed to help learners with special needs achieve a higher level of personal self-sufficiency and success in school and community than would be available if the student were only given access to a typical classroom education.<br><br>Common special needs include challenges with learning, communication challenges, emotional and behavioral disorders, physical disabilities, and developmental disorders. |
| Flynn effect | The Flynn effect is the name given to a substantial and long-sustained increase in intelligence test scores measured in many parts of the world. When intelligence quotient (IQ) tests are initially standardized using a sample of test-takers, by convention the average of the test results is set to 100 and their standard deviation is set to 15 or 16 IQ points. When IQ tests are revised, they are again standardized using a new sample of test-takers, usually born more recently than the first. |
| Malnutrition | Malnutrition is the condition that results from taking an unbalanced diet in which certain nutrients are lacking, in excess (too high an intake), or in the wrong proportions. A number of different nutrition disorders may arise, depending on which nutrients are under or overabundant in the diet.<br><br>The World Health Organization cites malnutrition as the gravest single threat to the world's public health. |
| Stereotype threat | Stereotype threat is the experience of anxiety or concern in a situation where a person has the potential to confirm a negative stereotype about their social group. Since its introduction into the scientific literature in 1995, stereotype threat has become one of the most widely studied topics in the field of social psychology. First described by social psychologist Claude Steele and his colleagues, stereotype threat has been shown to reduce the performance of individuals who belong to negatively stereotyped groups. |

| Test anxiety | Test anxiety involves a combination of physiological over-arousal, worry and dread about test performance, and often interferes with normal learning and lowers test performance. It is a physiological condition in which people experience extreme stress, anxiety, and discomfort during and/or before taking a test. Test anxiety is prevalent amongst the student populations of the world, and has been studied formally since the early 1950s. |
|---|---|
| Brain size | Brain size is one aspect of animal anatomy and evolution. Both overall brain size and the size of substructures have been analysed, and the question of links between size and functioning - particularly intelligence - has often proved controversial. Brain size is sometimes measured by weight and sometimes by volume (via MRI scans or by skull volume). |
| Longevity | The word 'longevity' is sometimes used as a synonym for 'life expectancy' in demography or to connote 'long life', especially when it concerns someone or something lasting longer than expected (an ancient tree, for example).<br><br>Reflections on longevity have usually gone beyond acknowledging the brevity of human life and have included thinking about methods to extend life. Longevity has been a topic not only for the scientific community but also for writers of travel, science fiction, and utopian novels. |
| Prefrontal cortex | The prefrontal cortex. is the anterior part of the frontal lobes of the brain, lying in front of the motor and premotor areas.<br><br>This brain region has been implicated in planning complex cognitive behavior, personality expression, decision making and moderating social behavior. |
| Convergent thinking | Convergent thinking is a term coined by Joy Paul Guilford as the opposite of divergent thinking. It generally means the ability to give the 'correct' answer to standard questions that do not require significant creativity, for instance in most tasks in school and on standardized multiple-choice tests for intelligence.<br><br>Convergent thinking is the the type of thinking that focuses on coming up with the single, well-established answer to a problem. |
| Divergent thinking | Divergent thinking is a thought process or method used to generate creative ideas by exploring many possible solutions. It is often used in conjunction with convergent thinking, which follows a particular set of logical steps to arrive at one solution, which in some cases is a 'correct' solution. Divergent thinking typically occurs in a spontaneous, free-flowing manner, such that many ideas are generated in an emergent cognitive fashion. |
| Insight | Insight is the understanding of a specific cause and effect in a specific context. |

Insight can be used with several related meanings:•a piece of information•the act or result of understanding the inner nature of things or of seeing intuitively in Greek called noesis•an introspection•the power of acute observation and deduction, penetration, discernment, perception called intellection or noesis•an understanding of cause and effect based on identification of relationships and behaviors within a model, context, or scenario

An insight that manifests itself suddenly, such as understanding how to solve a difficult problem, is sometimes called by the German word Aha-Erlebnis. The term was coined by the German psychologist and theoretical linguist Karl Bühler.

| | |
|---|---|
| Acculturation | Acculturation explains the process of cultural and psychological change that results following meeting between cultures. The effects of acculturation can be seen at multiple levels in both interacting cultures. At the group level, acculturation often results in changes to culture, customs, and social institutions. |
| Openness to experience | Openness to experience is one of five major domains which are used to describe human personality. Openness involves active imagination, aesthetic sensitivity, attentiveness to inner feelings, preference for variety, and intellectual curiosity. A great deal of psychometric research has demonstrated that these qualities are statistically correlated. |
| Mental disorder | A mental disorder is a psychological or behavioral pattern generally associated with subjective distress or disability that occurs in an individual, and which is not a part of normal development or culture. The recognition and understanding of mental health conditions has changed over time and across cultures, and there are still variations in the definition, assessment, and classification of mental disorders, although standard guideline criteria are widely accepted. A few mental disorders are diagnosed based on the harm to others, regardless of the subject's perception of distress. |
| Threshold hypothesis | The threshold hypothesis is a hypothesis concerning second language acquisition set forth in a study by Cummins (2000) that stated that a minimum threshold in language proficiency must be passed before a second-language speaker can reap any benefits from language. It also states that, in order to gain proficiency in a second language, the learner must also have passed a certain and age appropriate level of competence in his or her first language. |
| Cyberspace | Cyberspace is the electronic medium of computer networks, in which online communication takes place. |

The term 'cyberspace' was first used by the cyberpunk science fiction author William Gibson.

1. The _____ (formerly the American Association on Mental Retardation (AAMR)) is an American non-profit professional organization that advocates on behalf of those with mental retardation. AAMR has members in the United States and 55 other countries.

   a. American Association on Intellectual and Developmental Disabilities
   b. Posse Comitatus Act
   c. Wilkinson v Downton
   d. The Kallikak Family

2. _____ is an autosomal recessive metabolic genetic disorder characterized by a mutation in the gene for the hepatic enzyme phenylalanine hydroxylase (PAH), rendering it nonfunctional. This enzyme is necessary to metabolize the amino acid phenylalanine (Phe) to the amino acid tyrosine. When PAH activity is reduced, phenylalanine accumulates and is converted into phenylpyruvate (also known as phenylketone), which is detected in the urine.

   a. X-linked mental retardation
   b. Green children of Woolpit
   c. Posse Comitatus Act
   d. Phenylketonuria

3. _____, hereditary characteristics from parent organisms to their offspring; it underlies much of genetics. They were initially derived from the work of Gregor Johann Mendel published in 1865 and 1866 which was 're-discovered' in 1900, and were initially very controversial. When they were integrated with the chromosome theory of inheritance by Thomas Hunt Morgan in 1915, they became the core of classical genetics.

   a. Genetically modified mouse
   b. Green children of Woolpit
   c. Mendelian inheritance
   d. Wilkinson v Downton

4. An _____ is an innate component of a competency (the others being knowledge, understanding, learned or acquired abilities (skills) and attitude) to do a certain kind of work at a certain level. _____s may be physical or mental. The innate nature of _____ is in contrast to achievement, which represents knowledge or ability that is gained.

   a. Organized Crime Control Act
   b. Aptitude
   c. Uniform Determination of Death Act
   d. Aeron chair

5. . A _____ is a questionnaire or other standardized instrument designed to reveal aspects of an individual's character or psychological makeup. The first _____s were developed in the early 20th century and were intended to ease the process of personnel selection, particularly in the armed forces. Since these early efforts of these test, a wide variety of _____s have been developed, notably the Myers Briggs Type Indicator (MBTI), the MMPI, and a number of tests based on the Five Factor Model of personality.

   a. Positive affectivity

**Chapter 9. Intelligence and Psychological Testing**

b. Positive mental attitude

c. Personality test

d. Recklessness

**1.** a
**2.** d
**3.** c
**4.** b
**5.** c

*You can take the complete Chapter Practice Test*

**for Chapter 9. Intelligence and Psychological Testing**
on all key terms, persons, places, and concepts.

**Online 99 Cents**

*http://www.epub3.2.20111.9.cram101.com/*

**Use www.Cram101.com for all your study needs**

**including Cram101's online interactive problem solving labs in**

**chemistry, statistics, mathematics, and more.**

# Chapter 10. Motivation and Emotion

CHAPTER OUTLINE: KEY TERMS, PEOPLE, PLACES, CONCEPTS

_____ | Area studies

_____ | Homeostasis

_____ | Natural selection

_____ | Necker Cube

_____ | Case study

_____ | Gamma-Aminobutyric acid

_____ | Motivation

_____ | Reproductive success

_____ | Ventromedial nucleus

_____ | Gestalt psychology

_____ | Brainstem

_____ | Diabetes mellitus

_____ | Ghrelin

_____ | Insulin

_____ | Flynn effect

_____ | Environmental factor

_____ | Overeating

_____ | Palatability

_____ | Sensory-specific satiety

Mass index

Observational learning

Sodium chloride

Taste aversion

Erection

Parental investment

Sexual partner

Job performance

Testosterone

Ponzo illusion

Acquaintance rape

Homosexuality

Prevalence

Sexual orientation

Psychoanalytic theory

Hormone

Cannon-Bard theory

Thematic Apperception Test

Need for achievement

CHAPTER OUTLINE: KEY TERMS, PEOPLE, PLACES, CONCEPTS

| | Need for affiliation |
| --- | --- |
| | Projective test |
| | James-Lange theory |
| | Incentive |
| | Affective forecasting |
| | Electroconvulsive therapy |
| | Popular psychology |
| | Autonomic nervous system |
| | Endocrine system |
| | Fight or flight response |
| | Nervous system |
| | Poggendorff illusion |
| | Personality Assessment Inventory |
| | Amygdala |
| | Body language |
| | Limbic system |
| | Mirror neuron |
| | Prefrontal cortex |
| | Emotional expression |

Facial expression

Display rules

Two-factor theory

Subjective well-being

Subjectivity

Rating scale

Agreeableness

Job satisfaction

Marital status

Small talk

Unemployment

Hedonic treadmill

Circular reasoning

Non sequitur

Prenatal development

Major depressive disorder

Zygote

Placenta

Congenital disorder

CHAPTER OUTLINE: KEY TERMS, PEOPLE, PLACES, CONCEPTS

Miscarriage

Mendelian inheritance

Fetal alcohol syndrome

Microcephaly

Rorschach test

Birth weight

Chickenpox

Infant mortality

Maternal nutrition

Measles

Rubella

Childhood

Cohort effect

Personality development

Research design

Temperament

Reinforcement theory

Surrogacy

Toilet training

Cognitive development

Centration

Object permanence

Animal mind

Animism

Egocentrism

Language development

Private speech

Zone of proximal development

Moral reasoning

Adolescence

Conscience

Prosocial behavior

Puberty

Secondary sex characteristic

Generational change

Menarche

Neural development

Synaptic pruning

CHAPTER OUTLINE: KEY TERMS, PEOPLE, PLACES, CONCEPTS

Emerging adulthood

Adulthood

Cohabitation

Conscientiousness

Neuroticism

Openness to experience

Childlessness

Parenting

Menopause

Parkinsonism

Crystallized intelligence

Dementia

Hippocampus

Neurofibrillary tangle

Heredity

Masculinity

Verbal Behavior

Aggression

Nonverbal communication

# Chapter 10. Motivation and Emotion

| | Social behavior |
| | Nature versus nurture |
| | Cerebral hemisphere |
| | Corpus callosum |
| | Gender role |
| | Role model |
| | Socialization |

CHAPTER HIGHLIGHTS & NOTES: KEY TERMS, PEOPLE, PLACES, CONCEPTS

| Area studies | Area studies are interdisciplinary fields of research and scholarship pertaining to particular geographical, national/federal, or cultural regions. The term exists primarily as a general description for what are, in the practice of scholarship, many heterogeneous fields of research, encompassing both the social sciences and the humanities. Typical area studies programs involve history, political science, sociology, cultural studies, languages, geography, literature, and related disciplines. |
|---|---|
| Homeostasis | Homeostasis is the property of a system that regulates its internal environment and tends to maintain a stable, constant condition of properties such as temperature or pH. It can be either an open or closed system.<br><br>It was defined by Claude Bernard and later by Walter Bradford Cannon in 1926, 1929 and 1932.<br><br>Typically used to refer to a living organism, the concept came from that of milieu intérieur that was created by Claude Bernard and published in 1865. Multiple dynamic equilibrium adjustment and regulation mechanisms make homeostasis possible. |

| | |
|---|---|
| Natural selection | Natural selection is the process by which traits become more or less common in a population due to consistent effects upon the survival or reproduction of their bearers. It is a key mechanism of evolution. The natural genetic variation within a population of organisms may cause some individuals to survive and reproduce more successfully than others in their current environment. |
| Necker Cube | The Necker Cube is an optical illusion first published as a rhomboid in 1832 by Swiss crystallographer Louis Albert Necker. |
| | Ambiguity |
| | The Necker Cube is an ambiguous line drawing. |
| | The effect is interesting because each part of the picture is ambiguous by itself, yet the human visual system picks an interpretation of each part that makes the whole consistent. |
| Case study | A case study is a research method common in social science. It is based on an in-depth investigation of a single individual, group, or event. Case studies may be descriptive or explanatory. |
| Gamma-Aminobutyric acid | γ-Aminobutyric acid is the chief inhibitory neurotransmitter in the mammalian central nervous system. It plays a role in regulating neuronal excitability throughout the nervous system. In humans, GABA is also directly responsible for the regulation of muscle tone. |
| | Although chemically it is an amino acid, GABA is rarely referred to as such in the scientific or medical communities, because the term 'amino acid,' used without a qualifier, conventionally refers to the alpha amino acids, which GABA is not, nor is it ever incorporated into a protein. |
| | In spastic diplegia in humans, GABA absorption becomes impaired by nerves damaged from the condition's upper motor neuron lesion, which leads to hypertonia of the muscles signaled by those nerves that can no longer absorb GABA.Function Neurotransmitter |
| | In vertebrates, GABA acts at inhibitory synapses in the brain by binding to specific transmembrane receptors in the plasma membrane of both pre- and postsynaptic neuronal processes. This binding causes the opening of ion channels to allow the flow of either negatively charged chloride ions into the cell or positively charged potassium ions out of the cell. Depending on which ion channels open, the membrane potential is either hyperpolarized or depolarized. This action results in a negative change in the transmembrane potential, usually causing hyperpolarization. Two general classes of GABA receptor are known: $GABA_A$ in which the receptor is part of a ligand-gated ion channel complex, and $GABA_B$ metabotropic receptors, which are G protein-coupled receptors that open or close ion channels via intermediaries (G proteins). |

Neurons that produce GABA as their output are called GABAergic neurons, and have chiefly inhibitory action at receptors in the adult vertebrate. Medium Spiny Cells are a typical example of inhibitory CNS GABAergic cells. In contrast, GABA exhibits both excitatory and inhibitory actions in insects, mediating muscle activation at synapses between nerves and muscle cells, and also the stimulation of certain glands. In mammals, some GABAergic neurons, such as chandelier cells, are also able to excite their glutamatergic counterparts.

$GABA_A$ receptors are ligand-activated chloride channels; that is, when activated by GABA, they allow the flow of chloride ions across the membrane of the cell. Whether this chloride flow is excitatory/depolarizing (makes the voltage across the cell's membrane less negative), shunting (has no effect on the cell's membrane) or inhibitory/hyperpolarizing (makes the cell's membrane more negative) depends on the direction of the flow of chloride. When net chloride flows out of the cell, GABA is excitatory or depolarizing; when the net chloride flows into the cell, GABA is inhibitory or hyperpolarizing. When the net flow of chloride is close to zero, the action of GABA is shunting. Shunting inhibition has no direct effect on the membrane potential of the cell; however, it minimises the effect of any coincident synaptic input essentially by reducing the electrical resistance of the cell's membrane (in essence, equivalent to Ohm's law). A developmental switch in the molecular machinery controlling concentration of chloride inside the cell - and, hence, the direction of this ion flow - is responsible for the changes in the functional role of GABA between the neonatal and adult stages. That is to say, GABA's role changes from excitatory to inhibitory as the brain develops into adulthood. Brain development

For the past two decades, the theory of excitatory action of GABA early in development was unquestioned based on experiments in vitro, on brain slices. The main observation was that in the hippocampus and neocortex of the mammalian brain, GABA has primarily excitatory effects, and is in fact the major excitatory neurotransmitter in many regions of the brain before the maturation of glutamateergic synapses.

However, this theory has been questioned based on results showing that in brain slices of immature mice incubated in artificial cerebrospinal fluid (ACSF) (modified in a way that takes into account the normal composition of the neuronal milieu in sucklings by adding an energy substrate alternative to glucose, beta-hydroxybutyrate) GABA action shifts from excitatory to inhibitory mode. This effect has been later repeated when other energy substrates, pyruvate and lactate, supplemented glucose in the slices' media. The effects of beta-hydroxybutyrate were later confirmed for pyruvate and for lactate. However it was argued that the concentrations of the alternative energy substrates used in these experiments were non-physiological and the GABA-shift was instead caused by changes in pH resulting from the substrates acting as 'weak acids'.

These arguments were later rebutted by further findings showing that changes in pH even greater than that caused by energy substrates do not affect the GABA-shift described in the presence of energy substrate-fortified ACSF and that the mode of action of beta-hydroxybutyrate, pyruvate and lactate (assessed by measurement NAD(P)H and oxygen utilization) was energy metabolism-related.

In the developmental stages preceding the formation of synaptic contacts, GABA is synthesized by neurons and acts both as an autocrine (acting on the same cell) and paracrine (acting on nearby cells) signalling mediator.

GABA regulates the proliferation of neural progenitor cells the migration and differentiation the elongation of neurites and the formation of synapses.

GABA also regulates the growth of embryonic and neural stem cells. GABA can in?uence the development of neural progenitor cells via brain-derived neurotrophic factor (BDNF) expression. GABA activates the $GABA_A$ receptor, causing cell cycle arrest in the S-phase, limiting growth. Beyond the nervous system

GABAergic mechanisms have been demonstrated in various peripheral tissues and organs including, but not restricted to the intestine, stomach, pancreas, Fallopian tube, uterus, ovary, testis, kidney, urinary bladder, lung, and liver.

In 2007, an excitatory GABAergic system was described in the airway epithelium. The system activates following exposure to allergens and may participate in the mechanisms of asthma. GABAergic systems have also been found in the testis and in the eye lens. Structure and conformation

GABA is found mostly as a zwitterion, that is, with the carboxy group deprotonated and the amino group protonated. Its conformation depends on its environment. In the gas phase, a highly folded conformation is strongly favored because of the electrostatic attraction between the two functional groups. The stabilization is about 50 kcal/mol, according to quantum chemistry calculations. In the solid state, a more extended conformation is found, with a trans conformation at the amino end and a gauche conformation at the carboxyl end. This is due to the packing interactions with the neighboring molecules. In solution, five different conformations, some folded and some extended, are found as a result of solvation effects. The conformational flexibility of GABA is important for its biological function, as it has been found to bind to different receptors with different conformations. Many GABA analogues with pharmaceutical applications have more rigid structures in order to control the binding better. History

# Chapter 10. Motivation and Emotion

| | |
|---|---|
| Motivation | Motivation is a term that refers to a process that elicits, controls, and sustains certain behaviors. Motivation is a group of phenomena which affect the nature of an individual's behavior, the strength of the behavior, and the persistence of the behavior. For instance: An individual has not eaten, he or she feels hungry, as a response he or she eats and diminishes feelings of hunger. |
| Reproductive success | Reproductive success is defined as the passing of genes onto the next generation in a way that they too can pass those genes on. In practice, this is often a tally of the number of offspring produced by an individual. A more correct definition, which incorporates inclusive fitness, is the relative production of fertile offspring by a genotype. |
| Ventromedial nucleus | The ventromedial nucleus is a nucleus of the hypothalamus.<br><br>It has four subdivisions:•anterior (VMHa)•dorsomedial (VMHdm)•ventrolateral (VMHvl)•central (VMHc).<br><br>These subdivisions differ anatomically, neurochemically, and behaviorally. |
| Gestalt psychology | Gestalt psychology is holistic, parallel, and analog, with self-organizing tendencies. The principle maintains that the human eye sees objects in their entirety before perceiving their individual parts. Gestalt psychologists stipulate that perception is the product of complex interactions among various stimuli. |
| Brainstem | In vertebrate anatomy the brainstem is the posterior part of the brain, adjoining and structurally continuous with the spinal cord. The brain stem provides the main motor and sensory innervation to the face and neck via the cranial nerves. Though small, this is an extremely important part of the brain as the nerve connections of the motor and sensory systems from the main part of the brain to the rest of the body pass through the brain stem. |
| Diabetes mellitus | Diabetes mellitus is a group of metabolic diseases in which a person has high blood sugar, either because the body does not produce enough insulin, or because cells do not respond to the insulin that is produced. This high blood sugar produces the classical symptoms of polyuria (frequent urination), polydipsia (increased thirst) and polyphagia (increased hunger). |
| Ghrelin | Ghrelin is a hormone produced mainly by P/D1 cells lining the fundus of the human stomach and epsilon cells of the pancreas that stimulates hunger. Ghrelin levels increase before meals and decrease after meals. It is considered the counterpart of the hormone leptin, produced by adipose tissue, which induces satiation when present at higher levels. |
| Insulin | Insulin is a hormone that is central to regulating carbohydrate and fat metabolism in the body. Insulin causes cells in the liver, muscle, and fat tissue to take up glucose from the blood, storing it as glycogen in the liver and muscle. |

Insulin stops the use of fat as an energy source by inhibiting the release of glucagon. When insulin is absent, glucose is not taken up by body cells and the body begins to use fat as an energy source or gluconeogenesis; for example, by transfer of lipids from adipose tissue to the liver for mobilization as an energy source. As its level is a central metabolic control mechanism, its status is also used as a control signal to other body systems (such as amino acid uptake by body cells). In addition, it has several other anabolic effects throughout the body.

| | |
|---|---|
| Flynn effect | The Flynn effect is the name given to a substantial and long-sustained increase in intelligence test scores measured in many parts of the world. When intelligence quotient (IQ) tests are initially standardized using a sample of test-takers, by convention the average of the test results is set to 100 and their standard deviation is set to 15 or 16 IQ points. When IQ tests are revised, they are again standardized using a new sample of test-takers, usually born more recently than the first. |
| Environmental factor | Apart from the true monogenic genetic disorders, environmental factors may determine the development of disease in those genetically predisposed to a particular condition. Stress, physical and mental abuse, diet, exposure to toxins, pathogens, radiation and chemicals found in almost all personal care products and household cleaners are common environmental factors that determine a large segment of non-hereditary disease. Environmental factors such as the weather affect business interests. |
| Overeating | Overeating generally refers to the long-term consumption of excess food in relation to the energy that an organism expends (or expels via excretion), leading to weight gaining and often obesity. It may be regarded as an eating disorder.<br><br>This term may also be used to refer to specific episodes of over-consumption. |
| Palatability | Palatability is the hedonic reward provided by foods or fluids that are agreeable to the 'palate' in regard to the homeostatic satisfaction of nutritional, water, or energy needs. The palatability of a food or fluid, unlike its flavor or taste, varies with the state of an individual: it is lower after consumption and higher when deprived. Palatability of foods, however, can be learned. |
| Sensory-specific satiety | Sensory-specific satiety is a sensory hedonic phenomenon that refers to the declining satisfaction generated by the consumption of a certain type of food, and the consequent renewal in appetite resulting from the exposure to a new flavor or food. The phenomenon was first described in 1956 by the French physiologist Jacques Le Magnen. The term has been coined in 1981 by Barbara J. Rolls and Edmund T. Rolls. |
| Mass index | The mass index is an indicator, developed by Donald Dorsey, used in technical analysis to predict trend reversals. |

|  | It is based on the notion that there is a tendency for reversal when the price range widens, and therefore compares previous trading ranges (highs minus lows).<br><br>Mass index for a commodity is obtained by calculating its exponential moving average over a 9 day period and the exponential moving average of this average (a 'double' average), and summing the ratio of these two over a given amount of days (usually 25). |
|---|---|
| Observational learning | Observational learning is a type of learning that occurs as a function of observing, retaining and replicating novel behavior executed by others. It is argued that reinforcement has the effect of influencing which responses one will partake in, more than it influences the actual acquisition of the new response.<br><br>Although observational learning can take place at any stage in life, it is thought to be of greater importance during childhood, particularly as authority becomes important. |
| Sodium chloride | Sodium chloride, also known as salt, common salt, table salt, or halite, is an ionic compound with the formula NaCl. Sodium chloride is the salt most responsible for the salinity of the ocean and of the extracellular fluid of many multicellular organisms. As the major ingredient in edible salt, it is commonly used as a condiment and food preservative. |
| Taste aversion | Conditioned taste aversion, also known as Garcia effect (after Dr. John Garcia), and as 'Sauce-Bearnaise Syndrome', a term coined by Seligman and Hager, is an example of classical conditioning or Pavlovian conditioning. Conditioned taste aversion occurs when a subject associates the taste of a certain food with symptoms caused by a toxic, spoiled, or poisonous substance. Generally, taste aversion is caused after ingestion of the food causes nausea, sickness, or vomiting. |
| Erection | Penile erection is a physiological phenomenon where the penis becomes enlarged and firm. Penile erection is the result of a complex interaction of psychological, neural, vascular and endocrine factors, and is usually, though not exclusively, associated with sexual arousal. Penile erection can also occur due to a full urinary bladder. |
| Parental investment | Parental investment in evolutionary biology and evolutionary psychology, is any parental expenditure (time, energy etc). that benefits one offspring at a cost to parents' ability to invest in other components of fitness (Clutton-Brock 1991: 9; Trivers 1972). Components of fitness (Beatty 1992) include the wellbeing of existing offspring, parents' future reproduction, and inclusive fitness through aid to kin (Hamilton, 1964). |
| Sexual partner | Sexual partners are people who engage in consensual sexual activity together. The sexual partners can be of any gender or sexual orientation. |

| Job performance | Job performance is a commonly used, yet poorly defined concept in industrial and organizational psychology, the branch of psychology that deals with the workplace. It most commonly refers to whether a person performs their job well. Despite the confusion over how it should be exactly defined, performance is an extremely important criterion that relates to organizational outcomes and success. |
|---|---|
| Testosterone | Testosterone is a steroid hormone from the androgen group and is found in mammals, reptiles, birds, and other vertebrates. In mammals, testosterone is primarily secreted in the testes of males and the ovaries of females, although small amounts are also secreted by the adrenal glands. It is the principal male sex hormone and an anabolic steroid. |
| Ponzo illusion | The Ponzo illusion is a geometrical-optical illusion that was first demonstrated by the Italian psychologist Mario Ponzo (1882-1960) in 1913. He suggested that the human mind judges an object's size based on its background. He showed this by drawing two identical lines across a pair of converging lines, similar to railway tracks. The upper line looks longer because we interpret the converging sides according to linear perspective as parallel lines receding into the distance. |
| Acquaintance rape | Acquaintance rape is an assault or attempted assault usually committed by a new acquaintance involving sexual intercourse without mutual consent. <br><br> The term 'date rape' is widely used but can be misleading because the person who commits the crime might not be dating the victim. Rather, it could be an acquaintance or stranger. |
| Homosexuality | Homosexuality is romantic and/or sexual attraction or behavior between members of the same sex or gender. As a sexual orientation, homosexuality refers to 'an enduring pattern of or disposition to experience sexual, affectional, or romantic attractions' primarily or exclusively to people of the same sex; 'it also refers to an individual's sense of personal and social identity based on those attractions, behaviors expressing them, and membership in a community of others who share them.' <br><br> Homosexuality is one of the three main categories of sexual orientation, along with bisexuality and heterosexuality, within the heterosexual-homosexual continuum. The consensus of the behavioral and social sciences and the health and mental health professions is that homosexuality is a normal and positive variation in human sexual orientation, though many religious societies, including Catholicism, Mormonism, and Islam, and some psychological associations, such as NARTH, have traditionally taught that homosexual activity is sinful or dysfunctional. |

# Chapter 10. Motivation and Emotion

| | |
|---|---|
| Prevalence | In epidemiology, the prevalence of a health-related state (typically disease, but also other things like smoking or seatbelt use) in a statistical population is defined as the total number of cases of the risk factor in the population at a given time, or the total number of cases in the population, divided by the number of individuals in the population. It is used as an estimate of how common a disease is within a population over a certain period of time. It helps physicians or other health professionals understand the probability of certain diagnoses and is routinely used by epidemiologists, health care providers, government agencies and insurers. |
| Sexual orientation | Sexual orientation describes a pattern of emotional, romantic, or sexual attraction to men, women, both genders, neither gender, or another gender. According to the American Psychological Association, sexual orientation is enduring and also refers to a person's sense of 'personal and social identity based on those attractions, behaviors expressing them, and membership in a community of others who share them.' The consensus among most contemporary scholars in the field is that one's sexual orientation is not a choice. No simple, single cause for sexual orientation has been conclusively demonstrated, but research suggests that it is by a combination of genetic, hormonal, and environmental influences, with biological factors involving a complex interplay of genetic factors and the early uterine environment. |
| Psychoanalytic theory | Psychoanalytic theory refers to the definition and dynamics of personality development which underlie and guide psychoanalytic and psychodynamic psychotherapy. First laid out by Sigmund Freud, psychoanalytic theory has undergone many refinements since his work . Psychoanalytic theory came to full prominence as a critical force in the last third of the twentieth century as part of 'the flow of critical discourse after the 1960's. |
| Hormone | A hormone is a chemical released by a cell or a gland in one part of the body that sends out messages that affect cells in other parts of the organism. Only a small amount of hormone is required to alter cell metabolism. In essence, it is a chemical messenger that transports a signal from one cell to another. All multicellular organisms produce hormones; plant hormones are also called phytohormones. Hormones in animals are often transported in the blood. Cells respond to a hormone when they express a specific receptor for that hormone. The hormone binds to the receptor protein, resulting in the activation of a signal transduction mechanism that ultimately leads to cell type-specific responses. |
| Cannon-Bard theory | The Cannon-Bard theory, is a theory of emotion developed by physiologists Walter Cannon and Philip Bard, suggesting that individuals experience emotions and physiologically react simultaneously. These actions include changes in muscular tension, perspiration, etc. This theory challenges the James-Lange theory of emotion introduced in the late 19th century, which suggests that emotion results from one's 'bodily change,' rather than the other way around. |
| Thematic Apperception Test | The Thematic Apperception Test, is a projective psychological test. |

|  | Proponents of this technique assert that a person's responses to the TAT cards can provide information about his or her views of the self, the world, and interpersonal relationships. Historically, it has been among the most widely researched, taught, and used of such tests. |
|---|---|
| Need for achievement | Need for achievement refers to an individual's desire for significant accomplishment, mastering of skills, control, or high standards. The term was first used by Henry Murray and associated with a range of actions. These include: 'intense, prolonged and repeated efforts to accomplish something difficult. |
| Need for affiliation | The Need for affiliation is a term that was popularized by David McClelland and describes a person's need to feel a sense of involvement and 'belonging' within a social group; McClellend's thinking was strongly influenced by the pioneering work of Henry Murray who first identified underlying psychological human needs and motivational processes (1938). It was Murray who set out a taxonomy of needs, including achievement, power and affiliation--and placed these in the context of an integrated motivational model. People with a high need for affiliation require warm interpersonal relationships and approval from those with whom they have regular contact. |
| Projective test | In psychology, a projective test is a personality test designed to let a person respond to ambiguous stimuli, presumably revealing hidden emotions and internal conflicts. This is different from an 'objective test' in which responses are analyzed according to a universal standard (for example, a multiple choice exam). The responses to projective tests are content analyzed for meaning rather than being based on presuppositions about meaning, as is the case with objective tests. |
| James-Lange theory | The James-Lange theory refers to a hypothesis on the origin and nature of emotions and is one of the earliest theories of emotion, developed independently by two 19th-century scholars, William James and Carl Lange.<br><br>The theory states that within human beings, as a response to experiences in the world, the autonomic nervous system creates physiological events such as muscular tension, a rise in heart rate, perspiration, and dryness of the mouth. Emotions, then, are feelings which come about as a result of these physiological changes, rather than being their cause. James and Lange arrived at the theory independently. Lange specifically stated that vasomotor changes are emotions. |
| Incentive | In economics and sociology, an incentive is any factor (financial or non-financial) that enables or motivates a particular course of action, or counts as a reason for preferring one choice to the alternatives. It is an expectation that encourages people to behave in a certain way. |

# Chapter 10. Motivation and Emotion

| | |
|---|---|
| Affective forecasting | Affective forecasting is the prediction of one's affect (emotional state) in the future. As a process that influences preferences, decisions, and behavior, affective forecasting is studied by both psychologists and economists, with broad applications.<br><br>Kahneman and Snell began research on hedonic forecasts in the early 1990s, examining its impact on decision-making. |
| Electroconvulsive therapy | Electroconvulsive therapy formerly known as electroshock, is a psychiatric treatment in which seizures are electrically induced in anesthetized patients for therapeutic effect. Its mode of action is unknown. Today, ECT is most often recommended for use as a treatment for severe depression that has not responded to other treatment, and is also used in the treatment of mania and catatonia. |
| Popular psychology | The term popular psychology refers to concepts and theories about human mental life and behavior that are purportedly based on psychology and that attain popularity among the general population. The concept is closely related to the human potential movement of the 1950s and '60s.<br><br>The term 'pop psychologist' can be used to describe authors, consultants, lecturers and entertainers who are widely perceived as being psychologists, not because of their academic credentials, but because they have projected that image or have been perceived in that way in response to their work. |
| Autonomic nervous system | The autonomic nervous system is the part of the peripheral nervous system that acts as a control system functioning largely below the level of consciousness, and controls visceral functions. The Autonomic nervous system affects heart rate, digestion, respiration rate, salivation, perspiration, diameter of the pupils, micturition (urination), and sexual arousal. Whereas most of its actions are involuntary, some, such as breathing, work in tandem with the conscious mind. |
| Endocrine system | In physiology, the endocrine system is a system of glands, each of which secretes a type of hormone into the bloodstream to regulate the body. The endocrine system is an information signal system like the nervous system. Hormones are substances (chemical mediators) released from endocrine tissue into the bloodstream that attach to target tissue and allow communication among cells. |
| Fight or flight response | The fight or flight response was first described by Walter Bradford Cannon.<br><br>His theory states that animals react to threats with a general discharge of the sympathetic nervous system, priming the animal for fighting or fleeing. |

| | |
|---|---|
| Nervous system | The nervous system is an organ system containing a network of specialized cells called neurons that coordinate the actions of an animal and transmit signals between different parts of its body. In most animals the nervous system consists of two parts, central and peripheral. The central nervous system of vertebrates (such as humans) contains the brain, spinal cord, and retina. |
| Poggendorff illusion | The Poggendorff Illusion is a geometrical-optical illusion that involves the misperception of the position of one segment of a transverse line that has been interrupted by the contour of an intervening structure (here a rectangle). It is named after Poggendorff, the editor of the journal, who discovered it in the figures Johann Karl Friedrich Zöllner submitted when first reporting on what is now known as the Zöllner illusion, in 1860.<br><br>In the picture to the right, a straight black and red line is obscured by a grey rectangle. |
| Personality Assessment Inventory | Personality Assessment Inventory PhD, is a multi-scale test of psychological functioning that assesses constructs relevant to personality and psychopathology evaluation (e.g., depression, anxiety, aggression) in various contexts including psychotherapy, crisis/evaluation, forensic, personnel selection, pain/medical, and child custody assessment. The PAI has 22 non-overlapping scales, providing a comprehensive overview of psychopathology in adults. The PAI contains four kinds of scales: 1) validity scales, which measure the respondent's approach to the test, including faking good or bad, exaggeration, or defensiveness; 2) clinical scales, which correspond to psychiatric diagnostic categories; 3) treatment consideration scales, which assess factors that may relate to treatment of clinical disorders or other risk factors but which are not captured in psychiatric diagnoses (e.g., suicidal ideation); and 4) interpersonal scales, which provide indicators of interpersonal dimensions of personality functioning. |
| Amygdala | The amygdalae are almond-shaped groups of nuclei located deep within the medial temporal lobes of the brain in complex vertebrates, including humans. Shown in research to perform a primary role in the processing and memory of emotional reactions, the amygdalae are considered part of the limbic system.<br><br>The regions described as amygdala nuclei encompass several structures with distinct functional traits. |
| Body language | Body language is a form of non-verbal communication, which consists of body posture, gestures, facial expressions, and eye movements. Humans send and interpret such signals almost entirely subconsciously. |

# Chapter 10. Motivation and Emotion

| | |
|---|---|
| Limbic system | The limbic system is a set of brain structures including the hippocampus, amygdala, anterior thalamic nuclei, septum, limbic cortex and fornix, which seemingly support a variety of functions including emotion, behavior, long term memory, and olfaction. The term 'limbic' comes from the Latin limbus, for 'border' or 'edge'. Some scientists have suggested that the concept of the limbic system should be abandoned as obsolete, as it is grounded more in transient tradition than in facts. |
| Mirror neuron | A mirror neuron is a neuron that fires both when an animal acts and when the animal observes the same action performed by another. Thus, the neuron 'mirrors' the behavior of the other, as though the observer were itself acting. Such neurons have been directly observed in primate and other species including birds. |
| Prefrontal cortex | The prefrontal cortex. is the anterior part of the frontal lobes of the brain, lying in front of the motor and premotor areas.<br><br>This brain region has been implicated in planning complex cognitive behavior, personality expression, decision making and moderating social behavior. |
| Emotional expression | Emotional expressions in psychology are observable verbal and nonverbal behaviors that communicate an internal emotional or affective state. Examples of emotional expression are facial movements such as smiling or scowling, or behaviors like crying or laughing. Emotional expressions can occur with or without self-awareness. |
| Facial expression | A facial expression results from one or more motions or positions of the muscles of the face. These movements convey the emotional state of the individual to observers. Facial expressions are a form of nonverbal communication. |
| Display rules | Display rules are a social group's informal norms about when, where, and how one should express emotions.<br><br>Expressions of emotions vary to a great degree and hold significant meaning with great value of determining one's cultural and social identity. Display rules identify these expressions to a precise situation in a suitable context. |
| Two-factor theory | The Two-factor theory states that there are certain factors in the workplace that cause job satisfaction, while a separate set of factors cause dissatisfaction. It was developed by Frederick Herzberg, a psychologist, who theorized that job satisfaction and job dissatisfaction act independently of each other. |

| | |
|---|---|
| Subjective well-being | Subjective well-being refers to how people experience the quality of their lives and includes both emotional reactions and cognitive judgments. According to SWB, happiness is defined as a combination of life satisfaction and the relative frequency of positive and negative affect. SWB therefore encompasses moods and emotions as well as evaluations of one's satisfaction with general and specific areas of one's life. |
| Subjectivity | Subjectivity refers to the subject and his or her perspective, feelings, beliefs, and desires. In philosophy, the term is usually contrasted with objectivity.<br><br>Subjectivity may refer to the specific discerning interpretations of any aspect of experiences. |
| Rating scale | A rating scale is a set of categories designed to elicit information about a quantitative or a qualitative attribute. In the social sciences, common examples are the Likert scale and 1-10 rating scales in which a person selects the number which is considered to reflect the perceived quality of a product.<br><br>A rating scale is a method that requires the rater to assign a value, sometimes numeric, to the rated object, as a measure of some rated attribute. |
| Agreeableness | Agreeableness is a tendency to be pleasant and accommodating in social situations. In contemporary personality psychology, agreeableness is one of the five major dimensions of personality structure, reflecting individual differences in concern for cooperation and social harmony. People who score high on this dimension are empathetic, considerate, friendly, generous, and helpful. |
| Job satisfaction | Job satisfaction describes how content an individual is with his or her job. The happier people are within their job, the more satisfied they are said to be. Logic would dictate that the most satisfied ('happy') workers should be the best performers and vice versa. |
| Marital status | A person's marital status indicates whether the person is married. Questions about marital status appear on many polls and forms, including censuses and credit card applications.<br><br>In the simplest sense, the only possible answers are 'single' or 'married'. |
| Small talk | Small talk is an informal type of discourse that does not cover any functional topics of conversation or any transactions that need to be addressed. Small talk is conversation for its own sake, or '... comments on what is perfectly obvious.' The phenomenon of small talk was initially studied in 1923 by Bronislaw Malinowski, who coined the term 'phatic communication' to describe it. The ability to conduct small talk is a social skill; hence, small talk is some type of social communication. |

# Chapter 10. Motivation and Emotion

| | |
|---|---|
| Unemployment | Unemployment as defined by the International Labour Organization, occurs when people are without jobs and they have actively sought work within the past four weeks. The unemployment rate is a measure of the prevalence of unemployment and it is calculated as a percentage by dividing the number of unemployed individuals by all individuals currently in the labor force. In a 2011 news story, BusinessWeek reported, 'More than 200 million people globally are out of work, a record high, as almost two-thirds of advanced economies and half of developing countries are experiencing a slowdown in employment growth,' the group said. |
| Hedonic treadmill | The hedonic treadmill, is the supposed tendency of humans to quickly return to a relatively stable level of happiness despite major positive or negative events or life changes. According to this theory, as a person makes more money, expectations and desires rise in tandem, which results in no permanent gain in happiness. Brickman and Campbell coined the term in their essay 'Hedonic Relativism and Planning the Good Society' (1971), which appeared in M.H. Apley, ed., Adaptation Level Theory: A Symposium, New York: Academic Press, 1971, pp 287-302. The theory has consequences for understanding happiness as both an individual and a societal goal. |
| Circular reasoning | Circular reasoning is a formal logical fallacy in which the proposition to be proved is assumed implicitly or explicitly in one of the premises. For example:<br><br>'Only an untrustworthy person would run for office. The fact that politicians are untrustworthy is proof of this.'<br><br>Such an argument is fallacious, because it relies upon its own proposition -- 'politicians are untrustworthy' -- in order to support its central premise. |
| Non sequitur | Non sequitur, in formal logic, is an argument in which its conclusion does not follow from its premises. In a non sequitur, the conclusion can be either true or false, but the argument is fallacious because there is a disconnection between the premise and the conclusion. All formal fallacies are special cases of non sequitur. |
| Prenatal development | Prenatal development is the process in which a human embryo or fetus (or foetus) gestates during pregnancy, from fertilization until birth. Often, the terms fetal development, foetal development, or embryology are used in a similar sense. |
| Major depressive disorder | Major depressive disorder is a mental disorder characterized by an all-encompassing low mood accompanied by low self-esteem, and by loss of interest or pleasure in normally enjoyable activities. This cluster of symptoms (syndrome) was named, described and classified as one of the mood disorders in the 1980 edition of the American Psychiatric Association's diagnostic manual. The term 'depression' is ambiguous. |

| Zygote | A zygote is the initial cell formed when a new organism is produced by means of sexual reproduction. A zygote is synthesized from the union of two gametes, and constitutes the first stage in a unique organism's development. Zygotes are usually produced by a fertilization event between two haploid cells--an ovum from a female and a sperm cell from a male--which combine to form the single diploid cell. |
|---|---|
| Placenta | The placenta is an organ that connects the developing fetus to the uterine wall to allow nutrient uptake, waste elimination, and gas exchange via the mother's blood supply. Placentas are a defining characteristic of eutherian or 'placental' mammals, but are also found in some snakes and lizards with varying levels of development up to mammalian levels. The word placenta comes from the Latin for cake, from Greek plakóenta/plakoúnta, accusative of plakóeis/plakoús - πλακ?εις, πλακο?ς, 'flat, slab-like', in reference to its round, flat appearance in humans. |
| Congenital disorder | A congenital disorder, is a condition existing at birth and often before birth, or that develops during the first month of life (neonatal disease), regardless of causation. Of these diseases, those characterized by structural deformities are termed 'congenital anomalies'; that is a different concept (MeSH) which involves defects in or damage to a developing fetus.<br><br>A congenital disorder may be the result of genetic abnormalities, the intrauterine (uterus) environment, errors of morphogenesis, infection, or a chromosomal abnormality. |
| Miscarriage | Miscarriage is the spontaneous end of a pregnancy at a stage where the embryo or fetus is incapable of surviving independently, generally defined in humans at prior to 20 weeks of gestation. Miscarriage is the most common complication of early pregnancy. |
| Mendelian inheritance | Mendelian inheritance, hereditary characteristics from parent organisms to their offspring; it underlies much of genetics. They were initially derived from the work of Gregor Johann Mendel published in 1865 and 1866 which was 're-discovered' in 1900, and were initially very controversial. When they were integrated with the chromosome theory of inheritance by Thomas Hunt Morgan in 1915, they became the core of classical genetics. |
| Fetal alcohol syndrome | Fetal alcohol syndrome is a pattern of mental and physical defects that can develop in a fetus in association with high levels of alcohol consumption during pregnancy. Current research also implicates other lifestyle choices made by the prospective mother. Indications for lower levels of alcohol are inconclusive. |
| Microcephaly | Microcephaly is a neurodevelopmental disorder in which the circumference of the head is more than two standard deviations smaller than average for the person's age and sex. Microcephaly may be congenital or it may develop in the first few years of life. The disorder may stem from a wide variety of conditions that cause abnormal growth of the brain, or from syndromes associated with chromosomal abnormalities. |

# Chapter 10. Motivation and Emotion

| | |
|---|---|
| Rorschach test | The Rorschach test is a psychological test in which subjects' perceptions of inkblots are recorded and then analyzed using psychological interpretation, complex algorithms, or both. Some psychologists use this test to examine a person's personality characteristics and emotional functioning. It has been employed to detect underlying thought disorder, especially in cases where patients are reluctant to describe their thinking processes openly. |
| Birth weight | Birth weight is the body weight of a baby at its birth.<br><br>There have been numerous studies that have attempted, with varying degrees of success, to show links between birth weight and later-life conditions, including diabetes, obesity, tobacco smoking and intelligence. Determinants<br><br>There are basically two distinct determinants for birth weight:•The duration of gestation prior to birth, that is, the gestational age at which the child is born•The prenatal growth rate, generally measured in relation to what weight is expected for any gestational age.<br><br>The incidence of birth weight being outside what is normal is influenced by the parents in numerous ways, including:•Genetics•The health of the mother, particularly during the pregnancy•Environmental factors, including exposure of the mother to secondhand smoke•Economic status of the parents gives inconsistent study findings according to a review on 2010, and remains speculative as a determinant.•Other factors, like multiple births, where each baby is likely to be outside the AGA, one more so than the otherAbnormalities •A low birth weight can be caused either by a preterm birth (low gestational age at birth) or of the infant being small for gestational age (slow prenatal growth rate), or a combination of both.•A very large birth weight is usually caused by the infant having been large for gestational ageInfluence on adult life<br><br>Studies have been conducted to investigate how a person's birth weight can influence aspects of their future life. |
| Chickenpox | Chickenpox is a highly contagious illness caused by primary infection with varicella zoster virus (VZV). It usually starts with vesicular skin rash mainly on the body and head rather than at the periphery and becomes itchy, raw pockmarks, which mostly heal without scarring.<br><br>Chicken pox is an airborne disease spread easily through coughing or sneezing of ill individuals or through direct contact with secretions from the rash. |
| Infant mortality | In the field of public health, infant mortality is a commonly used statistical measure that is defined as the ratio of infant deaths to live births. |

|  | Traditionally, the most common cause worldwide was dehydration from diarrhea, however a variety of programs combating this problem have decreased the rate of children dying from dehydration. As a result, the most common cause is now pneumonia. |
| --- | --- |
| Maternal nutrition | Maternal nutrition is the dietary intake and habits of expectant mothers with dual emphasis on the health of the mother and the physical and mental development of infants. Nearly 24 per cent of babies are estimated to be born with lower than optimal weights at birth.<br><br>Pregnancy and child birth transform every aspect of expecting mother's lives. They should be very careful with their choices regarding what they eat. |
| Measles | Measles, is an infection of the respiratory system caused by a virus, specifically a paramyxovirus of the genus Morbillivirus. Morbilliviruses, like other paramyxoviruses, are enveloped, single-stranded, negative-sense RNA viruses. Symptoms include fever, cough, runny nose, red eyes and a generalized, maculopapular, erythematous rash. |
| Rubella | Rubella, commonly known as German measles, is a disease caused by the rubella virus. The name 'rubella' is derived from the Latin, meaning little red. Rubella is also known as German measles because the disease was first described by German physicians in the mid-eighteenth century. |
| Childhood | Childhood is the age span ranging from birth to adolescence. In developmental psychology, childhood is divided up into the developmental stages of toddlerhood (learning to walk), early childhood middle childhood and adolescence (puberty through post-puberty).<br><br>The term childhood is non-specific and can imply a varying range of years in human development. |
| Cohort effect | The term cohort effect is used in social science to describe variations in the characteristics of an area of study (such as the incidence of a characteristic or the age at onset) over time among individuals who are defined by some shared temporal experience or common life experience, such as year of birth, or year of exposure to radiation.<br><br>Cohort effects are important to epidemiologists searching for patterns in illnesses. Certain illnesses may be socially affected via the anticipation phenomenon, and cohort effects can be an indicator of this sort of phenomenon. |
| Personality development | An individual's personality is an aggregate conglomeration of decisions we've made throughout our lives (Bradshaw). There are inherent natural, genetic, and environmental factors that contribute to the development of our personality. |

According to process of socialization, 'personality also colors our values, beliefs, and expectations ... Hereditary factors that contribute to personality development do so as a result of interactions with the particular social environment in which people live.' There are several personality types as Katharine Cook Briggs and Isabel Briggs Myers illustrated in several personalities typology tests.

| | |
|---|---|
| Research design | Research design is considered as a 'blueprint' for research, dealing with at least four problems: which questions to study, which data are relevant, what data to collect, and how to analyze the results.. The best design depends on the research question as well as the orientation of the researcher. Every design has its positive and negative sides. |
| Temperament | In psychology, temperament refers to those aspects of an individual's personality, such as introversion or extroversion, that are often regarded as innate rather than learned. A great many classificatory schemes for temperament have been developed; none, though, has achieved general consensus in academia.<br><br>Historically, the concept of temperament was part of the theory of the four humours, with their corresponding four temperaments. |
| Reinforcement theory | Reinforcement theory is a limited effects media model applicable within the realm of communication. The theory generally states that people seek out and remember information that provides cognitive support for their pre-existing attitudes and beliefs. The main assumption that guides this theory is that people do not like to be wrong and often feel uncomfortable when their beliefs are challenged. |
| Surrogacy | Surrogacy is an arrangement in which a woman carries and delivers a child for another couple or person. This woman may be the child's genetic mother (called traditional surrogacy), or she may carry the pregnancy to delivery after having an embryo, to which she has no genetic relationship, transferred to her uterus (called gestational surrogacy). If the pregnant woman received compensation for carrying and delivering the child (besides medical and other reasonable expenses) the arrangement is called a commercial surrogacy, otherwise the arrangement is sometimes referred to as an altruistic surrogacy. |
| Toilet training | Toilet training, is the process of training a young child to use the toilet for urination and defecation, though training may start with a smaller toilet bowl-shaped device (often known as a potty). Cultural factors play a large part in what age is deemed appropriate, with the expectation for being potty trained ranging from 12 months for some tribes in Africa to 36 months in the modern United States. Most children can control their bowel before their bladder, boys typically start and finish later than girls, and it usually takes longer to learn to stay dry throughout the night. |

| Cognitive development | Cognitive development is a field of study in neuroscience and psychology focusing on a child's development in terms of information processing, conceptual resources, perceptual skill, language learning, and other aspects of brain development and cognitive psychology compared to an adult's point of view. A large portion of research has gone into understanding how a child imagines the world. Jean Piaget was a major force in the discovering of this field study, forming his 'theory of cognitive development'. |
|---|---|
| Centration | Centration is the tendency to focus on one aspect of a situation and neglect others. A term introduced by the Swiss psychologist Jean Piaget (1896-1980) to refer to the tendency of young children to focus attention on only one salient aspect of an object, situation, or problem at a time, to the exclusion of other potentially relevant aspects. A classic example is provided by an experiment first described by Piaget, in which a child watches while a number of objects are set out in a row and then moved closer together, and the child is asked whether there are now more objects, fewer objects, or the same number of objects. |
| Object permanence | Object permanence is the understanding that objects continue to exist even when they cannot be seen, heard, or touched. This is a fundamental understanding studied in the field of developmental psychology, the significant subfield of psychology that pertains to infants' and children's social and mental capacities and development. There is not yet scientific consensus on when this understanding emerges in human development. |
| Animal mind | The question of animal minds asks whether it is meaningful to describe a non-human animal as having a mind. <br><br> Discussion of this subject is frequently confused by the fact that some schools of philosophy and psychology (e.g. radical behaviorism) would question whether one should ascribe mind to anyone else (or even to oneself). Such an approach would naturally deny the existence of animal minds. |
| Animism | Animism refers to the belief that non-human entities are spiritual beings, or at least embody some kind of life-principle. <br><br> Animism encompasses religious beliefs that there is no separation between the uninspired or material world and souls or spirits exist not only in humans but also in all other animals, plants, rocks, natural phenomena such as thunder, geographic features such as mountains or rivers, or other entities of the natural environment. Animism may further attribute souls to abstract concepts such as words, true names or metaphors in mythology. |
| Egocentrism | In psychology, egocentrism is defined as·the incomplete differentiation of the self and the world, including other people and·the tendency to perceive, understand and interpret the world in terms of the self. An egocentric person cannot fully empathize, i.e. |

'put himself in other peoples' shoes', and believes everyone sees what she/he sees .

It appears that this egocentric stance towards the world is present mostly in younger children.

| | |
|---|---|
| Language development | Language development is a process starting early in human life, when a person begins to acquire language by learning it as it is spoken and by mimicry. Children's language development moves from simple to complex. Infants start without language. |
| Private speech | Children from two to about seven years old can be observed engaging in private speech -- speech spoken to oneself for communication, self-guidance, and self-regulation of behavior . Although it is audible, it is neither intended for nor directed at others . Private speech, although first studied by Vygotsky (1934/1986) and Piaget (1959), has received attention from researchers only in the past 30 years . |
| Zone of proximal development | The zone of proximal development often abbreviated ZPD, is the difference between what a learner can do without help and what he or she can do with help. It is a concept developed by Soviet psychologist and social constructivist Lev Vygotsky (1896 - 1934).<br><br>Vygotsky stated that a child follows an adult's example and gradually develops the ability to do certain tasks without help. |
| Moral reasoning | Moral reasoning is a study in psychology that overlaps with moral philosophy. It is also called moral development. Prominent contributors to theory include Lawrence Kohlberg and Elliot Turiel. |
| Adolescence | Adolescence is a transitional stage of physical and psychological human development generally occurring between puberty and legal adulthood (age of majority). The period of adolescence is most closely associated with the teenage years, although its physical, psychological and cultural expressions can begin earlier and end later. For example, although puberty has been historically associated with the onset of adolescent development, it now typically begins prior to the teenage years and there has been a normative shift of it occurring in preadolescence, particularly in females . |
| Conscience | Conscience is an aptitude, faculty, intuition, or judgment of the intellect that distinguishes right from wrong. Moral evaluations of this type may reference values or norms (principles and rules). In psychological terms conscience is often described as leading to feelings of remorse when a human does things that go against his/her moral values, and to feelings of rectitude or integrity when actions conform to such norms. |

| Prosocial behavior | Prosocial behavior, consists of actions which 'benefit other people or society as a whole,' 'such as helping, sharing, donating, co-operating, and volunteering.' These actions may be motivated by empathy and by concern about the welfare and rights of others, as well as for egoistic or practical concerns. Evidence suggests that prosociality is central to the well-being of social groups across a range of scales. Empathy is a strong motive in eliciting prosocial behavior, and has deep evolutionary roots. |
|---|---|
| Puberty | Puberty is the process of physical changes by which a child's body becomes an adult body capable of reproduction. Puberty is initiated by hormone signals from the brain to the gonads (the ovaries and testes). In response, the gonads produce a variety of hormones that stimulate the growth, function, or transformation of brain, bones, muscle, blood, skin, hair, breasts, and sex organs. |
| Secondary sex characteristic | Secondary sex characteristics are features that distinguish the two sexes of a species, but that are not directly part of the reproductive system. They are believed to be the product of sexual selection for traits which give an individual an advantage over its rivals in courtship and aggressive interactions. They are distinguished from the primary sex characteristics: the sex organs, which are directly necessary for reproduction to occur. |
| Generational change | Generational change is radical change that occurs in an organisation or a population as a result of its members being replaced over time by new members with different values or other characteristics.<br><br>Generational change generally presents both a real and a perceived crisis. In an organisation, the unspoken cultural values held by the longer serving members may be challenged, threatened or abandoned by newer members. |
| Menarche | Menarche is the first menstrual cycle, or first menstrual bleeding, in female human beings. From both social and medical perspectives it is often considered the central event of female puberty, as it signals the possibility of fertility.<br><br>Girls experience menarche at different ages. |
| Neural development | Neural development comprises the processes that generate, shape, and reshape the nervous system, from the earliest stages of embryogenesis to the final years of life. The study of neural development aims to describe the cellular basis of brain development and to address the underlying mechanisms. The field draws on both neuroscience and developmental biology to provide insight into the cellular and molecular mechanisms by which complex nervous systems develop. |

# Chapter 10. Motivation and Emotion

| | |
|---|---|
| Synaptic pruning | In neuroscience, synaptic pruning, neuronal pruning or axon pruning refer to neurological regulatory processes, which facilitate a change in neural structure by reducing the overall number of neurons and synapses, leaving more efficient synaptic configurations. Pruning is a process that is a general feature of mammalian neurological development. Pruning starts near the time of birth and is completed by the time of sexual maturation in humans. |
| Emerging adulthood | Emerging adulthood is a phase of the life span between adolescence and full-fledged adulthood, proposed by Jeffrey Arnett in a 2000 article in the American Psychologist. It primarily applies to young adults in developed countries who do not have children, do not live in their own home, or have sufficient income to become fully independent in their early to late 20's. Jeffrey Arnett says emerging adulthood is the period between 18 and 25 years of age where adolescents become more independent and explore various life possibilities. |
| Adulthood | An adult is a human being or living organism that is of relatively mature age, typically associated with sexual maturity and the attainment of reproductive age. In human context, the term has other subordinate meanings associated with social and legal concepts; for example, a legal adult is a legal concept for a person who has attained the age of majority and is therefore regarded as independent, self-sufficient, and responsible (contrast with 'minor'). Adulthood can be defined in terms of physiology, psychological adult development, law, personal character, or social status. |
| Cohabitation | Cohabitation is an arrangement whereby two people decide to live together on a longterm or permanent basis in an emotionally and/or sexually intimate relationship. The term is most frequently applied to couples who are not married. |
| Conscientiousness | Conscientiousness has many definitions. One is awareness, others are the trait of being painstaking and careful, or the quality of acting according to the dictates of one's conscience. It includes such elements as self-discipline, carefulness, thoroughness, organization, deliberation (the tendency to think carefully before acting), and need for achievement. |
| Neuroticism | Neuroticism is a fundamental personality trait in the study of psychology. It is an enduring tendency to experience negative emotional states. Individuals who score high on neuroticism are more likely than the average to experience such feelings as anxiety, anger, envy, guilt, and depressed mood. |
| Openness to experience | Openness to experience is one of five major domains which are used to describe human personality. Openness involves active imagination, aesthetic sensitivity, attentiveness to inner feelings, preference for variety, and intellectual curiosity. A great deal of psychometric research has demonstrated that these qualities are statistically correlated. |
| Childlessness | Childlessness describes a person who does not have any children. The causes of childlessness are many and it has great personal, social and political significance. |

| Parenting | Parenting is the process of promoting and supporting the physical, emotional, social, and intellectual development of a child from infancy to adulthood. Parenting refers to the activity of raising a child rather than the biological relationship.

In the case of humans, it is usually done by the biological parents of the child in question, although governments and society take a role as well. |
| --- | --- |
| Menopause | Menopause is a term used to describe the permanent cessation of the primary functions of the human ovaries: the ripening and release of ova and the release of hormones that cause both the creation of the uterine lining and the subsequent shedding of the uterine lining (a.k.a. the menses or the period). Menopause typically (but not always) occurs in women in midlife, during their late 40s or early 50s, and signals the end of the fertile phase of a woman's life.

The transition from reproductive to non-reproductive is the result of a reduction in female hormonal production by the ovaries. |
| Parkinsonism | Parkinsonism is a neurological syndrome characterized by tremor, hypokinesia, rigidity, and postural instability. The underlying causes of parkinsonism are numerous, and diagnosis can be complex. While the neurodegenerative condition Parkinson's disease (PD) is the most common cause of parkinsonism, a wide-range of other etiologies may lead to a similar set of symptoms, including some toxins, a few metabolic diseases, and a handful of non-PD neurological conditions. |
| Crystallized intelligence | In psychology, fluid and crystallized intelligence are factors of general intelligence originally identified by Raymond Cattell.

Fluid intelligence or fluid reasoning is the capacity to think logically and solve problems in novel situations, independent of acquired knowledge. It is the ability to analyze novel problems, identify patterns and relationships that underpin these problems and the extrapolation of these using logic.Crystallized intelligence is the ability to use skills, knowledge, and experience. It should not be equated with memory or knowledge, but it does rely on accessing information from long-term memory. |
| Dementia | Dementia is a serious loss of global cognitive ability in a previously unimpaired person, beyond what might be expected from normal aging. It may be static, the result of a unique global brain injury, or progressive, resulting in long-term decline due to damage or disease in the body. Although dementia is far more common in the geriatric population, it can occur before the age of 65, in which case it is termed 'early onset dementia'. |
| Hippocampus | The hippocampus is a major component of the brains of humans and other mammals. |

| | It belongs to the limbic system and plays important roles in long-term memory and spatial navigation. Like the cerebral cortex, with which it is closely associated, it is a paired structure, with mirror-image halves in the left and right sides of the brain. In humans and other primates, the hippocampus is located inside the medial temporal lobe, beneath the cortical surface. It contains two main interlocking parts: Ammon's horn and the dentate gyrus. |
|---|---|
| Neurofibrillary tangle | Neurofibrillary Tangles (NFTs) are aggregates of hyperphosphorylated tau protein that are most commonly known as a primary marker of Alzheimer's Disease. Their presence is also found in numerous other diseases known as Tauopathies. Little is known about their exact relationship to the different pathologies. |
| Heredity | Heredity is the passing of traits to offspring (from its parent or ancestors). This is the process by which an offspring cell or organism acquires or becomes predisposed to the characteristics of its parent cell or organism. Through heredity, variations exhibited by individuals can accumulate and cause some species to evolve. |
| Masculinity | Masculinity is, according The American Heritage Dictionary, someone or something that posses characteristics normally associated with males. The term can be used to describe any human, animal or object that has the quality of being masculine. When masculine is used to describe men, it can have degrees of comparison--more masculine, most masculine. |
| Verbal Behavior | Verbal Behavior is a 1957 book by psychologist B. F. Skinner, in which he analyzes human behavior, encompassing what is traditionally called language, linguistics, or speech. For Skinner, verbal behavior is simply behavior subject to the same controlling variables as any other operant behavior, although Skinner differentiates between verbal behavior which is mediated by other people, and that which is mediated by the natural world. The book Verbal Behavior is almost entirely theoretical, involving little experimental research in the work itself. |
| Aggression | Aggression, in its broadest sense, is behavior, or a disposition, that is forceful, hostile or attacking. It may occur either in retaliation or without provocation. In narrower definitions that are used in social sciences and behavioral sciences, aggression is an intention to cause harm or an act intended to increase relative social dominance. |
| Nonverbal communication | Nonverbal communication is usually understood as the process of communication through sending and receiving wordless messages. i.e., language is not the only source of communication, there are other means also. Messages can be communicated through gestures and touch (Haptic communication), by body language or posture, by facial expression and eye contact. |
| Social behavior | In physics, physiology and sociology, social behavior is behavior directed towards society, or taking place between, members of the same species. |

|  | Behavior such as predation which involves members of different species is not social. While many social behaviors are communication (provoke a response, or change in behavior, without acting directly on the receiver) communication between members of different species is not social behavior. |
| --- | --- |
| Nature versus nurture | The nature versus nurture debate concerns the relative importance of an individual's innate qualities ('nature,' i.e. nativism, or innatism) versus personal experiences ('nurture,' i.e. empiricism or behaviorism) in determining or causing individual differences in physical and behavioral traits.<br><br>'Nature versus nurture' in its modern sense was coined by the English Victorian polymath Francis Galton in discussion of the influence of heredity and environment on social advancement, although the terms had been contrasted previously, for example by Shakespeare (in his play, The Tempest: 4.1). Galton was influenced by the book On the Origin of Species written by his cousin, Charles Darwin. |
| Cerebral hemisphere | A cerebral hemisphere is one of the two regions of the eutherian brain that are delineated by the median plane, (medial longitudinal fissure). The brain can thus be described as being divided into left and right cerebral hemispheres. Each of these hemispheres has an outer layer of grey matter called the cerebral cortex that is supported by an inner layer of white matter. |
| Corpus callosum | The corpus callosum, is a wide, flat bundle of neural fibers beneath the cortex in the eutherian brain at the longitudinal fissure. It connects the left and right cerebral hemispheres and facilitates interhemispheric communication. It is the largest white matter structure in the brain, consisting of 200-250 million contralateral axonal projections. |
| Gender role | Gender roles refers to the set of social and behavioral norms that are widely considered to be socially appropriate for individuals of a specific sex in the context of a specific culture, which differ widely between cultures and over time. There are differences of opinion as to whether observed gender differences in behavior and personality characteristics are, at least in part, due to cultural or social factors, and therefore, the product of socialization experiences, or to what extent gender differences are due to biological and physiological differences.<br><br>Though some views on gender-based differentiation in the workplace and in interpersonal relationships has undergone profound changes, especially in Western countries, as a result of feminist influences, there are still considerable differences in gender roles in almost all societies. |
| Role model | The term role model generally means any 'person who serves as an example, whose behavior is emulated by others'. |

# Chapter 10. Motivation and Emotion

The term first appeared in Robert K. Merton's socialization research of medical students. Merton hypothesized that individuals compare themselves with reference groups of people who occupy the social role to which the individual aspires.

Socialization

Socialization is a term used by sociologists, social psychologists, anthropologists, politicians and educationalists to refer to the process of inheriting norms, customs and ideologies. It may provide the individual with the skills and habits necessary for participating within their own society; a society develops a culture through a plurality of shared norms, customs, values, traditions, social roles, symbols and languages. Socialization is thus 'the means by which social and cultural continuity are attained'.

CHAPTER QUIZ: KEY TERMS, PEOPLE, PLACES, CONCEPTS

1. _____ in evolutionary biology and evolutionary psychology, is any parental expenditure (time, energy etc). that benefits one offspring at a cost to parents' ability to invest in other components of fitness (Clutton-Brock 1991: 9; Trivers 1972). Components of fitness (Beatty 1992) include the wellbeing of existing offspring, parents' future reproduction, and inclusive fitness through aid to kin (Hamilton, 1964).

   a. Partially bivoltine
   b. Period of viability
   c. Plant reproduction
   d. Parental investment

2. In psychology, _____ refers to those aspects of an individual's personality, such as introversion or extroversion, that are often regarded as innate rather than learned. A great many classificatory schemes for _____ have been developed; none, though, has achieved general consensus in academia.

   Historically, the concept of _____ was part of the theory of the four humours, with their corresponding four _____s.

   a. Adroitness
   b. Facet
   c. Flexibility
   d. Temperament

3. . _____ is the process in which a human embryo or fetus (or foetus) gestates during pregnancy, from fertilization until birth. Often, the terms fetal development, foetal development, or embryology are used in a similar sense.

   a. Pregnancy over age 50

b. Prenatal development

c. Belly cast

d. Birthing ball

4. _____ is a group of metabolic diseases in which a person has high blood sugar, either because the body does not produce enough insulin, or because cells do not respond to the insulin that is produced. This high blood sugar produces the classical symptoms of polyuria (frequent urination), polydipsia (increased thirst) and polyphagia (increased hunger).

a. Green children of Woolpit

b. Cochlear nuclei

c. Diabetes mellitus

d. Dorsal column nuclei

5. _____ has many definitions. One is awareness, others are the trait of being painstaking and careful, or the quality of acting according to the dictates of one's conscience. It includes such elements as self-discipline, carefulness, thoroughness, organization, deliberation (the tendency to think carefully before acting), and need for achievement.

a. Dispositional affect

b. Conscientiousness

c. Grit

d. Habits of mind

**1.** d
**2.** d
**3.** b
**4.** c
**5.** b

---

## You can take the complete Chapter Practice Test

**for Chapter 10. Motivation and Emotion**
on all key terms, persons, places, and concepts.

### Online 99 Cents

### http://www.epub3.2.20111.10.cram101.com/

**Use www.Cram101.com for all your study needs**

**including Cram101's online interactive problem solving labs in**

**chemistry, statistics, mathematics, and more.**

# Chapter 11. Human Development Across the Personality

Personality Assessment Inventory

Agreeableness

Conscientiousness

Factor analysis

Neuroticism

Openness to experience

Cannon-Bard theory

Poggendorff illusion

Ponzo illusion

Rating scale

Socioeconomic status

Psychoanalysis

Psychoanalytic theory

Case study

Preconscious

Reality principle

Deese-Roediger-McDermott paradigm

Homosexuality

Motivated forgetting

CHAPTER OUTLINE: KEY TERMS, PEOPLE, PLACES, CONCEPTS

_____ | Rationalization

_____ | Reaction formation

_____ | Self-deception

_____ | Necker Cube

_____ | Anal stage

_____ | Analytical psychology

_____ | Collective unconscious

_____ | Gamma-Aminobutyric acid

_____ | Genital stage

_____ | Gratification

_____ | Latency stage

_____ | Oral stage

_____ | Penis envy

_____ | Personal unconscious

_____ | Personality development

_____ | Phallic stage

_____ | Puberty

_____ | Toilet training

_____ | Vienna Psychoanalytic Society

# Chapter 11. Human Development Across the Personality
CHAPTER OUTLINE: KEY TERMS, PEOPLE, PLACES, CONCEPTS

_____ | Inferiority complex

_____ | Behaviorism

_____ | Determinism

_____ | Cognitive switch theory

_____ | Reciprocal

_____ | Reciprocal determinism

_____ | Social cognitive theory

_____ | Social learning theory

_____ | Observational learning

_____ | Procrastination

_____ | Resistance

_____ | Role model

_____ | Self-efficacy

_____ | Substance abuse

_____ | Radical behaviorism

_____ | Animal mind

_____ | Humanism

_____ | Unconditional love

_____ | Self-actualization

Peak experience

Positive psychology

Introversion

Psychoticism

Neuroscience

Mendelian inheritance

Narcissistic Personality Inventory

Narcissism

Narcissistic personality disorder

Personality disorder

Mortality salience

Terror management theory

Collectivism

Socialization

Self-enhancement

Minnesota Multiphasic Personality Inventory

Personality test

Social desirability bias

Rorschach test

| | Thematic Apperception Test |
| --- | --- |
| | Projective test |
| | Popular psychology |
| | Hindsight |
| | Hindsight bias |

CHAPTER HIGHLIGHTS & NOTES: KEY TERMS, PEOPLE, PLACES, CONCEPTS

| Personality Assessment Inventory | Personality Assessment Inventory PhD, is a multi-scale test of psychological functioning that assesses constructs relevant to personality and psychopathology evaluation (e.g., depression, anxiety, aggression) in various contexts including psychotherapy, crisis/evaluation, forensic, personnel selection, pain/medical, and child custody assessment. The PAI has 22 non-overlapping scales, providing a comprehensive overview of psychopathology in adults. The PAI contains four kinds of scales: 1) validity scales, which measure the respondent's approach to the test, including faking good or bad, exaggeration, or defensiveness; 2) clinical scales, which correspond to psychiatric diagnostic categories; 3) treatment consideration scales, which assess factors that may relate to treatment of clinical disorders or other risk factors but which are not captured in psychiatric diagnoses (e.g., suicidal ideation); and 4) interpersonal scales, which provide indicators of interpersonal dimensions of personality functioning. |
| --- | --- |
| Agreeableness | Agreeableness is a tendency to be pleasant and accommodating in social situations. In contemporary personality psychology, agreeableness is one of the five major dimensions of personality structure, reflecting individual differences in concern for cooperation and social harmony. People who score high on this dimension are empathetic, considerate, friendly, generous, and helpful. |
| Conscientiousness | Conscientiousness has many definitions. One is awareness, others are the trait of being painstaking and careful, or the quality of acting according to the dictates of one's conscience. |

| | |
|---|---|
| Factor analysis | Factor analysis is a statistical method used to describe variability among observed, correlated variables in terms of a potentially lower number of unobserved variables called factors. In other words, it is possible, for example, that variations in three or four observed variables mainly reflect the variations in fewer such unobserved variables. Factor analysis searches for such joint variations in response to unobserved latent variables. |
| Neuroticism | Neuroticism is a fundamental personality trait in the study of psychology. It is an enduring tendency to experience negative emotional states. Individuals who score high on neuroticism are more likely than the average to experience such feelings as anxiety, anger, envy, guilt, and depressed mood. |
| Openness to experience | Openness to experience is one of five major domains which are used to describe human personality. Openness involves active imagination, aesthetic sensitivity, attentiveness to inner feelings, preference for variety, and intellectual curiosity. A great deal of psychometric research has demonstrated that these qualities are statistically correlated. |
| Cannon-Bard theory | The Cannon-Bard theory, is a theory of emotion developed by physiologists Walter Cannon and Philip Bard, suggesting that individuals experience emotions and physiologically react simultaneously. These actions include changes in muscular tension, perspiration, etc. This theory challenges the James-Lange theory of emotion introduced in the late 19th century, which suggests that emotion results from one's 'bodily change,' rather than the other way around. |
| Poggendorff illusion | The Poggendorff Illusion is a geometrical-optical illusion that involves the misperception of the position of one segment of a transverse line that has been interrupted by the contour of an intervening structure (here a rectangle). It is named after Poggendorff, the editor of the journal, who discovered it in the figures Johann Karl Friedrich Zöllner submitted when first reporting on what is now known as the Zöllner illusion, in 1860.<br><br>In the picture to the right, a straight black and red line is obscured by a grey rectangle. |
| Ponzo illusion | The Ponzo illusion is a geometrical-optical illusion that was first demonstrated by the Italian psychologist Mario Ponzo (1882-1960) in 1913. He suggested that the human mind judges an object's size based on its background. He showed this by drawing two identical lines across a pair of converging lines, similar to railway tracks. The upper line looks longer because we interpret the converging sides according to linear perspective as parallel lines receding into the distance. |
| Rating scale | A rating scale is a set of categories designed to elicit information about a quantitative or a qualitative attribute. In the social sciences, common examples are the Likert scale and 1-10 rating scales in which a person selects the number which is considered to reflect the perceived quality of a product. |

# Chapter 11. Human Development Across the Personality

| | |
|---|---|
| Socioeconomic status | Socioeconomic status is an economic and sociological combined total measure of a person's work experience and of an individual's or family's economic and social position relative to others, based on income, education, and occupation. When analyzing a family's Socioeconomic status, the household income earners' education and occupation are examined, as well as combined income, versus with an individual, when their own attributes are assessed. |
| Psychoanalysis | Psychoanalysis is a body of ideas developed by Austrian neurologist Sigmund Freud and continued by others. It is primarily devoted to the study of human psychological functioning and behavior, although it can also be applied to societies. Psychoanalysis has three main components:•a method of investigation of the mind and the way one thinks;•a systematized set of theories about human behavior;•a method of treatment of psychological or emotional illness.<br><br>Under the broad umbrella of psychoanalysis, there are at least 22 theoretical orientations regarding human mentation and development. |
| Psychoanalytic theory | Psychoanalytic theory refers to the definition and dynamics of personality development which underlie and guide psychoanalytic and psychodynamic psychotherapy. First laid out by Sigmund Freud, psychoanalytic theory has undergone many refinements since his work . Psychoanalytic theory came to full prominence as a critical force in the last third of the twentieth century as part of 'the flow of critical discourse after the 1960's. |
| Case study | A case study is a research method common in social science. It is based on an in-depth investigation of a single individual, group, or event. Case studies may be descriptive or explanatory. |
| Preconscious | In Freudian psychoanalysis, the word preconscious is applied to thoughts which are unconscious at the particular moment in question, but which are not repressed and are therefore available for recall and easily capable of becoming conscious.<br><br>'Preconscious' thoughts are thus 'unconscious' in a merely 'descriptive' sense, as opposed to a 'dynamic' one.<br><br>Classical psychoanalysis therefore permits itself to'<br><br>'distinguish two kinds of unconscious - one which is easily, under frequently occurring circumstances, transformed into something conscious, and another with which this transformation is difficult and takes place only subject to a considerable expenditure of effort or possibly never at all.' |
| Reality principle | In Freudian psychology, the reality principle is the psychoanalytic concept describing circumstantial reality compelling a man or a woman to defer instant gratification. |

The reality principle is the factual governor of the actions taken by the ego. Unlike the morality principle it does not always oppose the pleasure principle of the Id.

| | |
|---|---|
| Deese-Roediger-McDermott paradigm | The Deese-Roediger-McDermott (DRM) paradigm in cognitive psychology is an example of false memory. James Deese, an American psychologist and professor, first studied this paradigm in 1959. The DRM Paradigm refers to the tendency to falsely recall a target word from a set list of words centered around that target word. Henry L. Roediger III and Kathleen McDermott have done further research in more recent years to both confirm this phenomenon and find that it even extends into falsely recalling events, hence the name, the Deese-Roediger-McDermott paradigm. |
| Homosexuality | Homosexuality is romantic and/or sexual attraction or behavior between members of the same sex or gender. As a sexual orientation, homosexuality refers to 'an enduring pattern of or disposition to experience sexual, affectional, or romantic attractions' primarily or exclusively to people of the same sex; 'it also refers to an individual's sense of personal and social identity based on those attractions, behaviors expressing them, and membership in a community of others who share them.' |
| | Homosexuality is one of the three main categories of sexual orientation, along with bisexuality and heterosexuality, within the heterosexual-homosexual continuum. The consensus of the behavioral and social sciences and the health and mental health professions is that homosexuality is a normal and positive variation in human sexual orientation, though many religious societies, including Catholicism, Mormonism, and Islam, and some psychological associations, such as NARTH, have traditionally taught that homosexual activity is sinful or dysfunctional. |
| Motivated forgetting | Motivated forgetting is a debated concept referring to a psychological defence mechanism in which people forget unwanted memories, either consciously or unconsciously. There are times when memories are reminders of unpleasant experiences that make people angry, sad, anxious, ashamed or afraid. Motivated forgetting is a method in which people protect themselves by blocking the recall of these anxiety-arousing memories. |
| Rationalization | In psychology and logic, rationalization (also known as making excuses) is an unconscious defense mechanism in which perceived controversial behaviors or feelings are logically justified and explained in a rational or logical manner in order to avoid any true explanation, and are made consciously tolerable - or even admirable and superior - by plausible means. Rationalization encourages irrational or unacceptable behavior, motives, or feelings and often involves ad hoc hypothesizing. This process ranges from fully conscious (e.g. to present an external defense against ridicule from others) to mostly subconscious (e.g. to create a block against internal feelings of guilt). |

# Chapter 11. Human Development Across the Personality

| | |
|---|---|
| Reaction formation | In psychoanalytic theory, reaction formation is a defensive process (defense mechanism) in which anxiety-producing or unacceptable emotions and impulses are mastered by exaggeration (hypertrophy) of the directly opposing tendency.<br><br>Reaction formation depends on the hypothesis that'<br><br>'[t]he instincts and their derivatives may be arranged as pairs of opposites: life versus death, construction versus destruction, action versus passivity, dominance versus submission, and so forth. When one of the instincts produces anxiety by exerting pressure on the ego either directly or by way of the superego, the ego may try to sidetrack the offending impulse by concentrating upon its opposite.' |
| Self-deception | Self-deception is a process of denying or rationalizing away the relevance, significance, or importance of opposing evidence and logical argument. Self-deception involves convincing oneself of a truth (or lack of truth) so that one does not reveal any self-knowledge of the deception.<br><br>A consensus on the identification of self-deception remains elusive to contemporary philosophers, the result of the term's paradoxical elements and ambiguous paradigmatic cases. |
| Necker Cube | The Necker Cube is an optical illusion first published as a rhomboid in 1832 by Swiss crystallographer Louis Albert Necker.<br><br>Ambiguity<br><br>The Necker Cube is an ambiguous line drawing.<br><br>The effect is interesting because each part of the picture is ambiguous by itself, yet the human visual system picks an interpretation of each part that makes the whole consistent. |
| Anal stage | The anal stage, in Freudian psychology, is the period of human development occurring at about one to two years of age. Around this age, the child begins to toilet train, which brings about the child's fascination in the erogenous zone of the anus. The anal stage coincides with the start of the child's ability to control his anal sphincter, and therefore his ability to give or withhold gifts at will. |
| Analytical psychology | Analytical psychology is the school of psychology originating from the ideas of Swiss psychiatrist Carl Jung. His theoretical orientation has been advanced by his students and other thinkers who followed in his tradition. |

| | |
|---|---|
| Collective unconscious | Collective unconscious is a term of analytical psychology, coined by Carl Jung. It is proposed to be a part of the unconscious mind, expressed in humanity and all life forms with nervous systems, and describes how the structure of the psyche autonomously organizes experience. Jung distinguished the collective unconscious from the personal unconscious, in that the personal unconscious is a personal reservoir of experience unique to each individual, while the collective unconscious collects and organizes those personal experiences in a similar way with each member of a particular species. |
| Gamma-Aminobutyric acid | γ-Aminobutyric acid is the chief inhibitory neurotransmitter in the mammalian central nervous system. It plays a role in regulating neuronal excitability throughout the nervous system. In humans, GABA is also directly responsible for the regulation of muscle tone.<br><br>Although chemically it is an amino acid, GABA is rarely referred to as such in the scientific or medical communities, because the term 'amino acid,' used without a qualifier, conventionally refers to the alpha amino acids, which GABA is not, nor is it ever incorporated into a protein.<br><br>In spastic diplegia in humans, GABA absorption becomes impaired by nerves damaged from the condition's upper motor neuron lesion, which leads to hypertonia of the muscles signaled by those nerves that can no longer absorb GABA.Function Neurotransmitter<br><br>In vertebrates, GABA acts at inhibitory synapses in the brain by binding to specific transmembrane receptors in the plasma membrane of both pre- and postsynaptic neuronal processes. This binding causes the opening of ion channels to allow the flow of either negatively charged chloride ions into the cell or positively charged potassium ions out of the cell. Depending on which ion channels open, the membrane potential is either hyperpolarized or depolarized. This action results in a negative change in the transmembrane potential, usually causing hyperpolarization. Two general classes of GABA receptor are known: $GABA_A$ in which the receptor is part of a ligand-gated ion channel complex, and $GABA_B$ metabotropic receptors, which are G protein-coupled receptors that open or close ion channels via intermediaries (G proteins).<br><br>Neurons that produce GABA as their output are called GABAergic neurons, and have chiefly inhibitory action at receptors in the adult vertebrate. Medium Spiny Cells are a typical example of inhibitory CNS GABAergic cells. In contrast, GABA exhibits both excitatory and inhibitory actions in insects, mediating muscle activation at synapses between nerves and muscle cells, and also the stimulation of certain glands. In mammals, some GABAergic neurons, such as chandelier cells, are also able to excite their glutamatergic counterparts.<br><br>$GABA_A$ receptors are ligand-activated chloride channels; that is, when activated by GABA, they allow the flow of chloride ions across the membrane of the cell. |

Whether this chloride flow is excitatory/depolarizing (makes the voltage across the cell's membrane less negative), shunting (has no effect on the cell's membrane) or inhibitory/hyperpolarizing (makes the cell's membrane more negative) depends on the direction of the flow of chloride. When net chloride flows out of the cell, GABA is excitatory or depolarizing; when the net chloride flows into the cell, GABA is inhibitory or hyperpolarizing. When the net flow of chloride is close to zero, the action of GABA is shunting. Shunting inhibition has no direct effect on the membrane potential of the cell; however, it minimises the effect of any coincident synaptic input essentially by reducing the electrical resistance of the cell's membrane (in essence, equivalent to Ohm's law). A developmental switch in the molecular machinery controlling concentration of chloride inside the cell - and, hence, the direction of this ion flow - is responsible for the changes in the functional role of GABA between the neonatal and adult stages. That is to say, GABA's role changes from excitatory to inhibitory as the brain develops into adulthood. Brain development

For the past two decades, the theory of excitatory action of GABA early in development was unquestioned based on experiments in vitro, on brain slices. The main observation was that in the hippocampus and neocortex of the mammalian brain, GABA has primarily excitatory effects, and is in fact the major excitatory neurotransmitter in many regions of the brain before the maturation of glutamateergic synapses.

However, this theory has been questioned based on results showing that in brain slices of immature mice incubated in artificial cerebrospinal fluid (ACSF) (modified in a way that takes into account the normal composition of the neuronal milieu in sucklings by adding an energy substrate alternative to glucose, beta-hydroxybutyrate) GABA action shifts from excitatory to inhibitory mode. This effect has been later repeated when other energy substrates, pyruvate and lactate, supplemented glucose in the slices' media. The effects of beta-hydroxybutyrate were later confirmed for pyruvate and for lactate. However it was argued that the concentrations of the alternative energy substrates used in these experiments were non-physiological and the GABA-shift was instead caused by changes in pH resulting from the substrates acting as 'weak acids'. These arguments were later rebutted by further findings showing that changes in pH even greater than that caused by energy substrates do not affect the GABA-shift described in the presence of energy substrate-fortified ACSF and that the mode of action of beta-hydroxybutyrate, pyruvate and lactate (assessed by measurement NAD(P)H and oxygen utilization) was energy metabolism-related.

In the developmental stages preceding the formation of synaptic contacts, GABA is synthesized by neurons and acts both as an autocrine (acting on the same cell) and paracrine (acting on nearby cells) signalling mediator.

GABA regulates the proliferation of neural progenitor cells the migration and differentiation the elongation of neurites and the formation of synapses.

GABA also regulates the growth of embryonic and neural stem cells. GABA can in?uence the development of neural progenitor cells via brain-derived neurotrophic factor (BDNF) expression. GABA activates the $GABA_A$ receptor, causing cell cycle arrest in the S-phase, limiting growth. Beyond the nervous system

GABAergic mechanisms have been demonstrated in various peripheral tissues and organs including, but not restricted to the intestine, stomach, pancreas, Fallopian tube, uterus, ovary, testis, kidney, urinary bladder, lung, and liver.

In 2007, an excitatory GABAergic system was described in the airway epithelium. The system activates following exposure to allergens and may participate in the mechanisms of asthma. GABAergic systems have also been found in the testis and in the eye lens. Structure and conformation

GABA is found mostly as a zwitterion, that is, with the carboxy group deprotonated and the amino group protonated. Its conformation depends on its environment. In the gas phase, a highly folded conformation is strongly favored because of the electrostatic attraction between the two functional groups. The stabilization is about 50 kcal/mol, according to quantum chemistry calculations. In the solid state, a more extended conformation is found, with a trans conformation at the amino end and a gauche conformation at the carboxyl end. This is due to the packing interactions with the neighboring molecules. In solution, five different conformations, some folded and some extended, are found as a result of solvation effects. The conformational flexibility of GABA is important for its biological function, as it has been found to bind to different receptors with different conformations. Many GABA analogues with pharmaceutical applications have more rigid structures in order to control the binding better. History

Gamma-aminobutyric acid was first synthesized in 1883, and was first known only as a plant and microbe metabolic product.

| | |
|---|---|
| Genital stage | The genital stage in psychoanalysis is the term used by Sigmund Freud to describe the final stage of human psychosexual development. This stage begins at the start of puberty when sexual urges are once again awakened. Through the lessons learned during the previous stages, adolescents direct their sexual urges onto opposite sex peers, with the primary focus of pleasure of the genitals. |
| Gratification | Gratification is the pleasurable emotional reaction of happiness in response to a fulfillment of a desire or goal. |
| | Gratification, like all emotions, is a motivator of behavior and thus plays a role in the entire range of human social systems. Instant and Delayed Gratification |

# Chapter 11. Human Development Across the Personality

| | |
|---|---|
| Latency stage | In his model of the child's psychosexual development, Sigmund Freud describes five stages. Freud believed that the child discharges his/her libido (sexual energy) through a distinct body area that characterizes each stage.<br><br>The stages are:•the 'oral phase' (first stage)•the 'anal phase' (second stage)•the 'phallic phase' (third stage)•the 'latency phase' (fourth stage)•the 'genital phase' (fifth stage).<br><br>Because the latency stage is less of a stage and more of period between stages, it may begin at any time between the ages of 3 and 7 (whenever the child goes to school) and may continue until puberty, anywhere from the ages of 8 to 15 . |
| Oral stage | In Freudian psychoanalysis, the term oral stage denotes the first psychosexual development stage wherein the mouth of the infant is his or her primary erogenous zone. Spanning the life period from birth to the age of 21 months, the oral stage is the first of the five Freudian psychosexual development stages: (i) the Oral, (ii) the Anal, (iii) the Phallic, (iv) the Latent, and (v) the Genital. Moreover, because it is the infant's first human relationship -- biological (nutritive) and psychological (emotional) -- its duration depends upon the child-rearing mores of the mother's society. |
| Penis envy | Penis envy in Freudian psychoanalysis refers to the theorized reaction of a girl during her psychosexual development to the realization that she does not have a penis.<br><br>Freud considered this realization a defining moment in the development of gender and sexual identity for women. According to Freud, the parallel reaction in boys to the realization that girls do not have a penis is castration anxiety. |
| Personal unconscious | In analytical psychology, the personal unconscious is Carl Jung's term for the Freudian unconscious, as contrasted with the collective unconscious. Often referred to by him as 'No man's land,' the personal unconscious is located at the fringe of consciousness, between two worlds: 'the exterior or spacial world and the interior or psychic objective world' (Ellenberger, 707). As Charles Baudouin states, 'That the unconscious extends so far beyond consciousness is simply the counterpart of the fact that the exterior world extends so far beyond our visual field' (Ellenberger, 707). |
| Personality development | An individual's personality is an aggregate conglomeration of decisions we've made throughout our lives (Bradshaw). There are inherent natural, genetic, and environmental factors that contribute to the development of our personality. According to process of socialization, 'personality also colors our values, beliefs, and expectations ... |

| Phallic stage | In Freudian psychology, the Phallic stage is the third stage of psychosexual development, spanning the ages of three to six years, wherein the infant's libido (desire) centers upon his or her genitalia as the erogenous zone. When children become aware of their bodies, the bodies of other children, and the bodies of their parents, they gratify physical curiosity by undressing and exploring each other and their genitals, the center of the phallic stage, in course of which they learn the physical differences between 'male' and 'female', and the gender differences between 'boy' and 'girl', experiences which alter the psychologic dynamics of the parent and child relationship. The phallic stage is the third of five Freudian psychosexual development stages: (i) the Oral, (ii) the Anal, (iii) the Phallic, (iv) the Latent, and (v) the Genital. |
|---|---|
| Puberty | Puberty is the process of physical changes by which a child's body becomes an adult body capable of reproduction. Puberty is initiated by hormone signals from the brain to the gonads (the ovaries and testes). In response, the gonads produce a variety of hormones that stimulate the growth, function, or transformation of brain, bones, muscle, blood, skin, hair, breasts, and sex organs. |
| Toilet training | Toilet training, is the process of training a young child to use the toilet for urination and defecation, though training may start with a smaller toilet bowl-shaped device (often known as a potty). Cultural factors play a large part in what age is deemed appropriate, with the expectation for being potty trained ranging from 12 months for some tribes in Africa to 36 months in the modern United States. Most children can control their bowel before their bladder, boys typically start and finish later than girls, and it usually takes longer to learn to stay dry throughout the night. |
| Vienna Psychoanalytic Society | The Vienna Psychoanalytic Society was formerly known as the Wednesday Psychological Society. They commenced their meetings in Freud's apartment in 1902. By 1908 the group adopted its new name and was the international psychoanalytic authority of the time. |
| Inferiority complex | An inferiority complex, in the fields of psychology and psychoanalysis, is a feeling that one is inferior to others in some way. Such feelings can arise from an imagined or actual inferiority in the afflicted person. It is often subconscious, and is thought to drive afflicted individuals to overcompensate, resulting either in spectacular achievement or extreme schizotypal behavior, or both. Unlike a normal feeling of inferiority, which can act as an incentive for achievement (or promote discouragement), an inferiority complex is an advanced state of discouragement, often embedding itself into one's lifestyle, and sometimes resulting in a retreat from difficulties. |
| Behaviorism | Behaviorism also called the learning perspective (where any physical action is a behavior), is a philosophy of psychology based on the proposition that all things that organisms do--including acting, thinking and feeling--can and should be regarded as behaviors. The behaviorist school of thought maintains that behaviors as such can be described scientifically without recourse either to internal physiological events or to hypothetical constructs such as the mind. |

# Chapter 11. Human Development Across the Personality

| | |
|---|---|
| Determinism | Determinism is a philosophy stating that for everything that happens there are conditions such that, given them, nothing else could happen. Different versions of this theory depend upon various alleged connections, and interdependencies of things and events, asserting that these hold without exception. Deterministic theories throughout the history of philosophy have sprung from diverse motives and considerations, some of which overlap considerably. |
| Cognitive switch theory | Cognitive switch theory is a theory in gender role awareness. This theory states that all children are born neutral; sex is there but gender is not. The child thereafter becomes deliberate in filtering information that is biased toward the gender they believe they are. |
| Reciprocal | A reciprocal is a linguistic structure that marks a particular kind of relationship between two noun phrases. In a reciprocal construction, each of the participants occupies both the role of agent and patient with respect to each other. For example, the English sentence 'John and Mary cut each other's hair', contains a reciprocal structure: John cuts Mary's hair, and Mary cuts John's. |
| Reciprocal determinism | Reciprocal determinism is the theory set forth by psychologist Albert Bandura that a person's behavior both influences and is influenced by personal factors and the social environment. Bandura accepts the possibility of an individual's behavior being conditioned through the use of consequences. At the same time he asserts that a person's behavior (and personal factors, such as cognitive skills or attitudes) can impact the environment. |
| Social cognitive theory | Social cognitive theory, used in psychology, education, and communication, posits that portions of an individual's knowledge acquisition can be directly related to observing others within the context of social interactions, experiences, and outside media influences. In other words, people do not learn new behaviors solely by trying them and either succeeding or failing, but rather, the survival of humanity is dependent upon the replication of the actions of others. Depending on whether people are rewarded or punished for their behavior and the outcome of the behavior, that behavior may be modeled. |
| Social learning theory | Social learning theory is the theory that people learn new behavior through observational learning of the social factors in their environment. If people observe positive, desired outcomes in the observed behavior, then they are more likely to model, imitate, and adopt the behavior themselves. Modern theory is closely associated with Julian Rotter and Albert Bandura. |
| Observational learning | Observational learning is a type of learning that occurs as a function of observing, retaining and replicating novel behavior executed by others. It is argued that reinforcement has the effect of influencing which responses one will partake in, more than it influences the actual acquisition of the new response. |

| | |
|---|---|
| Procrastination | In psychology, procrastination refers to the act of replacing high-priority actions with tasks of lower priority, or doing something from which one derives enjoyment, and thus putting off important tasks to a later time. In accordance with Freud, the Pleasure principle (psychology) may be responsible for procrastination; humans do not prefer negative emotions and handing off a stressful task until a further date is enjoyable. The concept that humans work best under pressure provides additional enjoyment and motivation to postponing a task. |
| Resistance | 'Resistance' as initially used by Sigmund Freud, referred to patients blocking memories from conscious memory. This was a key concept, since the primary treatment method of Freud's talk therapy required making these memories available to the patient's consciousness.<br><br>'Resistance' expanded<br><br>Later, Freud described five different forms of resistance. |
| Role model | The term role model generally means any 'person who serves as an example, whose behavior is emulated by others'.<br><br>The term first appeared in Robert K. Merton's socialization research of medical students. Merton hypothesized that individuals compare themselves with reference groups of people who occupy the social role to which the individual aspires. |
| Self-efficacy | Self-efficacy is a term used in psychology, roughly corresponding to a person's belief in his/her own competence.<br><br>It has been defined as the belief that one is capable of performing in a certain manner to attain a certain set of goals. It is believed that our personalized ideas of self-efficacy affect our social interactions in almost every way. |
| Substance abuse | Substance abuse, refers to a maladaptive patterned use of a substance (drug) in which the user consumes the substance in amounts or with methods not condoned by medical professionals. Substance abuse/drug abuse is not limited to mood-altering or psycho-active drugs. Activity is also considered substance abuse when inappropriately used (as in steroids for performance enhancement in sports). |
| Radical behaviorism | Radical behaviorism is a philosophy developed by B.F. Skinner that underlies the experimental analysis of behavior approach to psychology. The term radical behaviorism applies to a particular school that emerged during the reign of behaviorism. However, radical behaviorism bears little resemblance to other schools of behaviorism, differing in the acceptance of mediating structures, the role of private events and emotions, and other areas. |

# Chapter 11. Human Development Across the Personality

| | |
|---|---|
| Animal mind | The question of animal minds asks whether it is meaningful to describe a non-human animal as having a mind.<br><br>Discussion of this subject is frequently confused by the fact that some schools of philosophy and psychology (e.g. radical behaviorism) would question whether one should ascribe mind to anyone else (or even to oneself). Such an approach would naturally deny the existence of animal minds. |
| Humanism | Humanism is an approach in study, philosophy, world view, or practice that focuses on human values and concerns, attaching prime importance to human rather than divine or supernatural matters. According to Greg M. Epstein, 'Humanism today can be categorized as a movement, a philosophy of life or worldview, or ... [a] lifestance.' In philosophy and social science, humanism is a perspective which affirms some notion of human nature, and is contrasted with anti-humanism.<br><br>Secular humanism is a secular ideology which espouses reason, ethics, and justice, whilst specifically rejecting supernatural and religious dogma as a basis of morality and decision-making. |
| Unconditional love | Unconditional love is a term that means to love someone regardless of the loved one's qualities or actions. The paradigm of unconditional love is a mother's love for her newborn.<br><br>Unconditional love is often used to describe the love in an idealized romantic relationship. |
| Self-actualization | Self-actualization is a term that has been used in various psychology theories, often in slightly different ways. The term was originally introduced by the organismic theorist Kurt Goldstein for the motive to realize one's full potential. In his view, it is the organism's master motive, the only real motive: 'the tendency to actualize itself as fully as possible is the basic drive...the drive of self-actualization.' Carl Rogers similarly wrote of 'the curative force in psychotherapy - man's tendency to actualize himself, to become his potentialities...to express and activate all the capacities of the organism.' However, the concept was brought most fully to prominence in Abraham Maslow's hierarchy of needs theory as the final level of psychological development that can be achieved when all basic and mental needs are fulfilled and the 'actualization' of the full personal potential takes place. |
| Peak experience | Peak experience is a term used to describe certain transpersonal and ecstatic states, particularly ones tinged with themes of euphoria, harmonization and interconnectedness. Participants characterize these experiences, and the revelations imparted therein, as possessing an ineffably mystical and spiritual quality or essence. |

| Positive psychology | Positive psychology is a recent branch of psychology whose purpose was summed up in 2000 by Martin Seligman and Mihaly Csikszentmihalyi: 'We believe that a psychology of positive human functioning will arise that achieves a scientific understanding and effective interventions to build thriving in individuals, families, and communities.' Positive psychologists seek 'to find and nurture genius and talent', and 'to make normal life more fulfilling', not simply to treat mental illness. The emerging field of Positive Psychology is intended to complement, not to replace traditional psychology.

By scientifically studying what has gone right, rather than wrong in both individuals and societies, Positive Psychology hopes to achieve a renaissance of sorts. |
|---|---|
| Introversion | Introversion - a notion introduced by Carl Gustav Jung in the work of Psychologische Typen (Psychological Types, 1921). In psychology, it means a personality trait involving a tendency to drive one's perceptions, actions, thoughts and emotions inside, resulting in reduced interest in activity directed to the outside world. |
| Psychoticism | Psychoticism is one of the three traits used by the psychologist Hans Eysenck in his P-E-N model (psychoticism, extraversion and neuroticism) model of personality.

High levels of this trait were believed by Eysenck to be linked to increased vulnerability to psychosis such as schizophrenia. He also believed that blood relatives of psychotics would show high levels of this trait, suggesting a genetic basis to the trait. |
| Neuroscience | Neuroscience is the scientific study of the nervous system. Traditionally, neuroscience has been seen as a branch of biology. However, it is currently an interdisciplinary science that collaborates with other fields such as chemistry, computer science, engineering, linguistics, mathematics, medicine and allied disciplines, philosophy, physics, and psychology. |
| Mendelian inheritance | Mendelian inheritance, hereditary characteristics from parent organisms to their offspring; it underlies much of genetics. They were initially derived from the work of Gregor Johann Mendel published in 1865 and 1866 which was 're-discovered' in 1900, and were initially very controversial. When they were integrated with the chromosome theory of inheritance by Thomas Hunt Morgan in 1915, they became the core of classical genetics. |
| Narcissistic Personality Inventory | The Narcissistic Personality Inventory is the most widely used measure of narcissism in social psychological research. Although several versions of the NPI have been proposed in the literature, a forty-item forced-choice version (Raskin & Terry, 1988) is the one most commonly employed in current research. The NPI is based on the DSM-III clinical criteria for narcissistic personality disorder (NPD), although it was designed to measure these features in the general population. |

# Chapter 11. Human Development Across the Personality

| | |
|---|---|
| Narcissism | Narcissism is the personality trait of egotism, vanity, conceit, or simple selfishness. Applied to a social group, it is sometimes used to denote elitism or an indifference to the plight of others.<br><br>The name 'narcissism' was coined by Freud after Narcissus who in Greek myth was a pathologically self-absorbed young man who fell in love with his own reflection in a pool. |
| Narcissistic personality disorder | Narcissistic personality disorder is a personality disorder in which the individual is described as being excessively preoccupied with issues of personal adequacy, power, prestige and vanity. This condition affects one percent of the population. First formulated in 1968, it was historically called megalomania, and it is closely linked to egocentrism. |
| Personality disorder | Personality disorders are a class of personality types and enduring behaviors associated with significant distress or disability, which appear to deviate from social expectations particularly in relating to others.<br><br>Personality disorders are included as mental disorders on Axis II of the Diagnostic manual of the American Psychiatric Association, and in the mental and behavioral disorders section of the ICD manual of the World Health Organization. Personality, defined psychologically, is the enduring behavioral and mental traits that distinguish human beings. |
| Mortality salience | Mortality salience is a term which describes awareness of one's eventual death.<br><br>Mortality salience has the potential to cause worldview defense, a psychological mechanism which strengthens people's connection with their in-group as a defense mechanism. This can lead to feelings of nationalism and racial bigotry being intensified. |
| Terror management theory | Terror Management Theory in social psychology, states that human behavior is mostly motivated by the fear of mortality. According to TMT theorists, symbols that create cultural worldviews are fiercely protected as representations of actual life. The Terror Management Theory posits that when people are reminded of their own deaths, they more readily enforce these symbols, often leading to punitive actions, violence, and war. |
| Collectivism | Collectivism is any philosophic, political, economic or social outlook that emphasizes the interdependence of every human in some collective group and the priority of group goals over individual goals. Collectivists usually focus on community, society or nation. Collectivism has been widely used to refer to a number of different political and economic philosophies, ranging from communalism and democracy to totalitarian nationalism. |
| Socialization | Socialization is a term used by sociologists, social psychologists, anthropologists, politicians and educationalists to refer to the process of inheriting norms, customs and ideologies. |

|  | It may provide the individual with the skills and habits necessary for participating within their own society; a society develops a culture through a plurality of shared norms, customs, values, traditions, social roles, symbols and languages. Socialization is thus 'the means by which social and cultural continuity are attained'. |
|---|---|
| Self-enhancement | Self-enhancement is a type of motivation that works to make people feel good about themselves and to maintain self-esteem. This motive becomes especially prominent in situations of threat, failure or blows to one's self-esteem. Self-enhancement involves a preference for positive over negative self-views. |
| Minnesota Multiphasic Personality Inventory | The Minnesota Multiphasic Personality Inventory is one of the most frequently used personality tests in mental health. The test is used by trained professionals to assist in identifying personality structure and psychopathology. Among its many uses, it is perhaps best known as the personality test that is used in conjunction with Secret and Top Secret security clearances required for many positions within United States federal agencies that incur an extensive responsibility for life and property, such as the Department of Defense, Central Intelligence Agency, and the Federal Aviation Administration. |
| Personality test | A personality test is a questionnaire or other standardized instrument designed to reveal aspects of an individual's character or psychological makeup. The first personality tests were developed in the early 20th century and were intended to ease the process of personnel selection, particularly in the armed forces. Since these early efforts of these test, a wide variety of personality tests have been developed, notably the Myers Briggs Type Indicator (MBTI), the MMPI, and a number of tests based on the Five Factor Model of personality. |
| Social desirability bias | Social desirability bias is the tendency of respondents to answer questions in a manner that will be viewed favorably by others. It can take the form of over-reporting good behavior or under-reporting bad behavior. The tendency poses a serious problem with conducting research with self-reports, especially questionnaires. |
| Rorschach test | The Rorschach test is a psychological test in which subjects' perceptions of inkblots are recorded and then analyzed using psychological interpretation, complex algorithms, or both. Some psychologists use this test to examine a person's personality characteristics and emotional functioning. It has been employed to detect underlying thought disorder, especially in cases where patients are reluctant to describe their thinking processes openly. |
| Thematic Apperception Test | The Thematic Apperception Test, is a projective psychological test. Proponents of this technique assert that a person's responses to the TAT cards can provide information about his or her views of the self, the world, and interpersonal relationships. Historically, it has been among the most widely researched, taught, and used of such tests. |

| | |
|---|---|
| Projective test | In psychology, a projective test is a personality test designed to let a person respond to ambiguous stimuli, presumably revealing hidden emotions and internal conflicts. This is different from an 'objective test' in which responses are analyzed according to a universal standard (for example, a multiple choice exam). The responses to projective tests are content analyzed for meaning rather than being based on presuppositions about meaning, as is the case with objective tests. |
| Popular psychology | The term popular psychology refers to concepts and theories about human mental life and behavior that are purportedly based on psychology and that attain popularity among the general population. The concept is closely related to the human potential movement of the 1950s and '60s.<br><br>The term 'pop psychologist' can be used to describe authors, consultants, lecturers and entertainers who are widely perceived as being psychologists, not because of their academic credentials, but because they have projected that image or have been perceived in that way in response to their work. |
| Hindsight | Hindsight, is the inclination to see events that have already occurred as being more predictable than they were before they took place. It is a multifaceted phenomenon that can affect different stages of designs, processes, contexts, and situations. Hindsight bias may cause memory distortion, where the recollection and reconstruction of content can lead to false theoretical outcomes. |
| Hindsight bias | Hindsight bias, is the inclination to see events that have already occurred as being more predictable than they were before they took place. It is a multifaceted phenomenon that can affect different stages of designs, processes, contexts, and situations. Hindsight bias may cause memory distortion, where the recollection and reconstruction of content can lead to false theoretical outcomes. |

1. In Freudian psychology, the _____ is the third stage of psychosexual development, spanning the ages of three to six years, wherein the infant's libido (desire) centers upon his or her genitalia as the erogenous zone. When children become aware of their bodies, the bodies of other children, and the bodies of their parents, they gratify physical curiosity by undressing and exploring each other and their genitals, the center of the _____, in course of which they learn the physical differences between 'male' and 'female', and the gender differences between 'boy' and 'girl', experiences which alter the psychologic dynamics of the parent and child relationship. The _____ is the third of five Freudian psychosexual development stages: (i) the Oral, (ii) the Anal, (iii) the Phallic, (iv) the Latent, and (v) the Genital.

    a. Pleasure principle
    b. Polycrates complex
    c. Polymorphous perversity
    d. Phallic stage

2. _____, used in psychology, education, and communication, posits that portions of an individual's knowledge acquisition can be directly related to observing others within the context of social interactions, experiences, and outside media influences. In other words, people do not learn new behaviors solely by trying them and either succeeding or failing, but rather, the survival of humanity is dependent upon the replication of the actions of others. Depending on whether people are rewarded or punished for their behavior and the outcome of the behavior, that behavior may be modeled.

    a. Solitary animal
    b. Somatic theory
    c. The Imp of the Perverse
    d. Social cognitive theory

3. _____ is a fundamental personality trait in the study of psychology. It is an enduring tendency to experience negative emotional states. Individuals who score high on _____ are more likely than the average to experience such feelings as anxiety, anger, envy, guilt, and depressed mood.

    a. Neuroticism
    b. Procrastination
    c. Psychological trauma
    d. Psychosomatic medicine

4. The _____, is a theory of emotion developed by physiologists Walter Cannon and Philip Bard, suggesting that individuals experience emotions and physiologically react simultaneously. These actions include changes in muscular tension, perspiration, etc. This theory challenges the James-Lange theory of emotion introduced in the late 19th century, which suggests that emotion results from one's 'bodily change,' rather than the other way around.

    a. Cannon-Bard theory
    b. Conceptual-act model of emotion
    c. Connectedness to nature scale
    d. Fanaticism

5. . The _____ in psychoanalysis is the term used by Sigmund Freud to describe the final stage of human psychosexual development. This stage begins at the start of puberty when sexual urges are once again awakened.

# Chapter 11. Human Development Across the Personality

Through the lessons learned during the previous stages, adolescents direct their sexual urges onto opposite sex peers, with the primary focus of pleasure of the genitals.

a. Healthy narcissism

b. Hypnoid state

c. Jointness

d. Genital stage

ANSWER KEY
Chapter 11. Human Development Across the Personality

1. d
2. d
3. a
4. a
5. d

---

## You can take the complete Chapter Practice Test

**for Chapter 11. Human Development Across the Personality**
on all key terms, persons, places, and concepts.

### Online 99 Cents

### http://www.epub3.2.20111.11.cram101.com/

**Use www.Cram101.com for all your study needs**

**including Cram101's online interactive problem solving labs in**

**chemistry, statistics, mathematics, and more.**

# Chapter 12. Social Behavior

CHAPTER OUTLINE: KEY TERMS, PEOPLE, PLACES, CONCEPTS

_____ | Case study

_____ | Impression formation

_____ | Social psychology

_____ | Attractiveness

_____ | Ethnic stereotype

_____ | Gamma-Aminobutyric acid

_____ | Psychoanalytic theory

_____ | Confirmation bias

_____ | Illusory correlation

_____ | Ingroup

_____ | Subjectivity

_____ | Fundamental attribution error

_____ | Hindsight bias

_____ | Collectivism

_____ | Interdependence

_____ | Dating

_____ | Factor analysis

_____ | Interpersonal attraction

_____ | Intimate relationship

Matching hypothesis

Job performance

Waist-hip ratio

Mendelian inheritance

Deception

Accessibility

Belief

Electroconvulsive therapy

Implicit attitude

Implicit Association Test

Persuasion

Racism

Exposure effect

Fear appeals

Mere Exposure effect

Cannon-Bard theory

Poggendorff illusion

Classical conditioning

Evaluative conditioning

CHAPTER OUTLINE: KEY TERMS, PEOPLE, PLACES, CONCEPTS

Observational learning

Operant conditioning

Resistance

Cognitive dissonance

Effort justification

Conformity

Social influence

Social

Ethics

Rating scale

Bystander effect

Diffusion of responsibility

Helping behavior

Decision making

Social loafing

Group cohesiveness

Group polarization

Groupthink

Social behavior

# Chapter 12. Social Behavior

Sexism

Conflict theory

Group conflict

Learning

Anecdotal evidence

Opinion

Flynn effect

Foot-in-the-door technique

CHAPTER HIGHLIGHTS & NOTES: KEY TERMS, PEOPLE, PLACES, CONCEPTS

| | |
|---|---|
| Case study | A case study is a research method common in social science. It is based on an in-depth investigation of a single individual, group, or event. Case studies may be descriptive or explanatory. |
| Impression formation | Impression formation in social psychology (sociology) refers to combining simultaneous experiences into emergent states that relate complexly to the sources. Research focuses mainly on impressions of individuals involved in social actions. However, studies also deal with impressions of an individual occupying an identity who simultaneously displays a status characteristic, psychological trait, mood, or emotion. |
| Social psychology | Social psychology (sociology), known as sociological social psychology, and sometimes as psychological sociology, is an area of sociology that focuses on social actions and on interrelations of personality, values, and mind with social structure and culture. |

Some of the major topics in this field are sociocultural change, social inequality and prejudice, leadership and intra-group behavior, social exchange, group conflict, impression formation and management, conversation structures, socialization, social constructionism, social norms and deviance, identity and roles, and emotional labor. The primary methods of data collection are sample surveys, field observations, vignette studies, field experiments, and controlled experiments.

| | |
|---|---|
| Attractiveness | Attractiveness or attraction refers to a quality that causes an interest or desire in something or someone. The term attraction may also refer to the object of the attraction itself, as in tourist attraction. |
| | Visual attractiveness |
| | Visual attractiveness or visual appeal is attraction produced primarily by visual stimuli. |
| Ethnic stereotype | An ethnic stereotype is a generalized representation of an ethnic group, composed of what are thought to be typical characteristics of members of the group. |
| | Ethnic stereotypes are commonly portrayed in ethnic jokes. |
| | Ethnic stereotypes•African Americans•Argentines•East Asians•Japanese•Hispanics and Latinos•Native Americans•South Asians•West and Central Asians•Arabs•Jews•Persians•White people•Irish•Italians•Polish people•French people•Chileans. |
| Gamma-Aminobutyric acid | γ-Aminobutyric acid is the chief inhibitory neurotransmitter in the mammalian central nervous system. It plays a role in regulating neuronal excitability throughout the nervous system. In humans, GABA is also directly responsible for the regulation of muscle tone. |
| | Although chemically it is an amino acid, GABA is rarely referred to as such in the scientific or medical communities, because the term 'amino acid,' used without a qualifier, conventionally refers to the alpha amino acids, which GABA is not, nor is it ever incorporated into a protein. |
| | In spastic diplegia in humans, GABA absorption becomes impaired by nerves damaged from the condition's upper motor neuron lesion, which leads to hypertonia of the muscles signaled by those nerves that can no longer absorb GABA.Function Neurotransmitter |
| | In vertebrates, GABA acts at inhibitory synapses in the brain by binding to specific transmembrane receptors in the plasma membrane of both pre- and postsynaptic neuronal processes. This binding causes the opening of ion channels to allow the flow of either negatively charged chloride ions into the cell or positively charged potassium ions out of the cell. |

Depending on which ion channels open, the membrane potential is either hyperpolarized or depolarized. This action results in a negative change in the transmembrane potential, usually causing hyperpolarization. Two general classes of GABA receptor are known: $GABA_A$ in which the receptor is part of a ligand-gated ion channel complex, and $GABA_B$ metabotropic receptors, which are G protein-coupled receptors that open or close ion channels via intermediaries (G proteins).

Neurons that produce GABA as their output are called GABAergic neurons, and have chiefly inhibitory action at receptors in the adult vertebrate. Medium Spiny Cells are a typical example of inhibitory CNS GABAergic cells. In contrast, GABA exhibits both excitatory and inhibitory actions in insects, mediating muscle activation at synapses between nerves and muscle cells, and also the stimulation of certain glands. In mammals, some GABAergic neurons, such as chandelier cells, are also able to excite their glutamatergic counterparts.

$GABA_A$ receptors are ligand-activated chloride channels; that is, when activated by GABA, they allow the flow of chloride ions across the membrane of the cell. Whether this chloride flow is excitatory/depolarizing (makes the voltage across the cell's membrane less negative), shunting (has no effect on the cell's membrane) or inhibitory/hyperpolarizing (makes the cell's membrane more negative) depends on the direction of the flow of chloride. When net chloride flows out of the cell, GABA is excitatory or depolarizing; when the net chloride flows into the cell, GABA is inhibitory or hyperpolarizing. When the net flow of chloride is close to zero, the action of GABA is shunting. Shunting inhibition has no direct effect on the membrane potential of the cell; however, it minimises the effect of any coincident synaptic input essentially by reducing the electrical resistance of the cell's membrane (in essence, equivalent to Ohm's law). A developmental switch in the molecular machinery controlling concentration of chloride inside the cell - and, hence, the direction of this ion flow - is responsible for the changes in the functional role of GABA between the neonatal and adult stages. That is to say, GABA's role changes from excitatory to inhibitory as the brain develops into adulthood. Brain development

For the past two decades, the theory of excitatory action of GABA early in development was unquestioned based on experiments in vitro, on brain slices. The main observation was that in the hippocampus and neocortex of the mammalian brain, GABA has primarily excitatory effects, and is in fact the major excitatory neurotransmitter in many regions of the brain before the maturation of glutamateergic synapses.

However, this theory has been questioned based on results showing that in brain slices of immature mice incubated in artificial cerebrospinal fluid (ACSF) (modified in a way that takes into account the normal composition of the neuronal milieu in sucklings by adding an energy substrate alternative to glucose, beta-hydroxybutyrate) GABA action shifts from excitatory to inhibitory mode. This effect has been later repeated when other energy substrates, pyruvate and lactate, supplemented glucose in the slices' media.

The effects of beta-hydroxybutyrate were later confirmed for pyruvate and for lactate. However it was argued that the concentrations of the alternative energy substrates used in these experiments were non-physiological and the GABA-shift was instead caused by changes in pH resulting from the substrates acting as 'weak acids'. These arguments were later rebutted by further findings showing that changes in pH even greater than that caused by energy substrates do not affect the GABA-shift described in the presence of energy substrate-fortified ACSF and that the mode of action of beta-hydroxybutyrate, pyruvate and lactate (assessed by measurement NAD(P)H and oxygen utilization) was energy metabolism-related.

In the developmental stages preceding the formation of synaptic contacts, GABA is synthesized by neurons and acts both as an autocrine (acting on the same cell) and paracrine (acting on nearby cells) signalling mediator.

GABA regulates the proliferation of neural progenitor cells the migration and differentiation the elongation of neurites and the formation of synapses.

GABA also regulates the growth of embryonic and neural stem cells. GABA can in?uence the development of neural progenitor cells via brain-derived neurotrophic factor (BDNF) expression. GABA activates the $GABA_A$ receptor, causing cell cycle arrest in the S-phase, limiting growth. Beyond the nervous system

GABAergic mechanisms have been demonstrated in various peripheral tissues and organs including, but not restricted to the intestine, stomach, pancreas, Fallopian tube, uterus, ovary, testis, kidney, urinary bladder, lung, and liver.

In 2007, an excitatory GABAergic system was described in the airway epithelium. The system activates following exposure to allergens and may participate in the mechanisms of asthma. GABAergic systems have also been found in the testis and in the eye lens. Structure and conformation

GABA is found mostly as a zwitterion, that is, with the carboxy group deprotonated and the amino group protonated. Its conformation depends on its environment. In the gas phase, a highly folded conformation is strongly favored because of the electrostatic attraction between the two functional groups. The stabilization is about 50 kcal/mol, according to quantum chemistry calculations. In the solid state, a more extended conformation is found, with a trans conformation at the amino end and a gauche conformation at the carboxyl end. This is due to the packing interactions with the neighboring molecules. In solution, five different conformations, some folded and some extended, are found as a result of solvation effects. The conformational flexibility of GABA is important for its biological function, as it has been found to bind to different receptors with different conformations. Many GABA analogues with pharmaceutical applications have more rigid structures in order to control the binding better. History

# Chapter 12. Social Behavior

| | |
|---|---|
| Psychoanalytic theory | Psychoanalytic theory refers to the definition and dynamics of personality development which underlie and guide psychoanalytic and psychodynamic psychotherapy. First laid out by Sigmund Freud, psychoanalytic theory has undergone many refinements since his work . Psychoanalytic theory came to full prominence as a critical force in the last third of the twentieth century as part of 'the flow of critical discourse after the 1960's. |
| Confirmation bias | Confirmation bias is a tendency for people to favor information that confirms their preconceptions or hypotheses regardless of whether the information is true. As a result, people gather evidence and recall information from memory selectively, and interpret it in a biased way. The biases appear in particular for emotionally significant issues and for established beliefs. |
| Illusory correlation | Illusory correlation is the phenomenon of seeing the relationship one expects in a set of data even when no such relationship exists. When people form false associations between membership in a statistical minority group and rare (typically negative) behaviors, this would be a common example of illusory correlation. This happens because the variables capture the attention simply because they are novel or deviant. |
| Ingroup | In sociology and social psychology, an ingroup is a social group to which an individual feels as though he or she belongs as a member of the group. People tend to hold positive attitudes towards members of their own groups, a phenomenon known as ingroup bias. The term originates from social identity theory which grew out of the work of social psychologist Henri Tajfel. |
| Subjectivity | Subjectivity refers to the subject and his or her perspective, feelings, beliefs, and desires. In philosophy, the term is usually contrasted with objectivity.

Subjectivity may refer to the specific discerning interpretations of any aspect of experiences. |
| Fundamental attribution error | In social psychology, the fundamental attribution error describes the tendency to over-value dispositional or personality-based explanations for the observed behaviors of others while under-valuing situational explanations for those behaviors. The fundamental attribution error is most visible when people explain the behavior of others. It does not explain interpretations of one's own behavior--where situational factors are often taken into consideration. |
| Hindsight bias | Hindsight bias, is the inclination to see events that have already occurred as being more predictable than they were before they took place. It is a multifaceted phenomenon that can affect different stages of designs, processes, contexts, and situations. Hindsight bias may cause memory distortion, where the recollection and reconstruction of content can lead to false theoretical outcomes. |

| | |
|---|---|
| Collectivism | Collectivism is any philosophic, political, economic or social outlook that emphasizes the interdependence of every human in some collective group and the priority of group goals over individual goals. Collectivists usually focus on community, society or nation. Collectivism has been widely used to refer to a number of different political and economic philosophies, ranging from communalism and democracy to totalitarian nationalism. |
| Interdependence | Interdependence is a relationship in which each member is mutually dependent on the others. This concept differs from a dependence relationship, where some members are dependent and some are not.<br><br>In an interdependent relationship, participants may be emotionally, economically, ecologically and/or morally reliant on and responsible to each other. |
| Dating | Dating is a form of human courtship consisting of social activities done by two persons with the aim of each assessing the other's suitability as a partner in an intimate relationship or as a spouse. While the term has several senses, it usually refers to the act of meeting and engaging in some mutually agreed upon social activity in public, together, as a couple. The protocols and practices of dating, and the terms used to describe it, vary considerably from country to country. |
| Factor analysis | Factor analysis is a statistical method used to describe variability among observed, correlated variables in terms of a potentially lower number of unobserved variables called factors. In other words, it is possible, for example, that variations in three or four observed variables mainly reflect the variations in fewer such unobserved variables. Factor analysis searches for such joint variations in response to unobserved latent variables. |
| Interpersonal attraction | Interpersonal attraction is the attraction between people which leads to friendships and romantic relationships. Interpersonal attraction, the process, is distinct from perceptions of physical attractiveness which involves views of what is and is not considered beautiful or attractive.<br><br>The study of interpersonal attraction is a major area of research in social psychology. |
| Intimate relationship | An intimate relationship is a particularly close interpersonal relationship, and the term is sometimes used euphemistically for a sexual relationship. The characteristics of an intimate relationship include an enduring behavioral interdependence, repeated interactions, emotional attachment and need fulfillment. Intimate relationships include friendships, dating relationships, spiritual relationships, and marital relationships and there are individual differences in both the quality and quantity of these relationships. |
| Matching hypothesis | The matching hypothesis is a popular psychological social psychology theory, proposed by Elaine Hatfield (Walster) and her colleagues in 1966 which suggests why people become attracted to their partner. |

|  | It claims that people are more likely to form long standing relationships with someone who is as equally physically attractive as they are. This is influenced by realistic choices, desire of the match and good probability of obtaining the date. |
|---|---|
| Job performance | Job performance is a commonly used, yet poorly defined concept in industrial and organizational psychology, the branch of psychology that deals with the workplace. It most commonly refers to whether a person performs their job well. Despite the confusion over how it should be exactly defined, performance is an extremely important criterion that relates to organizational outcomes and success. |
| Waist-hip ratio | Waist-hip ratio is the ratio of the circumference of the waist to that of the hips.<br><br>Measurement<br><br>Strictly, the waist circumference is measured at a level midway between the lowest rib and the iliac crest, and the hip circumference at the level of the great trochanters, with the legs close together. The waist-hip ratio equals the waist circumference divided by the hip circumference. |
| Mendelian inheritance | Mendelian inheritance, hereditary characteristics from parent organisms to their offspring; it underlies much of genetics. They were initially derived from the work of Gregor Johann Mendel published in 1865 and 1866 which was 're-discovered' in 1900, and were initially very controversial. When they were integrated with the chromosome theory of inheritance by Thomas Hunt Morgan in 1915, they became the core of classical genetics. |
| Deception | Deception, beguilement, deceit, bluff, mystification, and subterfuge are acts to propagate beliefs that are not true, or not the whole truth (as in half-truths or omission). Deception can involve dissimulation, propaganda, sleight of hand. It can employ distraction, camouflage or concealment. |
| Accessibility | Accessibility is a general term used to describe the degree to which a product, device, service, or environment is available to as many people as possible. Accessibility can be viewed as the 'ability to access' and possible benefit of some system or entity. Accessibility is often used to focus on people with disabilities or special needs and their right of access to entities, often through use of assistive technology. |
| Belief | Belief is the psychological state in which an individual holds a proposition or premise to be true.<br><br>Belief, knowledge and epistemology<br><br>The terms belief and knowledge are used differently in philosophy. |

| | |
|---|---|
| Electroconvulsive therapy | Electroconvulsive therapy formerly known as electroshock, is a psychiatric treatment in which seizures are electrically induced in anesthetized patients for therapeutic effect. Its mode of action is unknown. Today, ECT is most often recommended for use as a treatment for severe depression that has not responded to other treatment, and is also used in the treatment of mania and catatonia. |
| Implicit attitude | Implicit attitudes are the positive or negative thoughts, feelings, or actions towards objects which arise due to past experiences which one is either unaware of or which one cannot attribute to an identified previous experience. The commonly used definition of implicit attitude within cognitive and social psychology comes from Greenwald & Banaji's template for definitions of terms related to implicit cognition : <br><br> 'Implicit attitudes are introspectively unidentified traces of past experience that mediate favorable or unfavorable feeling, thought, or action toward social objects'. <br><br> Note that an attitude is differentiated from the concept of a stereotype in that it functions as a broad favorable or unfavorable characteristic towards a social object whereas a stereotype is a set of favorable and/or unfavorable characteristics which is applied to an individual based on social group membership. |
| Implicit Association Test | The Implicit Association Test is a measure within social psychology designed to detect the strength of a person's automatic association between mental representations of objects (concepts) in memory. The IAT was introduced in the scientific literature in 1998 by Anthony Greenwald, Debbie McGee, and Jordan Schwartz. The IAT is now widely used in social psychology research and is used to some extent in clinical, cognitive, and developmental psychology research. |
| Persuasion | Persuasion is the influence of beliefs, attitudes, intentions, motivations, or behaviors. <br><br> Persuasion methods are also sometimes referred to as persuasion tactics or persuasion strategies. Weapons of influence <br><br> Robert Cialdini, in his book on persuasion, defined six 'weapons of influence':•Reciprocity - People tend to return a favor. |
| Racism | Racism is generally understood as either belief that different racial groups are characterized by intrinsic characteristics or abilities and that some such groups are therefore naturally superior to others or as practices that discriminate against members of particular racial groups, for example by perpetuating unequal access to resources between groups. |

# Chapter 12. Social Behavior

The definition of racism is controversial both because there is little scholarly agreement about what the word 'race' means, and because there is also little agreement about what does and doesn't constitute discrimination. Some definitions would have it that any assumption that a person's behavior would be influenced by their racial categorization is racist, regardless of how seemingly benign such assumptions might be.

| | |
|---|---|
| Exposure effect | The exposure effect is a psychological phenomenon by which people tend to develop a preference for things merely because they are familiar with them. In social psychology, this effect is sometimes called the familiarity principle. In studies of interpersonal attraction, the more often a person is seen by someone, the more pleasing and likeable that person appears to be. |
| Fear appeals | Fear appeals have been predominantly studied in the context of education, marketing, and health awareness campaigns, with the intent to alter intentions and motivate individuals to act on a message. Much of the research has been directed at establishing the relevant variables in both the target of the message, as well as the message itself. Over the years, several models of the influence of fear appeals on persuasion, have been proposed. |
| Mere Exposure effect | The Mere Exposure Effect is a psychological phenomenon by which people tend to develop a preference for things merely because they are familiar with them. In social psychology, this effect is sometimes called the familiarity principle. In studies of interpersonal attraction, the more often a person is seen by someone, the more pleasing and likeable that person appears to be. |
| Cannon-Bard theory | The Cannon-Bard theory, is a theory of emotion developed by physiologists Walter Cannon and Philip Bard, suggesting that individuals experience emotions and physiologically react simultaneously. These actions include changes in muscular tension, perspiration, etc. This theory challenges the James-Lange theory of emotion introduced in the late 19th century, which suggests that emotion results from one's 'bodily change,' rather than the other way around. |
| Poggendorff illusion | The Poggendorff Illusion is a geometrical-optical illusion that involves the misperception of the position of one segment of a transverse line that has been interrupted by the contour of an intervening structure (here a rectangle). It is named after Poggendorff, the editor of the journal, who discovered it in the figures Johann Karl Friedrich Zöllner submitted when first reporting on what is now known as the Zöllner illusion, in 1860. |
| | In the picture to the right, a straight black and red line is obscured by a grey rectangle. |
| Classical conditioning | Introduction |
| | Classical conditioning is a form of learning in which one stimulus comes to signal the occurrence of a second stimulus. |

|  |  |
|---|---|
| | This is often brought about by pairing the two stimuli, as in Pavlov's classic experiments. Pavlov presented dogs with a ringing bell followed by food. |
| Evaluative conditioning | Evaluative conditioning concerns how we can come to like or dislike something through an association (association of ideas). |
| | If something that we have no strong feelings towards (such as an unfamiliar person, object, or picture, and so on) appears to us with something that we strongly dislike (such as a very unpleasant odour) then our feelings to that once innocuous item can change--we can come to dislike that thing too. The same can happen when something is paired with something else that we strongly like--we can come to like that item more. |
| Observational learning | Observational learning is a type of learning that occurs as a function of observing, retaining and replicating novel behavior executed by others. It is argued that reinforcement has the effect of influencing which responses one will partake in, more than it influences the actual acquisition of the new response. |
| | Although observational learning can take place at any stage in life, it is thought to be of greater importance during childhood, particularly as authority becomes important. |
| Operant conditioning | Operant conditioning is the use of a behavior's antecedent and/or its consequence to influence the occurrence and form of behavior. Operant conditioning is distinguished from classical conditioning (also called respondent conditioning) in that operant conditioning deals with the modification of 'voluntary behavior' or operant behavior. Operant behavior 'operates' on the environment and is maintained by its consequences, while classical conditioning deals with the conditioning of reflexive (reflex) behaviors which are elicited by antecedent conditions. |
| Resistance | 'Resistance' as initially used by Sigmund Freud, referred to patients blocking memories from conscious memory. This was a key concept, since the primary treatment method of Freud's talk therapy required making these memories available to the patient's consciousness. |
| | 'Resistance' expanded |
| | Later, Freud described five different forms of resistance. |
| Cognitive dissonance | Cognitive dissonance is a discomfort caused by holding conflicting cognitions (e.g., ideas, beliefs, values, emotional reactions) simultaneously. In a state of dissonance, people may feel surprise, dread, guilt, anger, or embarrassment. |

# Chapter 12. Social Behavior

| | |
|---|---|
| Effort justification | Effort Justification is an idea and paradigm in social psychology stemming from Festinger's theory of Cognitive Dissonance. Effort justification is people's tendency to attribute a greater value (greater than the objective value) to an outcome they had to put effort into acquiring or achieving.<br><br>Theory and Research<br><br>Cognitive Dissonance theory explains changes in people's attitudes or beliefs as the result of an attempt to reduce a dissonance (discrepancy) between contradicting ideas or cognitions. |
| Conformity | Conformity is the act of matching attitudes, beliefs, and behaviors to group norms. Norms are implicit rules shared by a group of individuals, that guide their interactions with others and among society or social group. This tendency to conform occurs in small groups and/or society as a whole, and may result from subtle unconscious influences, or direct and overt social pressure. |
| Social influence | Social influence occurs when one's emotions, opinions, or behaviors are affected by others. Social influence takes many forms and can be seen in conformity, socialization, peer pressure, obedience, leadership, persuasion, sales, and marketing. In 1958, Harvard psychologist, Herbert Kelman identified three broad varieties of social influence. |
| Social | The term social refers to a characteristic of living organisms as applied to populations humans and other animals. It always refers to the interaction of organisms with other organisms and to their collective co-existence, irrespective of whether they are aware of it or not, and irrespective of whether the interaction is voluntary or involuntary.<br><br>The word 'Social' derives from the Latin word socii ('allies'), it is particularly derived from the Italian Socii states that historically allied with the Roman Republic, though they famously rebelled against Rome in the Social War of 91-88 BC.Definition<br><br>In the absence of agreement about its meaning, the term 'social' is used in many different senses and regarded as a fuzzy concept, referring among other things to:<br><br>Attitudes, orientations, or behaviors which take the interests, intentions, or needs of other people into account (in contrast to anti-social behaviour) has played some role in defining the idea or the principle. |
| Ethics | Ethics, is a branch of philosophy that involves systematizing, defending, and recommending concepts of right and wrong behavior.<br><br>It is also a common term to refer to or define e.g. |

code of conduct, honourable behaviours, virtues, just actions, etc. Ethics may be either externally imposed (by e.g. society, professional organizations, schools, law enforcement, etc).

| | |
|---|---|
| Rating scale | A rating scale is a set of categories designed to elicit information about a quantitative or a qualitative attribute. In the social sciences, common examples are the Likert scale and 1-10 rating scales in which a person selects the number which is considered to reflect the perceived quality of a product.

A rating scale is a method that requires the rater to assign a value, sometimes numeric, to the rated object, as a measure of some rated attribute. |
| Bystander effect | The bystander effect are present. The probability of help has often appeared to be inversely related to the number of bystanders; in other words, the greater the number of bystanders, the less likely it is that any one of them will help. The mere presence of other bystanders greatly decreases intervention. |
| Diffusion of responsibility | Diffusion of responsibility is a sociopsychological phenomenon whereby a person is less likely to take responsibility for an action or inaction when others are present. Considered a form of attribution, the individual assumes that either others are responsible for taking action or have already done so. The phenomenon tends to occur in groups of people above a certain critical size and when responsibility is not explicitly assigned. |
| Helping behavior | Helping behavior refers to voluntary actions intended to help the others, with reward regarded or disregarded. It is a type of prosocial behavior (voluntary action intended to help or benefit another individual or group of individuals, such as sharing, comforting, rescuing and helping).

Altruism is distinguished from helping behavior. |
| Decision making | Decision making can be regarded as the mental processes (cognitive process) resulting in the selection of a course of action among several alternatives. Every decision making process produces a final choice. The output can be an action or an opinion of choice. |
| Social loafing | In the social psychology of groups, social loafing is the phenomenon of people exerting less effort to achieve a goal when they work in a group than when they work alone. This is seen as one of the main reasons groups are sometimes less productive than the combined performance of their members working as individuals, but should be distinguished from the coordination problems that groups sometime experience. Social loafing is also associated with two concepts that are typically used to explain why it occurs: The 'free-rider' theory and the resulting 'sucker effect', which is an individual's reduction in effort in order to avoid pulling the weight of a fellow group member. |

# Chapter 12. Social Behavior

| | |
|---|---|
| Group cohesiveness | 'Group cohesiveness' is the force bringing group members closer together. Cohesiveness has two dimensions: emotional (or personal) and task-related. The emotional aspect of cohesiveness, which was studied more often, is derived from the connection that members feel to other group members and to their group as a whole. |
| Group polarization | In social psychology, group polarization refers to the tendency for groups to make decisions that are more extreme than the initial inclination of its members. These more extreme decisions are towards greater risk if individual's initial tendency is to be risky and towards greater caution if individual's initial tendency is to be cautious. The phenomenon also holds that a group's attitude toward a situation may change in the sense that the individual's initial attitudes have strengthened and intensified after group discussion. |
| Groupthink | Groupthink is a type of thought within a deeply cohesive in-group whose members try to minimize conflict and reach consensus without critically testing, analyzing, and evaluating ideas. It is a second potential negative consequence of group cohesion.

Irving Janis studied a number of American Foreign policy 'disasters' such as failure to anticipate the Japanese attack on Pearl Harbor (1941); the Bay of Pigs fiasco (1961) when the US administration sought to overthrow Cuban Government of Fidel Castro; and the prosecution of the Vietnam War (1964-67) by President Lyndon Johnson. |
| Social behavior | In physics, physiology and sociology, social behavior is behavior directed towards society, or taking place between, members of the same species. Behavior such as predation which involves members of different species is not social. While many social behaviors are communication (provoke a response, or change in behavior, without acting directly on the receiver) communication between members of different species is not social behavior. |
| Sexism | Sexism, a term coined in the mid-20th century, is the belief or attitude that one sex is inherently superior to, more competent than, or more valuable than the other. It can also include this type of discrimination in regards to gender. Sexism primarily involves hatred of, or prejudice towards, either sex as a whole , or the application of stereotypes of masculinity in relation to men, or of femininity in relation to women. |
| Conflict theory | Conflict theories are perspectives in social science that emphasize the social, political or material inequality of a social group, that critique the broad socio-political system, or that otherwise detract from structural functionalism and ideological conservativism. Conflict theories draw attention to power differentials, such as class conflict, and generally contrast historically dominant ideologies.

Certain conflict theories set out to highlight the ideological aspects inherent in traditional thought. |

| | |
|---|---|
| Group conflict | Group conflict, is a pervasive feature common to all levels of social organization (e.g., sports teams, ethnic groups, nations, religions, gangs). Although group conflict is one of the most complex phenomena studied by social scientists, the history of the human race evidences a series of group-level conflicts that have gained notoriety over the years. For example, from 1820 to 1945, it has been estimated that at least 59 million persons were killed during conflicts between groups of one type or another. |
| Learning | Learning is acquiring new or modifying existing knowledge, behaviors, skills, values, or preferences and may involve synthesizing different types of information. The ability to learn is possessed by humans, animals and some machines. Progress over time tends to follow learning curves. |
| Anecdotal evidence | The expression anecdotal evidence refers to evidence from anecdotes. Because of the small sample, there is a larger chance that it may be true but unreliable due to cherry-picked or otherwise non-representative samples of typical cases.<br><br>Anecdotal evidence is considered dubious support of a claim; it is accepted only in lieu of more solid evidence. |
| Opinion | An opinion is a subjective statement or thought about an issue or topic, and is the result of emotion or interpretation of facts. An opinion may be supported by an argument, although people may draw opposing opinions from the same set of facts. Opinions rarely change without new arguments being presented. |
| Flynn effect | The Flynn effect is the name given to a substantial and long-sustained increase in intelligence test scores measured in many parts of the world. When intelligence quotient (IQ) tests are initially standardized using a sample of test-takers, by convention the average of the test results is set to 100 and their standard deviation is set to 15 or 16 IQ points. When IQ tests are revised, they are again standardized using a new sample of test-takers, usually born more recently than the first. |
| Foot-in-the-door technique | Foot-in-the-door technique is a compliance tactic that involves getting a person to agree to a large request by first setting them up by having that person agree to a modest request.<br><br>Classic FITD experiments<br><br>In an early study, a team of psychologists telephoned housewives in California and asked if the women would answer a few questions about the household products they used. Three days later, the psychologists called again. |

# Chapter 12. Social Behavior

1. A _____ is a research method common in social science. It is based on an in-depth investigation of a single individual, group, or event. Case studies may be descriptive or explanatory.

   a. History of scientific method
   b. Blind experiment
   c. Critical-Creative Thinking and Behavioral Research Laboratory
   d. Case study

2. _____ is the phenomenon of seeing the relationship one expects in a set of data even when no such relationship exists. When people form false associations between membership in a statistical minority group and rare (typically negative) behaviors, this would be a common example of _____. This happens because the variables capture the attention simply because they are novel or deviant.

   a. Illusory correlation
   b. Implicit cognition
   c. Inequity aversion
   d. Information bias

3. . γ-Aminobutyric acid is the chief inhibitory neurotransmitter in the mammalian central nervous system. It plays a role in regulating neuronal excitability throughout the nervous system. In humans, GABA is also directly responsible for the regulation of muscle tone.

   Although chemically it is an amino acid, GABA is rarely referred to as such in the scientific or medical communities, because the term 'amino acid,' used without a qualifier, conventionally refers to the alpha amino acids, which GABA is not, nor is it ever incorporated into a protein.

   In spastic diplegia in humans, GABA absorption becomes impaired by nerves damaged from the condition's upper motor neuron lesion, which leads to hypertonia of the muscles signaled by those nerves that can no longer absorb GABA.Function Neurotransmitter

   In vertebrates, GABA acts at inhibitory synapses in the brain by binding to specific transmembrane receptors in the plasma membrane of both pre- and postsynaptic neuronal processes. This binding causes the opening of ion channels to allow the flow of either negatively charged chloride ions into the cell or positively charged potassium ions out of the cell. Depending on which ion channels open, the membrane potential is either hyperpolarized or depolarized. This action results in a negative change in the transmembrane potential, usually causing hyperpolarization. Two general classes of GABA receptor are known: $GABA_A$ in which the receptor is part of a ligand-gated ion channel complex, and $GABA_B$ metabotropic receptors, which are G protein-coupled receptors that open or close ion channels via intermediaries (G proteins).

   Neurons that produce GABA as their output are called GABAergic neurons, and have chiefly inhibitory action at receptors in the adult vertebrate. Medium Spiny Cells are a typical example of inhibitory CNS GABAergic cells. In contrast, GABA exhibits both excitatory and inhibitory actions in insects, mediating muscle activation at synapses between nerves and muscle cells, and also the stimulation of certain glands. In mammals, some GABAergic neurons, such as chandelier cells, are also able to excite their glutamatergic counterparts.

$GABA_A$ receptors are ligand-activated chloride channels; that is, when activated by GABA, they allow the flow of chloride ions across the membrane of the cell. Whether this chloride flow is excitatory/depolarizing (makes the voltage across the cell's membrane less negative), shunting (has no effect on the cell's membrane) or inhibitory/hyperpolarizing (makes the cell's membrane more negative) depends on the direction of the flow of chloride. When net chloride flows out of the cell, GABA is excitatory or depolarizing; when the net chloride flows into the cell, GABA is inhibitory or hyperpolarizing. When the net flow of chloride is close to zero, the action of GABA is shunting. Shunting inhibition has no direct effect on the membrane potential of the cell; however, it minimises the effect of any coincident synaptic input essentially by reducing the electrical resistance of the cell's membrane (in essence, equivalent to Ohm's law). A developmental switch in the molecular machinery controlling concentration of chloride inside the cell - and, hence, the direction of this ion flow - is responsible for the changes in the functional role of GABA between the neonatal and adult stages. That is to say, GABA's role changes from excitatory to inhibitory as the brain develops into adulthood. Brain development

For the past two decades, the theory of excitatory action of GABA early in development was unquestioned based on experiments in vitro, on brain slices. The main observation was that in the hippocampus and neocortex of the mammalian brain, GABA has primarily excitatory effects, and is in fact the major excitatory neurotransmitter in many regions of the brain before the maturation of glutamateergic synapses.

However, this theory has been questioned based on results showing that in brain slices of immature mice incubated in artificial cerebrospinal fluid (ACSF) (modified in a way that takes into account the normal composition of the neuronal milieu in sucklings by adding an energy substrate alternative to glucose, beta-hydroxybutyrate) GABA action shifts from excitatory to inhibitory mode. This effect has been later repeated when other energy substrates, pyruvate and lactate, supplemented glucose in the slices' media. The effects of beta-hydroxybutyrate were later confirmed for pyruvate and for lactate. However it was argued that the concentrations of the alternative energy substrates used in these experiments were non-physiological and the GABA-shift was instead caused by changes in pH resulting from the substrates acting as 'weak acids'. These arguments were later rebutted by further findings showing that changes in pH even greater than that caused by energy substrates do not affect the GABA-shift described in the presence of energy substrate-fortified ACSF and that the mode of action of beta-hydroxybutyrate, pyruvate and lactate (assessed by measurement NAD(P)H and oxygen utilization) was energy metabolism-related.

In the developmental stages preceding the formation of synaptic contacts, GABA is synthesized by neurons and acts both as an autocrine (acting on the same cell) and paracrine (acting on nearby cells) signalling mediator.

GABA regulates the proliferation of neural progenitor cells the migration and differentiation the elongation of neurites and the formation of synapses.

GABA also regulates the growth of embryonic and neural stem cells. GABA can in?uence the development of neural progenitor cells via brain-derived neurotrophic factor (BDNF) expression. GABA activates the $GABA_A$ receptor, causing cell cycle arrest in the S-phase, limiting growth. Beyond the nervous system

GABAergic mechanisms have been demonstrated in various peripheral tissues and organs including, but not restricted to the intestine, stomach, pancreas, Fallopian tube, uterus, ovary, testis, kidney, urinary bladder, lung, and liver.

In 2007, an excitatory GABAergic system was described in the airway epithelium. The system activates following exposure to allergens and may participate in the mechanisms of asthma. GABAergic systems have also been found in the testis and in the eye lens. Structure and conformation

GABA is found mostly as a zwitterion, that is, with the carboxy group deprotonated and the amino group protonated. Its conformation depends on its environment. In the gas phase, a highly folded conformation is strongly favored because of the electrostatic attraction between the two functional groups. The stabilization is about 50 kcal/mol, according to quantum chemistry calculations. In the solid state, a more extended conformation is found, with a trans conformation at the amino end and a gauche conformation at the carboxyl end. This is due to the packing interactions with the neighboring molecules. In solution, five different conformations, some folded and some extended, are found as a result of solvation effects. The conformational flexibility of GABA is important for its biological function, as it has been found to bind to different receptors with different conformations. Many GABA analogues with pharmaceutical applications have more rigid structures in order to control the binding better. History

_____ was first synthesized in 1883, and was first known only as a plant and microbe metabolic product.

a. Gamma-Aminobutyric acid
b. Conditioned place preference
c. Dopaminergic
d. False neurotransmitter

4. _____, is the inclination to see events that have already occurred as being more predictable than they were before they took place. It is a multifaceted phenomenon that can affect different stages of designs, processes, contexts, and situations. _____ may cause memory distortion, where the recollection and reconstruction of content can lead to false theoretical outcomes.

a. Hindsight bias
b. Functional fixedness
c. Green children of Woolpit
d. Halo effect

5. In social psychology, _____ refers to the tendency for groups to make decisions that are more extreme than the initial inclination of its members. These more extreme decisions are towards greater risk if individual's initial tendency is to be risky and towards greater caution if individual's initial tendency is to be cautious. The phenomenon also holds that a group's attitude toward a situation may change in the sense that the individual's initial attitudes have strengthened and intensified after group discussion.

a. Group polarization
b. Herd mentality
c. Human Behavior and Evolution Society
d. Human nature

1. d
2. a
3. a
4. a
5. a

*You can take the complete Chapter Practice Test*

**for Chapter 12. Social Behavior**
on all key terms, persons, places, and concepts.

*Online 99 Cents*

*http://www.epub3.2.20111.12.cram101.com/*

**Use www.Cram101.com for all your study needs**

**including Cram101's online interactive problem solving labs in**

**chemistry, statistics, mathematics, and more.**

CHAPTER OUTLINE: KEY TERMS, PEOPLE, PLACES, CONCEPTS

Biopsychosocial model

Health psychology

Mortality rate

Subjectivity

Frustration

Approach-avoidance conflict

Behavior therapy

Rational emotive behavior therapy

Rating scale

Conformity

James-Lange theory

Annoyance

Anxiety

Apprehension

Grief

Resilience

Sadness

Popular psychology

Arousal

Autonomic nervous system

Fight or flight response

Nervous system

Startle reaction

Gamma-Aminobutyric acid

Adrenocorticotropic hormone

Catecholamine

Estrogen

Pituitary gland

Personality Assessment Inventory

Coping

Fatalism

Learned helplessness

Neurogenesis

Internet

Aggression

Case study

Catharsis

Deese-Roediger-McDermott paradigm

CHAPTER OUTLINE: KEY TERMS, PEOPLE, PLACES, CONCEPTS

_____ | Denial

_____ | Intellectualization

_____ | Self-deception

_____ | Ponzo illusion

_____ | Coping Strategies

_____ | Optimism

_____ | Positive illusions

_____ | Wishful thinking

_____ | Prefrontal cortex

_____ | Positive psychology

_____ | Cannon-Bard theory

_____ | Psychoanalytic theory

_____ | Hostility

_____ | Diabetes mellitus

_____ | Neuroticism

_____ | Social support

_____ | Life expectancy

_____ | Lung cancer

_____ | Prevalence

Tobacco

Physical fitness

Health effect

Safe sex

Transmission

Procrastination

Stress management

Forgiveness

Meditation

Base rate

Medical statistics

Sodium chloride

| Biopsychosocial model | The biopsychosocial model is a general model or approach that posits that biological, psychological (which entails thoughts, emotions, and behaviors), and social factors, all play a significant role in human functioning in the context of disease or illness. Indeed, health is best understood in terms of a combination of biological, psychological, and social factors rather than purely in biological terms. This is in contrast to the traditional, reductionist biomedical model of medicine that suggests every disease process can be explained in terms of an underlying deviation from normal function such as a pathogen, genetic or developmental abnormality, or injury. |
| --- | --- |
| Health psychology | Health psychology is concerned with understanding how biological, psychological, environmental, and cultural factors are involved in physical health and illness. Health psychologists work alongside other medical professionals in clinical settings, work on behavior change in public health promotion, teach at universities, and conduct research. Although its early beginnings can be traced to the kindred field of clinical psychology, four different divisions within health psychology and one allied field have developed over time. |
| Mortality rate | Mortality rate is a measure of the number of deaths (in general, or due to a specific cause) in some population, scaled to the size of that population, per unit time. Mortality rate is typically expressed in units of deaths per 1000 individuals per year; thus, a mortality rate of 9.5 in a population of 100,000 would mean 950 deaths per year in that entire population, or 0.95% out of the total. It is distinct from morbidity rate, which refers to the number of individuals in poor health during a given time period (the prevalence rate) or the number of newly appearing cases of the disease per unit of time (incidence rate). |
| Subjectivity | Subjectivity refers to the subject and his or her perspective, feelings, beliefs, and desires. In philosophy, the term is usually contrasted with objectivity.<br><br>Subjectivity may refer to the specific discerning interpretations of any aspect of experiences. |
| Frustration | Frustration is a common emotional response to opposition. Related to anger and disappointment, it arises from the perceived resistance to the fulfillment of individual will. The greater the obstruction, and the greater the will, the more the frustration is likely to be. |
| Approach-avoidance conflict | Approach-avoidance conflicts are choices regarding something positive, such as going out to a party, that has a negative valence (avoidance), such as getting grounded for being at the party. These decisions and the emotional state of ambivalence cause stress.<br><br>Approach-avoidance conflicts can occur when one goal contains both positive and negative characteristics. |

# Chapter 13. Stress, Coping, and Health

| | |
|---|---|
| Rational emotive behavior therapy | Rational emotive behavior therapy previously called rational therapy and rational emotive therapy, is a comprehensive, active-directive, philosophically and empirically based psychotherapy which focuses on resolving emotional and behavioral problems and disturbances and enabling people to lead happier and more fulfilling lives. REBT was created and developed by the American psychotherapist and psychologist Albert Ellis who was inspired by many of the teachings of Asian, Greek, Roman and modern philosophers. REBT is one form of cognitive behavior therapy (CBT) and was first expounded by Ellis in the mid-1950s; development continued until his death in 2007. |
| Rating scale | A rating scale is a set of categories designed to elicit information about a quantitative or a qualitative attribute. In the social sciences, common examples are the Likert scale and 1-10 rating scales in which a person selects the number which is considered to reflect the perceived quality of a product.<br><br>A rating scale is a method that requires the rater to assign a value, sometimes numeric, to the rated object, as a measure of some rated attribute. |
| Conformity | Conformity is the act of matching attitudes, beliefs, and behaviors to group norms. Norms are implicit rules shared by a group of individuals, that guide their interactions with others and among society or social group. This tendency to conform occurs in small groups and/or society as a whole, and may result from subtle unconscious influences, or direct and overt social pressure. |
| James-Lange theory | The James-Lange theory refers to a hypothesis on the origin and nature of emotions and is one of the earliest theories of emotion, developed independently by two 19th-century scholars, William James and Carl Lange.<br><br>The theory states that within human beings, as a response to experiences in the world, the autonomic nervous system creates physiological events such as muscular tension, a rise in heart rate, perspiration, and dryness of the mouth. Emotions, then, are feelings which come about as a result of these physiological changes, rather than being their cause. James and Lange arrived at the theory independently. Lange specifically stated that vasomotor changes are emotions. |
| Annoyance | Annoyance is an unpleasant mental state that is characterized by such effects as irritation and distraction from one's conscious thinking. It can lead to emotions such as frustration and anger. The property of being easily annoyed is called petulance, and something which annoys is called a nuisance. |
| Anxiety | Anxiety is a psychological and physiological state characterized by somatic, emotional, cognitive, and behavioral components. |

|  | The root meaning of the word anxiety is 'to vex or trouble'; in either the absence or presence of psychological stress, anxiety can create feelings of fear, worry, uneasiness and dread. Anxiety is considered to be a normal reaction to stress. |
|---|---|
| Apprehension | In psychology, apprehension (Lat. ad, 'to'; prehendere, 'to seize') is a term applied to a model of consciousness in which nothing is affirmed or denied of the object in question, but the mind is merely aware of ('seizes') it. |
|  | 'Judgment' (says Reid, ed. |
| Grief | Grief is a multi-faceted response to loss, particularly to the loss of someone or something to which a bond was formed. Although conventionally focused on the emotional response to loss, it also has physical, cognitive, behavioral, social, and philosophical dimensions. While the terms are often used interchangeably, bereavement often refers to the state of loss, and grief to the reaction to loss. |
| Resilience | Resilience is the property of a material to absorb energy when it is deformed elastically and then, upon unloading to have this energy recovered. In other words, it is the maximum energy per unit volume that can be elastically stored. It is represented by the area under the curve in the elastic region in the stress-strain curve. |
| Sadness | Sadness is an emotion characterized by feelings of disadvantage, loss, helplessness, sorrow, and rage. When sad, people often become outspoken, less energetic, and emotional. Crying is an indication of sadness. |
| Popular psychology | The term popular psychology refers to concepts and theories about human mental life and behavior that are purportedly based on psychology and that attain popularity among the general population. The concept is closely related to the human potential movement of the 1950s and '60s. |
|  | The term 'pop psychologist' can be used to describe authors, consultants, lecturers and entertainers who are widely perceived as being psychologists, not because of their academic credentials, but because they have projected that image or have been perceived in that way in response to their work. |
| Arousal | Arousal is a physiological and psychological state of being awake or reactive to stimuli. It involves the activation of the reticular activating system in the brain stem, the autonomic nervous system and the endocrine system, leading to increased heart rate and blood pressure and a condition of sensory alertness, mobility and readiness to respond. |

# Chapter 13. Stress, Coping, and Health

| | |
|---|---|
| Autonomic nervous system | The autonomic nervous system is the part of the peripheral nervous system that acts as a control system functioning largely below the level of consciousness, and controls visceral functions. The Autonomic nervous system affects heart rate, digestion, respiration rate, salivation, perspiration, diameter of the pupils, micturition (urination), and sexual arousal. Whereas most of its actions are involuntary, some, such as breathing, work in tandem with the conscious mind. |
| Fight or flight response | The fight or flight response was first described by Walter Bradford Cannon. His theory states that animals react to threats with a general discharge of the sympathetic nervous system, priming the animal for fighting or fleeing. This response was later recognized as the first stage of a general adaptation syndrome that regulates stress responses among vertebrates and other organisms. |
| Nervous system | The nervous system is an organ system containing a network of specialized cells called neurons that coordinate the actions of an animal and transmit signals between different parts of its body. In most animals the nervous system consists of two parts, central and peripheral. The central nervous system of vertebrates (such as humans) contains the brain, spinal cord, and retina. |
| Startle reaction | The startle reaction is the response of mind and body to a sudden unexpected stimulus, such as a flash of light, a loud noise (acoustic startle reflex), or a quick movement near the face. In human beings, the reaction includes physical movement away from the stimulus, a contraction of the muscles of the arms and legs, and often blinking. It also includes blood pressure, respiration, and breathing changes. The muscle reactions generally resolve themselves in a matter of seconds. The other responses take somewhat longer. An exaggerated startle reaction is called hyperexplexia (also hyperekplexia). The exaggerated startle response is often seen in patients with Posttraumatic stress disorder (PTSD). |
| Gamma-Aminobutyric acid | γ-Aminobutyric acid is the chief inhibitory neurotransmitter in the mammalian central nervous system. It plays a role in regulating neuronal excitability throughout the nervous system. In humans, GABA is also directly responsible for the regulation of muscle tone. Although chemically it is an amino acid, GABA is rarely referred to as such in the scientific or medical communities, because the term 'amino acid,' used without a qualifier, conventionally refers to the alpha amino acids, which GABA is not, nor is it ever incorporated into a protein. In spastic diplegia in humans, GABA absorption becomes impaired by nerves damaged from the condition's upper motor neuron lesion, which leads to hypertonia of the muscles signaled by those nerves that can no longer absorb GABA.Function Neurotransmitter |

In vertebrates, GABA acts at inhibitory synapses in the brain by binding to specific transmembrane receptors in the plasma membrane of both pre- and postsynaptic neuronal processes. This binding causes the opening of ion channels to allow the flow of either negatively charged chloride ions into the cell or positively charged potassium ions out of the cell. Depending on which ion channels open, the membrane potential is either hyperpolarized or depolarized. This action results in a negative change in the transmembrane potential, usually causing hyperpolarization. Two general classes of GABA receptor are known: $GABA_A$ in which the receptor is part of a ligand-gated ion channel complex, and $GABA_B$ metabotropic receptors, which are G protein-coupled receptors that open or close ion channels via intermediaries (G proteins).

Neurons that produce GABA as their output are called GABAergic neurons, and have chiefly inhibitory action at receptors in the adult vertebrate. Medium Spiny Cells are a typical example of inhibitory CNS GABAergic cells. In contrast, GABA exhibits both excitatory and inhibitory actions in insects, mediating muscle activation at synapses between nerves and muscle cells, and also the stimulation of certain glands. In mammals, some GABAergic neurons, such as chandelier cells, are also able to excite their glutamatergic counterparts.

$GABA_A$ receptors are ligand-activated chloride channels; that is, when activated by GABA, they allow the flow of chloride ions across the membrane of the cell. Whether this chloride flow is excitatory/depolarizing (makes the voltage across the cell's membrane less negative), shunting (has no effect on the cell's membrane) or inhibitory/hyperpolarizing (makes the cell's membrane more negative) depends on the direction of the flow of chloride. When net chloride flows out of the cell, GABA is excitatory or depolarizing; when the net chloride flows into the cell, GABA is inhibitory or hyperpolarizing. When the net flow of chloride is close to zero, the action of GABA is shunting. Shunting inhibition has no direct effect on the membrane potential of the cell; however, it minimises the effect of any coincident synaptic input essentially by reducing the electrical resistance of the cell's membrane (in essence, equivalent to Ohm's law). A developmental switch in the molecular machinery controlling concentration of chloride inside the cell - and, hence, the direction of this ion flow - is responsible for the changes in the functional role of GABA between the neonatal and adult stages. That is to say, GABA's role changes from excitatory to inhibitory as the brain develops into adulthood. Brain development

For the past two decades, the theory of excitatory action of GABA early in development was unquestioned based on experiments in vitro, on brain slices. The main observation was that in the hippocampus and neocortex of the mammalian brain, GABA has primarily excitatory effects, and is in fact the major excitatory neurotransmitter in many regions of the brain before the maturation of glutamateergic synapses.

# Chapter 13. Stress, Coping, and Health

However, this theory has been questioned based on results showing that in brain slices of immature mice incubated in artificial cerebrospinal fluid (ACSF) (modified in a way that takes into account the normal composition of the neuronal milieu in sucklings by adding an energy substrate alternative to glucose, beta-hydroxybutyrate) GABA action shifts from excitatory to inhibitory mode. This effect has been later repeated when other energy substrates, pyruvate and lactate, supplemented glucose in the slices' media. The effects of beta-hydroxybutyrate were later confirmed for pyruvate and for lactate. However it was argued that the concentrations of the alternative energy substrates used in these experiments were non-physiological and the GABA-shift was instead caused by changes in pH resulting from the substrates acting as 'weak acids'. These arguments were later rebutted by further findings showing that changes in pH even greater than that caused by energy substrates do not affect the GABA-shift described in the presence of energy substrate-fortified ACSF and that the mode of action of beta-hydroxybutyrate, pyruvate and lactate (assessed by measurement NAD(P)H and oxygen utilization) was energy metabolism-related.

In the developmental stages preceding the formation of synaptic contacts, GABA is synthesized by neurons and acts both as an autocrine (acting on the same cell) and paracrine (acting on nearby cells) signalling mediator.

GABA regulates the proliferation of neural progenitor cells the migration and differentiation the elongation of neurites and the formation of synapses.

GABA also regulates the growth of embryonic and neural stem cells. GABA can in?uence the development of neural progenitor cells via brain-derived neurotrophic factor (BDNF) expression. GABA activates the $GABA_A$ receptor, causing cell cycle arrest in the S-phase, limiting growth. Beyond the nervous system

GABAergic mechanisms have been demonstrated in various peripheral tissues and organs including, but not restricted to the intestine, stomach, pancreas, Fallopian tube, uterus, ovary, testis, kidney, urinary bladder, lung, and liver.

In 2007, an excitatory GABAergic system was described in the airway epithelium. The system activates following exposure to allergens and may participate in the mechanisms of asthma. GABAergic systems have also been found in the testis and in the eye lens. Structure and conformation

GABA is found mostly as a zwitterion, that is, with the carboxy group deprotonated and the amino group protonated. Its conformation depends on its environment. In the gas phase, a highly folded conformation is strongly favored because of the electrostatic attraction between the two functional groups.

The stabilization is about 50 kcal/mol, according to quantum chemistry calculations. In the solid state, a more extended conformation is found, with a trans conformation at the amino end and a gauche conformation at the carboxyl end. This is due to the packing interactions with the neighboring molecules. In solution, five different conformations, some folded and some extended, are found as a result of solvation effects. The conformational flexibility of GABA is important for its biological function, as it has been found to bind to different receptors with different conformations. Many GABA analogues with pharmaceutical applications have more rigid structures in order to control the binding better. History

Gamma-aminobutyric acid was first synthesized in 1883, and was first known only as a plant and microbe metabolic product.

| | |
|---|---|
| Adrenocorticotropic hormone | Adrenocorticotropic hormone is a polypeptide tropic hormone produced and secreted by the anterior pituitary gland. It is an important component of the hypothalamic-pituitary-adrenal axis and is often produced in response to biological stress (along with corticotropin-releasing hormone from the hypothalamus). Its principal effects are increased production and release of corticosteroids and, as its name suggests, cortisol from the adrenal cortex. |
| Catecholamine | Catecholamines are 'fight-or-flight' hormones released by the adrenal glands in response to stress. They are part of the sympathetic nervous system. They are called catecholamines because they contain a catechol or 3,4-dihydroxyphenyl group. |
| Estrogen | Estrogens (AmE), oestrogens , are a group of compounds named for their importance in the estrous cycle of humans and other animals, and functioning as the primary female sex hormones. Natural estrogens are steroid hormones, while some synthetic ones are non-steroidal. |
| Pituitary gland | In vertebrate anatomy the pituitary gland, is an endocrine gland about the size of a pea and weighing 0.5 g (0.02 oz)., in humans. It is a protrusion off the bottom of the hypothalamus at the base of the brain, and rests in a small, bony cavity (sella turcica) covered by a dural fold (diaphragma sellae). The pituitary is functionally connected to the hypothalamus by the median eminence via a small tube called the infundibular stem (Pituitary Stalk). |
| Personality Assessment Inventory | Personality Assessment Inventory PhD, is a multi-scale test of psychological functioning that assesses constructs relevant to personality and psychopathology evaluation (e.g., depression, anxiety, aggression) in various contexts including psychotherapy, crisis/evaluation, forensic, personnel selection, pain/medical, and child custody assessment. The PAI has 22 non-overlapping scales, providing a comprehensive overview of psychopathology in adults. |

# Chapter 13. Stress, Coping, and Health

| | |
|---|---|
| Coping | Coping has been defined in psychological terms by Susan Folkman and Richard Lazarus as 'constantly changing cognitive and behavioral efforts to manage specific external and/or internal demands that are appraised as taxing' or 'exceeding the resources of the person'.<br><br>Coping is thus expending conscious effort to solve personal and interpersonal problems, and seeking to master, minimize or tolerate stress or conflict. Psychological coping mechanisms are commonly termed coping strategies or coping skills. |
| Fatalism | Fatalism is a philosophical doctrine emphasizing the subjugation of all events or actions to fate.<br><br>Fatalism generally refers to several of the following ideas:•Though the word 'fatalism' is commonly used to refer to an attitude of resignation in the face of some future event or events which are thought to be inevitable, philosophers usually use the word to refer to the view that we are powerless to do anything other than what we actually do. Included in this is that man has no power to influence the future, or indeed, his own actions. |
| Learned helplessness | Learned helplessness is a technical term that refers to the condition of a human or animal that has learned to behave helplessly, failing to respond even though there are opportunities for it to help itself by avoiding unpleasant circumstances or by gaining positive rewards. Learned helplessness theory is the view that clinical depression and related mental illnesses may result from a perceived absence of control over the outcome of a situation. Organisms which have been ineffective and less sensitive in determining the consequences of their behavior are defined as having acquired learned helplessness. |
| Neurogenesis | Neurogenesis is the process by which neurons are generated from neural stem and progenitor cells. Most active during pre-natal development, neurogenesis is responsible for populating the growing brain with neurons. Recently neurogenesis was shown to continue in several small parts of the brain of mammals: the hippocampus and the subventricular zone. |
| Internet | The Internet is a global system of interconnected computer networks that use the standard Internet Protocol Suite (TCP/IP) to serve billions of users worldwide. It is a network of networks that consists of millions of private, public, academic, business, and government networks, of local to global scope, that are linked by a broad array of electronic, wireless and optical networking technologies. The Internet carries a vast range of information resources and services, such as the inter-linked hypertext documents of the World Wide Web (WWW) and the infrastructure to support electronic mail. |
| Aggression | Aggression, in its broadest sense, is behavior, or a disposition, that is forceful, hostile or attacking. It may occur either in retaliation or without provocation. |

| | |
|---|---|
| Case study | A case study is a research method common in social science. It is based on an in-depth investigation of a single individual, group, or event. Case studies may be descriptive or explanatory. |
| Catharsis | Catharsis is a Greek word meaning 'cleansing' or 'purging'. It is derived from the verb καθα?ρειν, kathairein, 'to purify, purge,' and it is related to the adjective καθαρ?ς, katharos, 'pure or clean.' |
| | Catharsis is a term in dramatic art that describes the 'emotional cleansing' sometimes depicted in a play as occurring for one or more of its characters, as well as the same phenomenon as (an intended) part of the audience's experience. It describes an extreme change in emotion, occurring as the result of experiencing strong feelings (such as sorrow, fear, pity, or even laughter). |
| Deese-Roediger-McDermott paradigm | The Deese-Roediger-McDermott (DRM) paradigm in cognitive psychology is an example of false memory. James Deese, an American psychologist and professor, first studied this paradigm in 1959. The DRM Paradigm refers to the tendency to falsely recall a target word from a set list of words centered around that target word. Henry L. Roediger III and Kathleen McDermott have done further research in more recent years to both confirm this phenomenon and find that it even extends into falsely recalling events, hence the name, the Deese-Roediger-McDermott paradigm. |
| Denial | Denial is a defense mechanism postulated by Sigmund Freud, in which a person is faced with a fact that is too uncomfortable to accept and rejects it instead, insisting that it is not true despite what may be overwhelming evidence. The subject may use:•simple denial - deny the reality of the unpleasant fact altogether•minimisation - admit the fact but deny its seriousness (a combination of denial and rationalization)•projection - admit both the fact and seriousness but deny responsibility. |
| Intellectualization | Intellectualization is a defense mechanism where reasoning is used to block confrontation with an unconscious conflict and its associated emotional stress, by 'using excessive and abstract ideation to avoid difficult feelings'. It involves removing one's self, emotionally, from a stressful event. Intellectualization may accompany, but 'differs from rationalization, which is justification of irrational behavior through cliches, stories, and pat explanation'. |
| Self-deception | Self-deception is a process of denying or rationalizing away the relevance, significance, or importance of opposing evidence and logical argument. Self-deception involves convincing oneself of a truth (or lack of truth) so that one does not reveal any self-knowledge of the deception. |

# Chapter 13. Stress, Coping, and Health

| | |
|---|---|
| Ponzo illusion | The Ponzo illusion is a geometrical-optical illusion that was first demonstrated by the Italian psychologist Mario Ponzo (1882-1960) in 1913. He suggested that the human mind judges an object's size based on its background. He showed this by drawing two identical lines across a pair of converging lines, similar to railway tracks. The upper line looks longer because we interpret the converging sides according to linear perspective as parallel lines receding into the distance. |
| Coping Strategies | Coping Strategies is treatment designed for posttraumatic stress disorder within United States Armed Forces personnel and their families by the charitable organization Patriot Outreach. It is primarily distributed through CD-ROM, consisting of a customized mindfulness exercise audio program entitled 'Be Still and Know', as well as additional programs on overcoming stress, fear and pain, and field manuals and other resources. The treatment is considered effective by military personnel and has received praise. |
| Optimism | Optimism is a mental attitude that interprets situations and events as being best (optimized), meaning that in some way for factors that may not be fully comprehended, the present moment is in an optimum state. The concept is typically extended to include the attitude of hope for future conditions unfolding as optimal as well. The more broad concept of optimism is the understanding that all of nature, past, present and future, operates by laws of optimization along the lines of Hamilton's principle of optimization in the realm of physics. |
| Positive illusions | Positive illusions are unrealistically favorable attitudes that people have towards themselves. Positive illusions are a form of self-deception or self-enhancement that feel good, maintain self-esteem or stave off discomfort at least in the short term. There are three broad kinds: inflated assessment of one's own abilities, unrealistic optimism about the future and an illusion of control. |
| Wishful thinking | Wishful thinking is the formation of beliefs and making decisions according to what might be pleasing to imagine instead of by appealing to evidence, rationality or reality. Studies have consistently shown that holding all else equal, subjects will predict positive outcomes to be more likely than negative outcomes . |
| | Christopher Booker described wishful thinking in terms of'the fantasy cycle' ... a pattern that recurs in personal lives, in politics, in history - and in storytelling. |
| Prefrontal cortex | The prefrontal cortex. is the anterior part of the frontal lobes of the brain, lying in front of the motor and premotor areas. |
| | This brain region has been implicated in planning complex cognitive behavior, personality expression, decision making and moderating social behavior. |

| Positive psychology | Positive psychology is a recent branch of psychology whose purpose was summed up in 2000 by Martin Seligman and Mihaly Csikszentmihalyi: 'We believe that a psychology of positive human functioning will arise that achieves a scientific understanding and effective interventions to build thriving in individuals, families, and communities.' Positive psychologists seek 'to find and nurture genius and talent', and 'to make normal life more fulfilling', not simply to treat mental illness. The emerging field of Positive Psychology is intended to complement, not to replace traditional psychology. |
| --- | --- |
| | By scientifically studying what has gone right, rather than wrong in both individuals and societies, Positive Psychology hopes to achieve a renaissance of sorts. |
| Cannon-Bard theory | The Cannon-Bard theory, is a theory of emotion developed by physiologists Walter Cannon and Philip Bard, suggesting that individuals experience emotions and physiologically react simultaneously. These actions include changes in muscular tension, perspiration, etc. This theory challenges the James-Lange theory of emotion introduced in the late 19th century, which suggests that emotion results from one's 'bodily change,' rather than the other way around. |
| Psychoanalytic theory | Psychoanalytic theory refers to the definition and dynamics of personality development which underlie and guide psychoanalytic and psychodynamic psychotherapy. First laid out by Sigmund Freud, psychoanalytic theory has undergone many refinements since his work . Psychoanalytic theory came to full prominence as a critical force in the last third of the twentieth century as part of 'the flow of critical discourse after the 1960's. |
| Hostility | Hostility is a form of angry internal rejection or denial in psychology. It is a part of personal construct psychology, developed by George Kelly. In everyday speech it is more commonly used as a synonym for anger and aggression. |
| Diabetes mellitus | Diabetes mellitus is a group of metabolic diseases in which a person has high blood sugar, either because the body does not produce enough insulin, or because cells do not respond to the insulin that is produced. This high blood sugar produces the classical symptoms of polyuria (frequent urination), polydipsia (increased thirst) and polyphagia (increased hunger). |
| Neuroticism | Neuroticism is a fundamental personality trait in the study of psychology. It is an enduring tendency to experience negative emotional states. Individuals who score high on neuroticism are more likely than the average to experience such feelings as anxiety, anger, envy, guilt, and depressed mood. |
| Social support | Social support can be defined and measured in many ways. It can loosely be defined as feeling that one is cared for by and has assistance available from other people and that one is part of a supportive social network. |

# Chapter 13. Stress, Coping, and Health

| | |
|---|---|
| Life expectancy | Life expectancy is the expected (in the statistical sense) number of years of life remaining at a given age. It is denoted by $e_x$, which means the average number of subsequent years of life for someone now aged x, according to a particular mortality experience. (In technical literature, this symbol means the average number of complete years of life remaining, excluding fractions of a year. |
| Lung cancer | Lung cancer is a disease which consists of uncontrolled cell growth in tissues of the lung. This growth may lead to metastasis, which is the invasion of adjacent tissue and infiltration beyond the lungs. The vast majority of primary lung cancers are carcinomas, derived from epithelial cells. Lung cancer, the most common cause of cancer-related death in men and women, is responsible for 1.3 million deaths worldwide annually, as of 2004. The most common symptoms are shortness of breath, coughing (including coughing up blood), and weight loss. |
| Prevalence | In epidemiology, the prevalence of a health-related state (typically disease, but also other things like smoking or seatbelt use) in a statistical population is defined as the total number of cases of the risk factor in the population at a given time, or the total number of cases in the population, divided by the number of individuals in the population. It is used as an estimate of how common a disease is within a population over a certain period of time. It helps physicians or other health professionals understand the probability of certain diagnoses and is routinely used by epidemiologists, health care providers, government agencies and insurers. |
| Tobacco | Tobacco is an agricultural product processed from the leaves of plants in the genus Nicotiana. It can be consumed, used as an organic pesticide and, in the form of nicotine tartrate, used in some medicines. It is most commonly used as a recreational drug, and is a valuable cash crop for countries such as Cuba, China and the United States. |
| Physical fitness | Physical fitness comprises two related concepts: general fitness (a state of health and well-being), and specific fitness (a task-oriented definition based on the ability to perform specific aspects of sports or occupations). Physical fitness is generally achieved through correct nutrition, exercise, and enough rest.<br><br>In previous years, fitness was commonly defined as the capacity to carry out the day's activities without undue fatigue. |
| Health effect | Health effects are changes in health resulting from exposure to a source. Health effects are an important consideration in many areas, such as hygiene, pollution studies, workplace safety, nutrition and health sciences in general. Some of the major environmental sources of health effects are air pollution, water pollution, soil contamination, noise pollution and over-illumination. |
| Safe sex | Safe sex is defined as sexual activity engaged in by people who have taken precautions to protect themselves against sexually transmitted diseases (STDs) such as AIDS. |

It is also referred to as safer sex, or protected sex, while unsafe sex or unprotected sex is sexual activity engaged in without precautions. Some sources prefer the term safer sex to more precisely reflect the fact that these practices reduce, but do not completely eliminate, the risk of disease transmission. In recent years, the term 'sexually transmitted infections' (STIs) has been preferred over 'STDs,' as it has a broader range of meaning; a person may be infected, and may potentially infect others, without showing signs of disease.

| | |
|---|---|
| Transmission | A machine consists of a power source and a power transmission system, which provides controlled application of the power. Merriam-Webster defines transmission as: an assembly of parts including the speed-changing gears and the propeller shaft by which the power is transmitted from an engine to a live axle. Often transmission refers simply to the gearbox that uses gears and gear trains to provide speed and torque conversions from a rotating power source to another device. |
| Procrastination | In psychology, procrastination refers to the act of replacing high-priority actions with tasks of lower priority, or doing something from which one derives enjoyment, and thus putting off important tasks to a later time. In accordance with Freud, the Pleasure principle (psychology) may be responsible for procrastination; humans do not prefer negative emotions and handing off a stressful task until a further date is enjoyable. The concept that humans work best under pressure provides additional enjoyment and motivation to postponing a task. |
| Stress management | Stress management refers to a wide spectrum of techniques and psychotherapies aimed at controlling a person's levels of stress, especially chronic stress, usually for the purpose of improving everyday functioning. |
| | In this context, the term 'stress' refers only to a stress with significant negative consequences, or distress in the terminology advocated by Hans Selye, rather than what he calls eustress, a stress whose consequences are helpful or otherwise positive. |
| | Stress produces numerous symptoms which vary according to persons, situations, and severity. |
| Forgiveness | Forgiveness is typically defined as the process of concluding resentment, indignation or anger as a result of a perceived offense, difference or mistake, and/or ceasing to demand punishment or restitution. The Oxford English Dictionary defines forgiveness as 'to grant free pardon and to give up all claim on account of an offense or debt'. The concept and benefits of forgiveness have been explored in religious thought, the social sciences and medicine. |
| Meditation | Meditation is any form of a family of practices in which practitioners train their minds or self-induce a mode of consciousness to realize some benefit. |

Meditation is generally an inwardly oriented, personal practice, which individuals do by themselves. Prayer beads or other ritual objects are commonly used during meditation.

| Base rate | In probability and statistics, base rate generally refers to the (base) class probabilities unconditioned on featural evidence, frequently also known as prior probabilities. In plainer words, if it were the case that 1% of the public were 'medical professionals', and 99% of the public were not 'medical professionals', then the base rate of medical professionals is simply 1%. |

In science, particularly medicine, the base rate is critical for comparison.

| Medical statistics | Medical statistics deals with applications of statistics to medicine and the health sciences, including epidemiology, public health, forensic medicine, and clinical research. Medical statistics has been a recognized branch of statistics in the UK for more than 40 years but the term does not appear to have come into general use in North America, where the wider term 'biostatistics' is more commonly used. |

Constantly newer and newer statistical ratios are being developed to help measure the changing Patterns of various disease and health conditions.

| Sodium chloride | Sodium chloride, also known as salt, common salt, table salt, or halite, is an ionic compound with the formula NaCl. Sodium chloride is the salt most responsible for the salinity of the ocean and of the extracellular fluid of many multicellular organisms. As the major ingredient in edible salt, it is commonly used as a condiment and food preservative. |

1. _____ is the expected (in the statistical sense) number of years of life remaining at a given age. It is denoted by $e_x$, which means the average number of subsequent years of life for someone now aged x, according to a particular mortality experience. (In technical literature, this symbol means the average number of complete years of life remaining, excluding fractions of a year.

    a. Life extension
    b. Lighting for the elderly
    c. Lipofuscin
    d. Life expectancy

2. Coping has been defined in psychological terms by Susan Folkman and Richard Lazarus as 'constantly changing cognitive and behavioral efforts to manage specific external and/or internal demands that are appraised as taxing' or 'exceeding the resources of the person'.

   Coping is thus expending conscious effort to solve personal and interpersonal problems, and seeking to master, minimize or tolerate stress or conflict. Psychological coping mechanisms are commonly termed _____ strategies or _____ skills.

    a. Coping
    b. Lateral strain
    c. Psychoneuroimmunology
    d. Procrastination

3. _____ is the formation of beliefs and making decisions according to what might be pleasing to imagine instead of by appealing to evidence, rationality or reality. Studies have consistently shown that holding all else equal, subjects will predict positive outcomes to be more likely than negative outcomes .

   Christopher Booker described _____ in terms of'the fantasy cycle' ... a pattern that recurs in personal lives, in politics, in history - and in storytelling.

    a. Green children of Woolpit
    b. Theory of indispensable attributes
    c. Pulfrich effect
    d. Wishful thinking

4. _____s are changes in health resulting from exposure to a source. _____s are an important consideration in many areas, such as hygiene, pollution studies, workplace safety, nutrition and health sciences in general. Some of the major environmental sources of _____s are air pollution, water pollution, soil contamination, noise pollution and over-illumination.

    a. Health intervention
    b. Diversified technique
    c. stair climbing
    d. Health effect

5. _____s are choices regarding something positive, such as going out to a party, that has a negative valence (avoidance), such as getting grounded for being at the party. These decisions and the emotional state of ambivalence cause stress.

_____s can occur when one goal contains both positive and negative characteristics.

a. Attentional blink
b. Attribute substitution
c. Approach-avoidance conflict
d. Entrainment

**1.** d
**2.** a
**3.** d
**4.** d
**5.** c

---

## You can take the complete Chapter Practice Test

### for Chapter 13. Stress, Coping, and Health
on all key terms, persons, places, and concepts.

## Online 99 Cents

## *http://www.epub3.2.20111.13.cram101.com/*

**Use www.Cram101.com for all your study needs**

**including Cram101's online interactive problem solving labs in**

**chemistry, statistics, mathematics, and more.**

CHAPTER OUTLINE: KEY TERMS, PEOPLE, PLACES, CONCEPTS

| | Demonic possession |

| | Exorcism |

| | Medical model |

| | Psychopathology |

| | Rating scale |

| | Case study |

| | Etiology |

| | Social stigma |

| | Transvestic fetishism |

| | Major depressive disorder |

| | Personal distress |

| | Diagnostic and Statistical Manual of Mental Disorders |

| | Mendelian inheritance |

| | Mental disorder |

| | Eating disorder |

| | Personality disorder |

| | Somatoform disorder |

| | Substance-related disorder |

| | Area studies |

Internet

Comorbidity

Epidemiology

Prevalence

Acrophobia

Agoraphobia

Anxiety disorder

Claustrophobia

Gamma-Aminobutyric acid

Generalized anxiety disorder

Panic attack

Panic disorder

Posttraumatic stress disorder

Ponzo illusion

Personality Assessment Inventory

Anxiety sensitivity

Avoidance response

Serotonin

Social phobia

Ames room

Dissociative amnesia

Dissociative disorder

Memory loss

Child abuse

Dissociative identity disorder

James-Lange theory

Anhedonia

Bipolar disorder

Mood disorder

Mood swing

Postpartum depression

Norepinephrine

Cortisol

Explanatory style

Hypothalamus

Learned helplessness

Pituitary gland

Auditory hallucination

Delusion

Hallucination

Schizophrenia

Disorganized schizophrenia

Emergence

Paranoid schizophrenia

Persecution

Dopamine

Prefrontal cortex

Expressed emotion

Prenatal development

Antisocial personality disorder

Avoidant personality disorder

Borderline personality disorder

Dependent personality disorder

Histrionic personality disorder

Narcissistic personality disorder

Obsessive-compulsive personality disorder

Paranoid personality disorder

CHAPTER OUTLINE: KEY TERMS, PEOPLE, PLACES, CONCEPTS

Schizoid personality disorder

Schizotypal personality disorder

Disinhibition

Genetic predisposition

Involuntary commitment

Anorexia nervosa

Flynn effect

Amenorrhoea

Binge eating

Bulimia nervosa

Osteoporosis

Overeating

Poggendorff illusion

Point prevalence

Representativeness heuristic

Availability heuristic

Conjunction fallacy

Hindsight bias

# Chapter 14. Psychological Disorders

| Demonic possession | Demonic possession is the supposed control over a human by a malevolent supernatural being or evil spirit. Descriptions of demonic possessions often include erased memories or personalities, convulsions, 'fits' and fainting as if one were dying. Other descriptions include access to hidden knowledge (gnosis) and foreign languages (glossolalia), drastic changes in vocal intonation and facial structure, the sudden appearance of injuries (scratches, bite marks) or lesions, and superhuman strength. |
|---|---|
| Exorcism | Exorcism is the religious practice of evicting demons or other spiritual entities from a person or place which they are believed to have possessed. Depending on the spiritual beliefs of the exorcist, this may be done by causing the entity to swear an oath, performing an elaborate ritual, or simply by commanding it to depart in the name of a higher power. The term became prominent in early Christianity from the early 2nd century onward as the casting out of demons. Nevertheless, the practice is quite ancient and part of the belief system of many cultures and religions. |
| Medical model | Medical model is the term cited by psychiatrist Ronald D. Laing in his The Politics of the Family and Other Essays (1971), for the 'set of procedures in which all doctors are trained.' This set includes complaint, history, physical examination, ancillary tests if needed, diagnosis, treatment, and prognosis with and without treatment. Sociologist Erving Goffman, in his Asylums, favorably compared the medical model, which was a post-Industrial Revolution occurrence, with the conduct in the tinkering trades (watch, radio, TV repair). The medical model is an approach to pathology that aims to find medical treatments for diagnosed symptoms and syndromes and treats the human body as a very complex mechanism (hence, Goffman's tinkering trade analogy). |
| Psychopathology | Psychopathology is the study of mental illness, mental distress, and abnormal/maladaptive behavior. The term is most commonly used within psychiatry where pathology refers to disease processes. Abnormal psychology is a similar term used more frequently in the non-medical field of psychology. |
| Rating scale | A rating scale is a set of categories designed to elicit information about a quantitative or a qualitative attribute. In the social sciences, common examples are the Likert scale and 1-10 rating scales in which a person selects the number which is considered to reflect the perceived quality of a product. |
| | A rating scale is a method that requires the rater to assign a value, sometimes numeric, to the rated object, as a measure of some rated attribute. |
| Case study | A case study is a research method common in social science. It is based on an in-depth investigation of a single individual, group, or event. |

| Etiology | Etiology (alternatively aetiology, aitiology ) is the study of causation, or origination.

In medicine, the term refers to the causes of diseases or pathologies. Where no etiology can be ascertained, then the disorder is said to be idiopathic. |
| --- | --- |
| Social stigma | Social stigma is a severe social disapproval of personal characteristics or beliefs that are perceived to be against cultural norms. Erving Goffman defined stigma as the process by which is normal.

The three forms of stigma recognised by Goffman include: The experience of a mental illness (or the imposition of such a diagnosis); a physical form of deformity or an undesired differentness; or an association with a particular race, religion, belief etc. |
| Transvestic fetishism | Transvestic fetishism is a psychiatric diagnosis applied to those who are thought to have an excessive sexual or erotic interest in cross-dressing; this interest is often expressed in autoerotic behavior. It differs from cross-dressing for entertainment or other purposes that do not involve sexual arousal and is categorized as a paraphilia in the Diagnostic and Statistical Manual of the American Psychiatric Association. (Sexual arousal in response to donning sex-typical clothing is homeovestism). |
| Major depressive disorder | Major depressive disorder is a mental disorder characterized by an all-encompassing low mood accompanied by low self-esteem, and by loss of interest or pleasure in normally enjoyable activities. This cluster of symptoms (syndrome) was named, described and classified as one of the mood disorders in the 1980 edition of the American Psychiatric Association's diagnostic manual. The term 'depression' is ambiguous. |
| Personal distress | Personal distress is an aversive, self-focused emotional reaction (e.g., anxiety, worry, discomfort) to the apprehension or comprehension of another's emotional state or condition. This negative affective state often occurs as a result of emotional contagion when there is confusion between self and other. Unlike empathy, personal distress does not have to be congruent with the other's state, and often leads to a self-oriented, egoistic reaction to reduce it, by withdrawing from the stressor, for example, thereby decreasing the likelihood of prosocial behavior. |
| Diagnostic and Statistical Manual of Mental Disorders | The Diagnostic and Statistical Manual of Mental Disorders published by the American Psychiatric Association provides a common language and standard criteria for the classification of mental disorders. It is used in the United States and in varying degrees around the world, by clinicians, researchers, psychiatric drug regulation agencies, health insurance companies, pharmaceutical companies, and policy makers. The current version is the DSM-IV-TR (fourth edition, text revision). |

# Chapter 14. Psychological Disorders

| | |
|---|---|
| Mendelian inheritance | Mendelian inheritance, hereditary characteristics from parent organisms to their offspring; it underlies much of genetics. They were initially derived from the work of Gregor Johann Mendel published in 1865 and 1866 which was 're-discovered' in 1900, and were initially very controversial. When they were integrated with the chromosome theory of inheritance by Thomas Hunt Morgan in 1915, they became the core of classical genetics. |
| Mental disorder | A mental disorder is a psychological or behavioral pattern generally associated with subjective distress or disability that occurs in an individual, and which is not a part of normal development or culture. The recognition and understanding of mental health conditions has changed over time and across cultures, and there are still variations in the definition, assessment, and classification of mental disorders, although standard guideline criteria are widely accepted. A few mental disorders are diagnosed based on the harm to others, regardless of the subject's perception of distress. |
| Eating disorder | Eating disorders refer to a group of conditions defined by abnormal eating habits that may involve either insufficient or excessive food intake to the detriment of an individual's physical and mental health. Bulimia nervosa, anorexia nervosa, and binge eating disorder are the most common specific forms in the United Kingdom. Though primarily thought of as affecting females (an estimated 5-10 million being affected in the U.K)., eating disorders affect males as well Template:An estimated 10 - 15% of people with eating disorders are males (Gorgan, 1999). |
| Personality disorder | Personality disorders are a class of personality types and enduring behaviors associated with significant distress or disability, which appear to deviate from social expectations particularly in relating to others. Personality disorders are included as mental disorders on Axis II of the Diagnostic manual of the American Psychiatric Association, and in the mental and behavioral disorders section of the ICD manual of the World Health Organization. Personality, defined psychologically, is the enduring behavioral and mental traits that distinguish human beings. |
| Somatoform disorder | In psychology, a somatoform disorder is a mental disorder characterized by physical symptoms that suggest physical illness or injury - symptoms that cannot be explained fully by a general medical condition, direct effect of a substance, or attributable to another mental disorder (e.g. panic disorder). The symptoms that result from a somatoform disorder are due to mental factors. In people who have a somatoform disorder, medical test results are either normal or do not explain the person's symptoms. |
| Substance-related disorder | A substance-related disorder is an umbrella term used to describe several different conditions (such as intoxication, harmful use/abuse, dependence, withdrawal, and psychoses or amnesia associated with the use of the substance) associated with several different substances (such as alcohol or opioids). |

A substance related disorder is a condition in which 'an individual uses or abuses a substance to the point where it leads to maladaptive behaviours, manifested by at least one symptom that interferes with normal life functioning within a 12 month period.'. In order to be diagnosed with substance dependence an individual must display at least three of the following for a 12 month period: 'development of tolerance to the substance, withdrawal symptoms, persistent desire/unsuccessful attempts to stop using the substance, ingestion of larger amounts of substance, declined life functioning, and persistent use of substance.' Substance abuse has been found to be most common among people 18 to 25 years of age and is also more common in males than females and in urban residents compared to those who live in rural areas.

**Area studies**

Area studies are interdisciplinary fields of research and scholarship pertaining to particular geographical, national/federal, or cultural regions. The term exists primarily as a general description for what are, in the practice of scholarship, many heterogeneous fields of research, encompassing both the social sciences and the humanities. Typical area studies programs involve history, political science, sociology, cultural studies, languages, geography, literature, and related disciplines.

**Internet**

The Internet is a global system of interconnected computer networks that use the standard Internet Protocol Suite (TCP/IP) to serve billions of users worldwide. It is a network of networks that consists of millions of private, public, academic, business, and government networks, of local to global scope, that are linked by a broad array of electronic, wireless and optical networking technologies. The Internet carries a vast range of information resources and services, such as the inter-linked hypertext documents of the World Wide Web (WWW) and the infrastructure to support electronic mail.

**Comorbidity**

In medicine, comorbidity is either the presence of one or more disorders (or diseases) in addition to a primary disease or disorder, or the effect of such additional disorders or diseases.

In medicine

In medicine, comorbidity describes the effect of all other diseases an individual patient might have other than the primary disease of interest.

Many tests attempt to standardize the 'weight' or value of comorbid conditions, whether they are secondary or tertiary illnesses.

**Epidemiology**

Epidemiology is the study of disease patterns in a society. It is the cornerstone method of public health research, and helps inform evidence-based medicine for identifying risk factors for disease and determining optimal treatment approaches to clinical practice and for preventive medicine.

# Chapter 14. Psychological Disorders

| | |
|---|---|
| Prevalence | In epidemiology, the prevalence of a health-related state (typically disease, but also other things like smoking or seatbelt use) in a statistical population is defined as the total number of cases of the risk factor in the population at a given time, or the total number of cases in the population, divided by the number of individuals in the population. It is used as an estimate of how common a disease is within a population over a certain period of time. It helps physicians or other health professionals understand the probability of certain diagnoses and is routinely used by epidemiologists, health care providers, government agencies and insurers. |
| Acrophobia | Acrophobia is an extreme or irrational fear of heights. It belongs to a category of specific phobias, called space and motion discomfort that share both similar etiology and options for treatment.<br><br>Most people experience a degree of natural fear when exposed to heights, especially if there is little or no protection. |
| Agoraphobia | Agoraphobia is an anxiety disorder characterized by anxiety in situations where it is perceived to be difficult or embarrassing to escape. These situations can include, but are not limited to, wide-open spaces, and uncontrollable social situations such as may be met in shopping malls, airports, and on bridges. Agoraphobia is defined within the DSM-IV TR as a subset of panic disorder, involving the fear of incurring a panic attack in those environments. |
| Anxiety disorder | Anxiety disorder is a blanket term covering several different forms of a type of mental illness of abnormal and pathological fear and anxiety. Conditions now considered anxiety disorders only came under the aegis of psychiatry near the end of the 19th century. Gelder, Mayou & Geddes (2005) explain that anxiety disorders are classified in two groups: continuous symptoms and episodic symptoms. |
| Claustrophobia | Claustrophobia is the fear of having no escape and being closed in small spaces or rooms (opposite: claustrophilia). It is typically classified as an anxiety disorder and often results in panic attack, and can be the result of many situations or stimuli, including elevators crowded to capacity, windowless rooms, and even tight-necked clothing. The onset of claustrophobia has been attributed to many factors, including a reduction in the size of the amygdala, classical conditioning, or a genetic predisposition to fear small spaces. |
| Gamma-Aminobutyric acid | γ-Aminobutyric acid is the chief inhibitory neurotransmitter in the mammalian central nervous system. It plays a role in regulating neuronal excitability throughout the nervous system. In humans, GABA is also directly responsible for the regulation of muscle tone.<br><br>Although chemically it is an amino acid, GABA is rarely referred to as such in the scientific or medical communities, because the term 'amino acid,' used without a qualifier, conventionally refers to the alpha amino acids, which GABA is not, nor is it ever incorporated into a protein. |

In spastic diplegia in humans, GABA absorption becomes impaired by nerves damaged from the condition's upper motor neuron lesion, which leads to hypertonia of the muscles signaled by those nerves that can no longer absorb GABA.Function Neurotransmitter

In vertebrates, GABA acts at inhibitory synapses in the brain by binding to specific transmembrane receptors in the plasma membrane of both pre- and postsynaptic neuronal processes. This binding causes the opening of ion channels to allow the flow of either negatively charged chloride ions into the cell or positively charged potassium ions out of the cell. Depending on which ion channels open, the membrane potential is either hyperpolarized or depolarized. This action results in a negative change in the transmembrane potential, usually causing hyperpolarization. Two general classes of GABA receptor are known: $GABA_A$ in which the receptor is part of a ligand-gated ion channel complex, and $GABA_B$ metabotropic receptors, which are G protein-coupled receptors that open or close ion channels via intermediaries (G proteins).

Neurons that produce GABA as their output are called GABAergic neurons, and have chiefly inhibitory action at receptors in the adult vertebrate. Medium Spiny Cells are a typical example of inhibitory CNS GABAergic cells. In contrast, GABA exhibits both excitatory and inhibitory actions in insects, mediating muscle activation at synapses between nerves and muscle cells, and also the stimulation of certain glands. In mammals, some GABAergic neurons, such as chandelier cells, are also able to excite their glutamatergic counterparts.

$GABA_A$ receptors are ligand-activated chloride channels; that is, when activated by GABA, they allow the flow of chloride ions across the membrane of the cell. Whether this chloride flow is excitatory/depolarizing (makes the voltage across the cell's membrane less negative), shunting (has no effect on the cell's membrane) or inhibitory/hyperpolarizing (makes the cell's membrane more negative) depends on the direction of the flow of chloride. When net chloride flows out of the cell, GABA is excitatory or depolarizing; when the net chloride flows into the cell, GABA is inhibitory or hyperpolarizing. When the net flow of chloride is close to zero, the action of GABA is shunting. Shunting inhibition has no direct effect on the membrane potential of the cell; however, it minimises the effect of any coincident synaptic input essentially by reducing the electrical resistance of the cell's membrane (in essence, equivalent to Ohm's law). A developmental switch in the molecular machinery controlling concentration of chloride inside the cell - and, hence, the direction of this ion flow - is responsible for the changes in the functional role of GABA between the neonatal and adult stages. That is to say, GABA's role changes from excitatory to inhibitory as the brain develops into adulthood. Brain development

For the past two decades, the theory of excitatory action of GABA early in development was unquestioned based on experiments in vitro, on brain slices.

The main observation was that in the hippocampus and neocortex of the mammalian brain, GABA has primarily excitatory effects, and is in fact the major excitatory neurotransmitter in many regions of the brain before the maturation of glutamateergic synapses.

However, this theory has been questioned based on results showing that in brain slices of immature mice incubated in artificial cerebrospinal fluid (ACSF) (modified in a way that takes into account the normal composition of the neuronal milieu in sucklings by adding an energy substrate alternative to glucose, beta-hydroxybutyrate) GABA action shifts from excitatory to inhibitory mode. This effect has been later repeated when other energy substrates, pyruvate and lactate, supplemented glucose in the slices' media. The effects of beta-hydroxybutyrate were later confirmed for pyruvate and for lactate. However it was argued that the concentrations of the alternative energy substrates used in these experiments were non-physiological and the GABA-shift was instead caused by changes in pH resulting from the substrates acting as 'weak acids'. These arguments were later rebutted by further findings showing that changes in pH even greater than that caused by energy substrates do not affect the GABA-shift described in the presence of energy substrate-fortified ACSF and that the mode of action of beta-hydroxybutyrate, pyruvate and lactate (assessed by measurement NAD(P)H and oxygen utilization) was energy metabolism-related.

In the developmental stages preceding the formation of synaptic contacts, GABA is synthesized by neurons and acts both as an autocrine (acting on the same cell) and paracrine (acting on nearby cells) signalling mediator.

GABA regulates the proliferation of neural progenitor cells the migration and differentiation the elongation of neurites and the formation of synapses.

GABA also regulates the growth of embryonic and neural stem cells. GABA can in?uence the development of neural progenitor cells via brain-derived neurotrophic factor (BDNF) expression. GABA activates the $GABA_A$ receptor, causing cell cycle arrest in the S-phase, limiting growth. Beyond the nervous system

GABAergic mechanisms have been demonstrated in various peripheral tissues and organs including, but not restricted to the intestine, stomach, pancreas, Fallopian tube, uterus, ovary, testis, kidney, urinary bladder, lung, and liver.

In 2007, an excitatory GABAergic system was described in the airway epithelium. The system activates following exposure to allergens and may participate in the mechanisms of asthma. GABAergic systems have also been found in the testis and in the eye lens. Structure and conformation

GABA is found mostly as a zwitterion, that is, with the carboxy group deprotonated and the amino group protonated. Its conformation depends on its environment. In the gas phase, a highly folded conformation is strongly favored because of the electrostatic attraction between the two functional groups. The stabilization is about 50 kcal/mol, according to quantum chemistry calculations. In the solid state, a more extended conformation is found, with a trans conformation at the amino end and a gauche conformation at the carboxyl end. This is due to the packing interactions with the neighboring molecules. In solution, five different conformations, some folded and some extended, are found as a result of solvation effects. The conformational flexibility of GABA is important for its biological function, as it has been found to bind to different receptors with different conformations. Many GABA analogues with pharmaceutical applications have more rigid structures in order to control the binding better. History

Gamma-aminobutyric acid was first synthesized in 1883, and was first known only as a plant and microbe metabolic product.

| | |
|---|---|
| Generalized anxiety disorder | Generalized anxiety disorder is an anxiety disorder that is characterized by excessive, uncontrollable and often irrational worry about everyday things that is disproportionate to the actual source of worry. This excessive worry often interferes with daily functioning, as individuals suffering GAD typically anticipate disaster, and are overly concerned about everyday matters such as health issues, money, death, family problems, friend problems, relationship problems or work difficulties. Individuals often exhibit a variety of physical symptoms, including fatigue, fidgeting, headaches, nausea, numbness in hands and feet, muscle tension, muscle aches, difficulty swallowing, bouts of difficulty breathing, difficulty concentrating, trembling, twitching, irritability, agitation, sweating, restlessness, insomnia, hot flashes, and rashes and inability to fully control the anxiety (ICD-10). |
| Panic attack | Panic attacks are periods of intense fear or apprehension that are of sudden onset and of relatively brief duration. Panic attacks usually begin abruptly, reach a peak within 10 minutes, and subside over the next several hours. Often, those afflicted will experience significant anticipatory anxiety and limited symptom attacks in between attacks, in situations where attacks have previously occurred. |
| Panic disorder | Panic disorder is an anxiety disorder characterized by recurring severe panic attacks. It may also include significant behavioral changes lasting at least a month and of ongoing worry about the implications or concern about having other attacks. The latter are called anticipatory attacks (DSM-IVR). |
| Posttraumatic stress disorder | Posttraumatic stress disorder is a severe anxiety disorder that can develop after exposure to any event that results in psychological trauma. |

# Chapter 14. Psychological Disorders

|  |  |
|---|---|
|  | This event may involve the threat of death to oneself or to someone else, or to one's own or someone else's physical, sexual, or psychological integrity, overwhelming the individual's ability to cope. As an effect of psychological trauma, PTSD is less frequent and more enduring than the more commonly seen acute stress response. |
| Ponzo illusion | The Ponzo illusion is a geometrical-optical illusion that was first demonstrated by the Italian psychologist Mario Ponzo (1882-1960) in 1913. He suggested that the human mind judges an object's size based on its background. He showed this by drawing two identical lines across a pair of converging lines, similar to railway tracks. The upper line looks longer because we interpret the converging sides according to linear perspective as parallel lines receding into the distance. |
| Personality Assessment Inventory | Personality Assessment Inventory PhD, is a multi-scale test of psychological functioning that assesses constructs relevant to personality and psychopathology evaluation (e.g., depression, anxiety, aggression) in various contexts including psychotherapy, crisis/evaluation, forensic, personnel selection, pain/medical, and child custody assessment. The PAI has 22 non-overlapping scales, providing a comprehensive overview of psychopathology in adults. The PAI contains four kinds of scales: 1) validity scales, which measure the respondent's approach to the test, including faking good or bad, exaggeration, or defensiveness; 2) clinical scales, which correspond to psychiatric diagnostic categories; 3) treatment consideration scales, which assess factors that may relate to treatment of clinical disorders or other risk factors but which are not captured in psychiatric diagnoses (e.g., suicidal ideation); and 4) interpersonal scales, which provide indicators of interpersonal dimensions of personality functioning. |
| Anxiety sensitivity | Anxiety sensitivity refers to the fear of sensations experienced in anxiety-related situations. In other terms, bodily sensations related to anxiety are misattributed as a negative experience causing more intense sensations. For example, a person may fear having an increased heart rate because they believe that will increase their chance of having a heart attack. |
| Avoidance response | An avoidance response is a form of escape behavior present in animals in which the subject evades an aversive event. This can be due to anxiety or a frightening situation. Avoidance response is a response that is not necessarily conditioned before being exposed to in the stressful or fearful situation; the stimuli could be neutral. |
| Serotonin | Serotonin is a monoamine neurotransmitter. Biochemically derived from tryptophan, serotonin is primarily found in the gastrointestinal (GI) tract, platelets, and in the central nervous system (CNS) of animals including humans. It is a well-known contributor to feelings of well-being; therefore it is also known as a 'happiness hormone' despite not being a hormone. |
| Social phobia | Social Phobia is distinguished by an irrational fear of public humiliation or embarrassment. |

|  | It is one of several phobia disorders, which are all typified by excessive, specific, and consistent fear and avoidance of an object, activity, or situation. People with social phobia may avoid doing activities in public such as eating or speaking, as well as using public bathrooms. |
|---|---|
| Ames room | An Ames room is a distorted room that is used to create an optical illusion. Probably influenced by the writings of Hermann Helmholtz, it was invented by American ophthalmologist Adelbert Ames, Jr. in 1934, and constructed in the following year. |
| Dissociative amnesia | Dissociative amnesia is a memory disorder characterized by extreme memory loss that is caused by extensive psychological stress. As well as, abnormal memory functioning in the absence of structural brain damage or a known neurobiological cause; severe cases are very rare. Psychogenic amnesia is defined by (a) the presence of retrograde amnesia (the inability to retrieve stored memories leading up to the onset of amnesia), and (b) an absence of anterograde amnesia (the inability to form new long term memories). Dissociative amnesia is due to psychological rather than physiological causes and can sometimes be helped by therapy. |
| Dissociative disorder | Dissociative disorders can be defined as conditions that involve disruptions or breakdowns of memory, awareness, identity and/or perception. People with dissociative disorders use dissociation, a defense mechanism, pathologically and involuntarily. Dissociative disorders are thought to primarily be caused by psychological trauma. |
| Memory loss | Memory loss can be partial or total and it is normal when it comes with aging. Sudden memory loss is usually a result of brain trauma and it may be permanent or temporary. When it is caused by medical conditions such as Alzheimer's disease, the memory loss is gradual and tends to be permanent. |
| Child abuse | Child abuse is the physical, sexual, emotional mistreatment, or neglect of children. In the United States, the Centers for Disease Control and Prevention (CDC) define child maltreatment as any act or series of acts of commission or omission by a parent or other caregiver that results in harm, potential for harm, or threat of harm to a child. Most child abuse occurs in a child's home, with a smaller amount occurring in the organizations, schools or communities the child interacts with. |
| Dissociative identity disorder | Dissociative identity disorder is a psychiatric diagnosis. According to the Diagnostic and Statistical Manual of Mental Disorders (DSM) its essential feature '...is the presence of two or more distinct identities or personality states...that recurrently take control of behavior.' The diagnosis requires that at least two personalities (one may be the host) routinely take control of the individual's behavior with an associated memory loss that goes beyond normal forgetfulness; in addition, symptoms cannot be the temporary effects of drug use or a general medical condition. |

# Chapter 14. Psychological Disorders

| | |
|---|---|
| James-Lange theory | The James-Lange theory refers to a hypothesis on the origin and nature of emotions and is one of the earliest theories of emotion, developed independently by two 19th-century scholars, William James and Carl Lange.<br><br>The theory states that within human beings, as a response to experiences in the world, the autonomic nervous system creates physiological events such as muscular tension, a rise in heart rate, perspiration, and dryness of the mouth. Emotions, then, are feelings which come about as a result of these physiological changes, rather than being their cause. James and Lange arrived at the theory independently. Lange specifically stated that vasomotor changes are emotions. |
| Anhedonia | In psychology and psychiatry, anhedonia is defined as the inability to experience pleasure from activities usually found enjoyable, e.g. exercise, hobbies, sexual activities or social interactions. While earlier definitions of anhedonia emphasized pleasurable experience, more recent models have highlighted the need to consider different aspects of enjoyable behavior, such as motivation or desire to engage in an activity ('motivational anhedonia'), as compared to the level of enjoyment of the activity itself ('consummatory anhedonia') .<br><br>Anhedonia can be a characteristic of mental disorders including mood disorders, schizoaffective disorder, schizoid personality disorder and schizophrenia. |
| Bipolar disorder | Bipolar disorder, also referred to as bipolar affective disorder or manic depression, is a psychiatric diagnosis that describes a category of mood disorders defined by the presence of one or more episodes of abnormally elevated energy levels, cognition, and mood with or without one or more depressive episodes. The elevated moods are clinically referred to as mania or, if milder, hypomania. Individuals who experience manic episodes also commonly experience depressive episodes, or symptoms, or mixed episodes in which features of both mania and depression are present at the same time. |
| Mood disorder | Mood disorder is the term designating a group of diagnoses in the Diagnostic and Statistical Manual of Mental Disorders (DSM IV TR) classification system where a disturbance in the person's mood is hypothesized to be the main underlying feature. The classification is known as mood (affective) disorders in ICD 10.<br><br>English psychiatrist Henry Maudsley proposed an overarching category of affective disorder. |
| Mood swing | A mood swing is an extreme or rapid change in mood. When these changes start to become controlling, mood swings can start to affect the way someone functions.<br><br>Mood swings that last for days or even weeks. |

| Postpartum depression | Postpartum depression also called postnatal depression, is a form of clinical depression which can affect women, and less frequently men, typically after childbirth. Studies report prevalence rates among women from 5% to 25%, but methodological differences among the studies make the actual prevalence rate unclear. Among men, in particular new fathers, the incidence of postpartum depression has been estimated to be between 1.2% and 25.5%. |
|---|---|
| Norepinephrine | Norepinephrine is a catecholamine with multiple roles including as a hormone and a neurotransmitter. <br><br> As a stress hormone, norepinephrine affects parts of the brain, such as the amygdala, where attention and responses are controlled. Along with epinephrine, norepinephrine also underlies the fight-or-flight response, directly increasing heart rate, triggering the release of glucose from energy stores, and increasing blood flow to skeletal muscle. It increases the brain's oxygen supply. Norepinephrine can also suppress neuroinflammation when released diffusely in the brain from the locus ceruleus. |
| Cortisol | Cortisol is a steroid hormone, or glucocorticoid, produced by the adrenal gland. It is released in response to stress and a low level of blood glucocorticoids. Its primary functions are to increase blood sugar through gluconeogenesis; suppress the immune system; and aid in fat, protein and carbohydrate metabolism. |
| Explanatory style | Explanatory style is a psychological attribute that indicates how people explain to themselves why they experience a particular event, either positive or negative. Psychologists have identified three components in explanatory style:•Personal. This involves how one explains where the cause of an event arises. |
| Hypothalamus | The Hypothalamus is a portion of the brain that contains a number of small nuclei with a variety of functions. One of the most important functions of the hypothalamus is to link the nervous system to the endocrine system via the pituitary gland (hypophysis). <br><br> The hypothalamus is located below the thalamus, just above the brain stem. |
| Learned helplessness | Learned helplessness is a technical term that refers to the condition of a human or animal that has learned to behave helplessly, failing to respond even though there are opportunities for it to help itself by avoiding unpleasant circumstances or by gaining positive rewards. Learned helplessness theory is the view that clinical depression and related mental illnesses may result from a perceived absence of control over the outcome of a situation. Organisms which have been ineffective and less sensitive in determining the consequences of their behavior are defined as having acquired learned helplessness. |

# Chapter 14. Psychological Disorders

| | |
|---|---|
| Pituitary gland | In vertebrate anatomy the pituitary gland, is an endocrine gland about the size of a pea and weighing 0.5 g (0.02 oz)., in humans. It is a protrusion off the bottom of the hypothalamus at the base of the brain, and rests in a small, bony cavity (sella turcica) covered by a dural fold (diaphragma sellae). The pituitary is functionally connected to the hypothalamus by the median eminence via a small tube called the infundibular stem (Pituitary Stalk). |
| Auditory hallucination | An auditory hallucination, is a form of hallucination that involves perceiving sounds without auditory stimulus. A common form involves hearing one or more talking voices. This may be associated with psychotic disorders such as schizophrenia or mania, and holds special significance in diagnosing these conditions. |
| Delusion | A delusion is a belief that is either mistaken or not substantiated and is held with very strong feelings or opinions and expressed forcefully. In psychiatry, it is defined to be a belief that is pathological (the result of an illness or illness process) and is held despite evidence to the contrary. As a pathology, it is distinct from a belief based on false or incomplete information, dogma, stupidity, poor memory, illusion, or other effects of perception. |
| Hallucination | A hallucination, in the broadest sense of the word, is a perception in the absence of a stimulus. In a stricter sense, hallucinations are defined as perceptions in a conscious and awake state in the absence of external stimuli which have qualities of real perception, in that they are vivid, substantial, and located in external objective space. The latter definition distinguishes hallucinations from the related phenomena of dreaming, which does not involve wakefulness; illusion, which involves distorted or misinterpreted real perception; imagery, which does not mimic real perception and is under voluntary control; and pseudohallucination, which does not mimic real perception, but is not under voluntary control. |
| Schizophrenia | Schizophrenia is a mental disorder characterized by a disintegration of thought processes and of emotional responsiveness. It most commonly manifests as auditory hallucinations, paranoid or bizarre delusions, or disorganized speech and thinking, and it is accompanied by significant social or occupational dysfunction. The onset of symptoms typically occurs in young adulthood, with a global lifetime prevalence of about 0.3-0.7%. |
| Disorganized schizophrenia | Disorganized schizophrenia, is a subtype of schizophrenia, as defined in the Diagnostic and Statistical Manual of Mental Disorders, DSM-IV code 295.10.<br><br>Disorganized schizophrenia is thought to be an extreme expression of the disorganization syndrome that has been hypothesised to be one aspect of a three-factor model of symptoms in schizophrenia, the other factors being reality distortion (involving delusions and hallucinations) and psychomotor poverty (poverty of speech, lack of spontaneous movement and various aspects of blunting of emotion). Presentation |

| Emergence | In philosophy, systems theory, science, and art, emergence is the way complex systems and patterns arise out of a multiplicity of relatively simple interactions. Emergence is central to the theories of integrative levels and of complex systems. |
| --- | --- |
| | The concept has been in use since at least the time of Aristotle. |
| Paranoid schizophrenia | Paranoid schizophrenia is a sub-type of schizophrenia. In the United States, it is defined in the Diagnostic and Statistical Manual of Mental Disorders, DSM-IV code 295.30. It is the most common type of schizophrenia. |
| | Aspects |
| | Paranoid schizophrenia is manifested primarily through impaired thought processes, in which the central focus is on distorted perceptions or paranoid behavior and thinking. |
| Persecution | Persecution is the systematic mistreatment of an individual or group by another group. The most common forms are religious persecution, ethnic persecution, and political persecution, though there is naturally some overlap between these terms. The inflicting of suffering, harassment, isolation, imprisonment, fear, pain or exclusion |
| | International law |
| | As part of the Nuremberg Principles, crimes against humanity are part of international law. |
| Dopamine | Dopamine, a simple organic chemical in the catecholamine family, plays a number of important physiological roles in the bodies of animals. Its name derives from its chemical structure, which consists of an amine group ($NH_2$) linked to a catechol structure called dihydroxyphenethylamine, the decarboxyalted form of dihydroxyphenylalanine (acronym DOPA). In the brain, dopamine functions as a neurotransmitter--a chemical released by nerve cells to send signals to other nerve cells. |
| Prefrontal cortex | The prefrontal cortex. is the anterior part of the frontal lobes of the brain, lying in front of the motor and premotor areas. |
| | This brain region has been implicated in planning complex cognitive behavior, personality expression, decision making and moderating social behavior. |
| Expressed emotion | Expressed emotion is a qualitative measure of the 'amount' of emotion displayed, typically in the family setting, usually by a family or care takers. Theoretically, a high level of EE in the home can worsen the prognosis in patients with mental illness, (Brown et al., 1962, 1972) or act as a potential risk factor for the development of psychiatric disease. |

# Chapter 14. Psychological Disorders

CHAPTER HIGHLIGHTS & NOTES: KEY TERMS, PEOPLE, PLACES, CONCEPTS

| | |
|---|---|
| Prenatal development | Prenatal development is the process in which a human embryo or fetus (or foetus) gestates during pregnancy, from fertilization until birth. Often, the terms fetal development, foetal development, or embryology are used in a similar sense. |
| Antisocial personality disorder | Antisocial personality disorder is described by the American Psychiatric Association's Diagnostic and Statistical Manual, fourth edition (DSM-IV-TR), as an Axis II personality disorder characterized by '...a pervasive pattern of disregard for, and violation of, the rights of others that begins in childhood or early adolescence and continues into adulthood.'<br><br>The World Health Organization's International Statistical Classification of Diseases and Related Health Problems', tenth edition (ICD-10), defines a conceptually similar disorder to antisocial personality disorder called (F60.2) Dissocial personality disorder.<br><br>The American Psychiatric Association's Diagnostic and Statistical Manual of Mental Disorders incorporated various concepts of psychopathy/sociopathy/antisocial personality in early versions but, starting with the DSM-III in 1980, used instead the term Antisocial Personality Disorder and focused on earlier behavior instead of using personality judgements. The World Health Organization's ICD incorporates a similar diagnosis of Dissocial Personality Disorder. |
| Avoidant personality disorder | Avoidant personality disorder is a personality disorder recognized in the Diagnostic and Statistical Manual of Mental Disorders handbook in a person characterized by a pervasive pattern of social inhibition, feelings of inadequacy, extreme sensitivity to negative evaluation, and avoidance of social interaction.<br><br>People with avoidant personality disorder often consider themselves to be socially inept or personally unappealing and avoid social interaction for fear of being ridiculed, humiliated, rejected, or disliked. Avoidant personality disorder is usually first noticed in early adulthood. |
| Borderline personality disorder | Borderline personality disorder is a personality disorder described as a prolonged disturbance of personality function in a person (generally over the age of eighteen years, although it is also found in adolescents), characterized by depth and variability of moods. The disorder typically involves unusual levels of instability in mood; black and white thinking, or splitting; the disorder often manifests itself in idealization and devaluation episodes, as well as chaotic and unstable interpersonal relationships, self-image, identity, and behavior; as well as a disturbance in the individual's sense of self. In extreme cases, this disturbance in the sense of self can lead to periods of dissociation. |
| Dependent personality disorder | Dependent personality disorder formerly known as asthenic personality disorder, is a personality disorder that is characterized by a pervasive psychological dependence on other people. This personality disorder is a long-term (chronic) condition in which people depend on others to meet their emotional and physical needs, with depending on themselves a minority. |

| | |
|---|---|
| Histrionic personality disorder | Histrionic personality disorder is defined by the American Psychiatric Association as a personality disorder characterized by a pattern of excessive emotionality and attention-seeking, including an excessive need for approval and inappropriately seductive behavior, usually beginning in early adulthood. These individuals are lively, dramatic, vivacious, enthusiastic, and flirtatious. HPD is most commonly found in the United States and affects four times as many women as men. |
| Narcissistic personality disorder | Narcissistic personality disorder is a personality disorder in which the individual is described as being excessively preoccupied with issues of personal adequacy, power, prestige and vanity. This condition affects one percent of the population. First formulated in 1968, it was historically called megalomania, and it is closely linked to egocentrism. |
| Obsessive-compulsive personality disorder | Obsessive-compulsive personality disorder is a personality disorder characterized by a pervasive pattern of preoccupation with orderliness, perfectionism, and mental and interpersonal control at the expense of flexibility, openness, and efficiency. |

The primary symptoms of obsessive\ compulsive\ personality\ disorder can include preoccupation with remembering and paying attention to minute details and facts, following rules and regulations, compulsion to make lists and schedules, as well as rigidity/inflexibility of beliefs and/or exhibition of perfectionism that interferes with task-completion. Symptoms may cause extreme distress and interfere with a person's occupational and social functioning. According to the National Institute for Mental Health:

Most patients spend their early life avoiding symptoms and developing techniques to avoid dealing with these strenuous issues. Obsession

Some, but not all, patients with obsessive\ compulsive\ personality\ disorder show an obsessive need for cleanliness. This obsessive\ compulsive\ personality\ disorder trait is not to be confused with domestic efficiency; over-attention to related details may instead make these (and other) activities of daily living difficult to accomplish. Though obsessive behavior is in part a way to control anxiety, tension often remains. In the case of a hoarder, attention effectively to clean the home may be hindered by the amount of clutter that the hoarder resolves later to organize.

While there are superficial similarities between the list-making and obsessive aspects of Asperger's syndrome and obsessive\ compulsive\ personality\ disorder, the former is different from obsessive\ compulsive\ personality\ disorder especially regarding affective behaviors, including (but not limited to) empathy, social coping, and general social skills.

Perception of own and others' actions and beliefs tend to be polarised (i.e., 'right' or 'wrong', with little or no margin between the two) for people with this disorder.

# Chapter 14. Psychological Disorders

As might be expected, such rigidity places strain on interpersonal relationships, with frustration sometimes turning into anger and even violence. This is known as disinhibition. People with obsessive\ compulsive\ personality\ disorder often tend to general pessimism and/or underlying form(s) of depression. This can at times become so serious that suicide is a risk. Indeed, one study suggests that personality disorders are a significant substrate to psychiatric morbidity. They may cause more problems in functioning than a major depressive episode. Causes

Research into the familial tendency of obsessive\ compulsive\ personality\ disorder may be illuminated by DNA studies. Two studies suggest that people with a particular form of the DRD3 gene are highly likely to develop obsessive\ compulsive\ personality\ disorder and depression, particularly if they are male. Genetic concomitants, however, may lie dormant until triggered by events in the lives of those who are predisposed to obsessive\ compulsive\ personality\ disorder. These events could include trauma faced during childhood, such as physical, emotional or sexual abuse, or other types of psychological trauma. Diagnosis DSM

The Diagnostic and Statistical Manual of Mental Disorders fourth edition, (DSM IV-TR = 301.4), a widely used manual for diagnosing mental disorders, defines obsessive-compulsive personality disorder (in Axis II Cluster C) as:A pervasive pattern of preoccupation with orderliness, perfectionism, and mental and interpersonal control, at the expense of flexibility, openness, and efficiency, beginning by early adulthood and present in a variety of contexts. It is a requirement of DSM-IV that a diagnosis of any specific personality disorder also satisfies a set of general personality disorder criteria.Criticism

Since DSM IV-TR was published in 2000, some studies have found fault with its obsessive\ compulsive\ personality\ disorder coverage. A 2004 study challenged the usefulness of all but three of the criteria: perfectionism, rigidity and stubbornness, and miserliness. A study in 2007 found that obsessive\ compulsive\ personality\ disorder is etiologically distinct from avoidant and dependent personality disorders, suggesting it is incorrectly categorized as a Cluster C disorder. WHO

The World Health Organization's ICD-10 uses the term (F60.5) Anankastic personality disorder. It is characterized by at least three of the following:•feelings of excessive doubt and caution;•preoccupation with details, rules, lists, order, organization or schedule;•perfectionism that interferes with task completion;•excessive conscientiousness, scrupulousness, and undue preoccupation with productivity to the exclusion of pleasure and interpersonal relationships;•excessive pedantry and adherence to social conventions;•rigidity and stubbornness;•unreasonable insistence by the individual that others submit exactly to his or her way of doing things, or unreasonable reluctance to allow others to do things;•intrusion of insistent and unwelcome thoughts or impulses.Includes: •compulsive and obsessional personality (disorder)•obsessive-compulsive personality disorderExcludes: •obsessive-compulsive disorder

| | |
|---|---|
| Paranoid personality disorder | Paranoid personality disorder is a mental disorder characterized by paranoia and a pervasive, long-standing suspiciousness and generalized mistrust of others. Individuals with this personality disorder may be hypersensitive, easily feel slighted, and habitually relate to the world by vigilant scanning of the environment for clues or suggestions that may validate their fears or biases. Paranoid individuals are eager observers. |
| Schizoid personality disorder | Schizoid personality disorder is a personality disorder characterized by a lack of interest in social relationships, a tendency towards a solitary lifestyle, secretiveness, emotional coldness, and apathy. Affected individuals may also demonstrate a simultaneous rich, elaborate, and exclusively internal fantasy world, although this is often more suggestive of schizotypal personality disorder.<br><br>SPD is not the same as schizophrenia, although they share some similar characteristics such as detachment or blunted affect; there is increased prevalence of the disorder in families with schizophrenia. |
| Schizotypal personality disorder | Schizotypal personality disorder is a personality disorder characterized by a need for social isolation, anxiety in social situations, odd behavior and thinking, and often unconventional beliefs. People with this disorder feel extreme discomfort with maintaining close relationships with people, and therefore they often don't. They frequently misinterpret situations as being strange or having unusual meaning for them. |
| Disinhibition | Disinhibition is a term in psychology used to describe a lack of restraint manifested in several ways, including disregard for social conventions, impulsivity, and poor risk assessment. Disinhibition affects motor, instinctual, emotional, cognitive and perceptual aspects with signs and symptoms similar to the diagnostic criteria for mania. Hypersexuality, hyperphagia, and aggressive outbursts are indicative of disinhibited instinctual drives. |
| Genetic predisposition | A genetic predisposition is a genetic affectation which influences the phenotype of an individual organism within a species or population but by definition that phenotype can also be modified by the environmental conditions. In the rest of the population, conditions cannot have that effect. Genetic testing is able to identify individuals who are genetically predisposed to certain health problems. |
| Involuntary commitment | Involuntary commitment is court-ordered into treatment in a hospital (inpatient) or in the community (outpatient).<br><br>Criteria for civil commitment are established by law, which varies between nations and, in the U.S., from state to state. Commitment proceedings often follow a period of emergency hospitalization during which an individual with acute psychiatric symptoms is confined for a relatively short duration (e.g. |

# Chapter 14. Psychological Disorders

| | |
|---|---|
| Anorexia nervosa | The differential diagnoses of anorexia nervosa (AN) include various medical and psychological conditions which may be misdiagnosed as (AN), in some cases these conditions may be comorbid with anorexia nervosa (AN). The misdiagnosis of AN is not uncommon. In one instance a case of achalasia was misdiagnosed as AN and the patient spent two months confined to a psychiatric hospital. |
| Flynn effect | The Flynn effect is the name given to a substantial and long-sustained increase in intelligence test scores measured in many parts of the world. When intelligence quotient (IQ) tests are initially standardized using a sample of test-takers, by convention the average of the test results is set to 100 and their standard deviation is set to 15 or 16 IQ points. When IQ tests are revised, they are again standardized using a new sample of test-takers, usually born more recently than the first. |
| Amenorrhoea | Amenorrhoea amenorrhea (AmE), or amenorrha, is the absence of a menstrual period in a woman of reproductive age. Physiological states of amenorrhoea are seen during pregnancy and lactation (breastfeeding), the latter also forming the basis of a form of contraception known as the lactational amenorrhoea method. Outside of the reproductive years there is absence of menses during childhood and after menopause. |
| Binge eating | Binge eating is a pattern of disordered eating which consists of episodes of uncontrollable eating. It is sometimes as a symptom of binge eating disorder. During such binges, a person rapidly consumes an excessive amount of food. Most people who have eating binges try to hide this behavior from others, and often feel ashamed about being overweight or depressed about their overeating. |
| Bulimia nervosa | Bulimia nervosa is an eating disorder characterized by restraining of food intake for a period of time followed by an over intake or binging period that results in feelings of guilt and low self-esteem. The median age of onset is 18. Sufferers attempt to overcome these feelings in a number of ways. The most common form is defensive vomiting, sometimes called purging; fasting, the use of laxatives, enemas, diuretics, and over exercising are also common. |
| Osteoporosis | Osteoporosis is a disease of bones that leads to an increased risk of fracture. In osteoporosis the bone mineral density (BMD) is reduced, bone microarchitecture is deteriorating, and the amount and variety of proteins in bone is altered. Osteoporosis is defined by the World Health Organization (WHO) as a bone mineral density that is 2.5 standard deviations or more below the mean peak bone mass (average of young,healthy adults) as measured by DXA; the term 'established osteoporosis' includes the presence of a fragility fracture. |
| Overeating | Overeating generally refers to the long-term consumption of excess food in relation to the energy that an organism expends (or expels via excretion), leading to weight gaining and often obesity. It may be regarded as an eating disorder. |

| Poggendorff illusion | The Poggendorff Illusion is a geometrical-optical illusion that involves the misperception of the position of one segment of a transverse line that has been interrupted by the contour of an intervening structure (here a rectangle). It is named after Poggendorff, the editor of the journal, who discovered it in the figures Johann Karl Friedrich Zöllner submitted when first reporting on what is now known as the Zöllner illusion, in 1860.<br><br>In the picture to the right, a straight black and red line is obscured by a grey rectangle. |
|---|---|
| Point prevalence | In epidemiology, point prevalence is a measure of the proportion of people in a population who have a disease or condition at a particular time, such as a particular date. It is like a snap shot of the disease in time. It can be used for statistics on the occurrence of chronic diseases. |
| Representativeness heuristic | The representativeness heuristic is used when making judgments about the probability of an event under uncertainty (Kahneman & Tversky, 1972). It was first proposed by Amos Tversky and Daniel Kahneman who defined representativeness as 'the degree to which [an event] (i) is similar in essential characteristics to its parent population and (ii) reflects the salient features of the process by which it is generated' (Kahneman & Tversky, 1982, p. 33). When people rely on representativeness to make judgements, they are likely to judge wrongly because the fact that something is more representative does not make it more likely (Tversky & Kahneman, 1982). |
| Availability heuristic | The availability heuristic is a mental shortcut that uses the ease with which examples come to mind to make judgements about the probability of events. The availability heuristic operates on the notion that 'if you can think of it, it must be important.' The availability of consequences associated with an action is positively related to perceptions of the magnitude of the consequences of that action. In other words, the easier it is to recall the consequences of something, the bigger we perceive these consequences to be. |
| Conjunction fallacy | The conjunction fallacy is a logical fallacy that occurs when it is assumed that specific conditions are more probable than a single general one.<br><br>The most often-cited example of this fallacy originated with Amos Tversky and Daniel Kahneman:'<br><br>Linda is 31 years old, single, outspoken, and very bright. She majored in philosophy.' |
| Hindsight bias | Hindsight bias, is the inclination to see events that have already occurred as being more predictable than they were before they took place. It is a multifaceted phenomenon that can affect different stages of designs, processes, contexts, and situations. Hindsight bias may cause memory distortion, where the recollection and reconstruction of content can lead to false theoretical outcomes. |

# Chapter 14. Psychological Disorders

1. An _____ is a form of escape behavior present in animals in which the subject evades an aversive event. This can be due to anxiety or a frightening situation. _____ is a response that is not necessarily conditioned before being exposed to in the stressful or fearful situation; the stimuli could be neutral.

   a. Axon reflex
   b. Avoidance response
   c. Escape reflex
   d. Extensor digitorum reflex

2. _____ is the study of disease patterns in a society. It is the cornerstone method of public health research, and helps inform evidence-based medicine for identifying risk factors for disease and determining optimal treatment approaches to clinical practice and for preventive medicine. In the study of communicable and non-communicable diseases, epidemiologists are involved in outbreak investigation to study design, data collection, statistical analysis, documentation of results and submission for publication.

   a. Epidemiology
   b. Foerster's syndrome
   c. Hallucinogen persisting perception disorder
   d. Mechanisms of schizophrenia

3. A _____ is a research method common in social science. It is based on an in-depth investigation of a single individual, group, or event. Case studies may be descriptive or explanatory.

   a. Case study
   b. Blind experiment
   c. Critical-Creative Thinking and Behavioral Research Laboratory
   d. Cybermethodology

4. _____ is the supposed control over a human by a malevolent supernatural being or evil spirit. Descriptions of _____s often include erased memories or personalities, convulsions, 'fits' and fainting as if one were dying. Other descriptions include access to hidden knowledge (gnosis) and foreign languages (glossolalia), drastic changes in vocal intonation and facial structure, the sudden appearance of injuries (scratches, bite marks) or lesions, and superhuman strength.

   a. Fasting
   b. Demonic possession
   c. General Confession
   d. Genuflection

5. . _____ is court-ordered into treatment in a hospital (inpatient) or in the community (outpatient).

   Criteria for civil commitment are established by law, which varies between nations and, in the U.S., from state to state. Commitment proceedings often follow a period of emergency hospitalization during which an individual with acute psychiatric symptoms is confined for a relatively short duration (e.g.

72 hours) in a treatment facility for evaluation and stabilization by mental health professionals - who may then determine whether further civil commitment is appropriate or necessary.

a. Involuntary commitment
b. Love Is...
c. Mirror stage
d. Name of the Father

1. b
2. a
3. a
4. b
5. a

---

## You can take the complete Chapter Practice Test

### for Chapter 14. Psychological Disorders
on all key terms, persons, places, and concepts.

## Online 99 Cents

## *http://www.epub3.2.20111.14.cram101.com/*

**Use www.Cram101.com for all your study needs**

**including Cram101's online interactive problem solving labs in**

**chemistry, statistics, mathematics, and more.**

CHAPTER OUTLINE: KEY TERMS, PEOPLE, PLACES, CONCEPTS

_____ Psychotherapy

_____ Psychiatrist

_____ Mendelian inheritance

_____ Ethnic group

_____ Gamma-Aminobutyric acid

_____ Mental health

_____ Personality test

_____ Rating scale

_____ Social worker

_____ Psychoanalysis

_____ Deese-Roediger-McDermott paradigm

_____ Personality Assessment Inventory

_____ Person-centered therapy

_____ Unconditional positive regard

_____ Ponzo illusion

_____ Positive psychology

_____ Positive Psychotherapy

_____ Couples therapy

_____ Family therapy

Social skill

Behavior therapy

Behaviorism

Classical conditioning

Systematics

Systematic desensitization

Aversion therapy

Electroconvulsive therapy

Exposure therapy

Virtual reality

Attention deficit disorder

Behavior modification

Case study

Cognitive therapy

Interpersonal skills

Rational emotive behavior therapy

Social anxiety

Mental disorder

Alprazolam

CHAPTER OUTLINE: KEY TERMS, PEOPLE, PLACES, CONCEPTS

Benzodiazepine

Chlorpromazine

Decision making

Diazepam

Haloperidol

Problem solving

Schizophrenia

Tranquilizer

Atypical antipsychotic

Clozapine

Fluoxetine

Fluphenazine

Olanzapine

Paroxetine

Quetiapine

Reuptake

Selective serotonin reuptake inhibitor

Serotonin

Sertraline

Tardive dyskinesia

Norepinephrine

Mood stabilizer

Parkinsonism

Prefrontal cortex

Transcranial magnetic stimulation

Geriatrics

Interpersonal psychotherapy

Cognitive behavioral therapy

Halfway house

Human services

Multimodal therapy

Regression toward the mean

Quackery

Prenatal development

Insomnia

CHAPTER HIGHLIGHTS & NOTES: KEY TERMS, PEOPLE, PLACES, CONCEPTS

| | |
|---|---|
| Psychotherapy | Psychotherapy, is an intentional interpersonal relationship used by trained psychotherapists to aid a client or patient in problems of living.<br><br>It is a talking therapy and aims to increase the individual's sense of their own well-being. Psychotherapists employ a range of techniques based on experiential relationship building, dialogue, communication and behavior change that are designed to improve the mental health of a client or patient, or to improve group relationships (such as in a family). |
| Psychiatrist | A psychiatrist is a physician who specializes. in psychiatry and is certified in treating mental disorders. All psychiatrists are trained in diagnostic evaluation and in psychotherapy. |
| Mendelian inheritance | Mendelian inheritance, hereditary characteristics from parent organisms to their offspring; it underlies much of genetics. They were initially derived from the work of Gregor Johann Mendel published in 1865 and 1866 which was 're-discovered' in 1900, and were initially very controversial. When they were integrated with the chromosome theory of inheritance by Thomas Hunt Morgan in 1915, they became the core of classical genetics. |
| Ethnic group | An ethnic group is a group of people whose members identify with each other, through a common heritage, often consisting of a common language, a common culture (often including a shared religion) and an ideology that stresses common ancestry or endogamy.<br><br>Members of an ethnic group are conscious of belonging to an ethnic group; moreover ethnic identity is further marked by the recognition from others of a group's distinctiveness. Processes that result in the emergence of such identification are called ethnogenesis. |
| Gamma-Aminobutyric acid | γ-Aminobutyric acid is the chief inhibitory neurotransmitter in the mammalian central nervous system. It plays a role in regulating neuronal excitability throughout the nervous system. In humans, GABA is also directly responsible for the regulation of muscle tone.<br><br>Although chemically it is an amino acid, GABA is rarely referred to as such in the scientific or medical communities, because the term 'amino acid,' used without a qualifier, conventionally refers to the alpha amino acids, which GABA is not, nor is it ever incorporated into a protein.<br><br>In spastic diplegia in humans, GABA absorption becomes impaired by nerves damaged from the condition's upper motor neuron lesion, which leads to hypertonia of the muscles signaled by those nerves that can no longer absorb GABA.Function Neurotransmitter<br><br>In vertebrates, GABA acts at inhibitory synapses in the brain by binding to specific transmembrane receptors in the plasma membrane of both pre- and postsynaptic neuronal processes. This binding causes the opening of ion channels to allow the flow of either negatively charged chloride ions into the cell or positively charged potassium ions out of the cell. |

# Chapter 15. Treatment of Psychological Disorders

Depending on which ion channels open, the membrane potential is either hyperpolarized or depolarized. This action results in a negative change in the transmembrane potential, usually causing hyperpolarization. Two general classes of GABA receptor are known: $GABA_A$ in which the receptor is part of a ligand-gated ion channel complex, and $GABA_B$ metabotropic receptors, which are G protein-coupled receptors that open or close ion channels via intermediaries (G proteins).

Neurons that produce GABA as their output are called GABAergic neurons, and have chiefly inhibitory action at receptors in the adult vertebrate. Medium Spiny Cells are a typical example of inhibitory CNS GABAergic cells. In contrast, GABA exhibits both excitatory and inhibitory actions in insects, mediating muscle activation at synapses between nerves and muscle cells, and also the stimulation of certain glands. In mammals, some GABAergic neurons, such as chandelier cells, are also able to excite their glutamatergic counterparts.

$GABA_A$ receptors are ligand-activated chloride channels; that is, when activated by GABA, they allow the flow of chloride ions across the membrane of the cell. Whether this chloride flow is excitatory/depolarizing (makes the voltage across the cell's membrane less negative), shunting (has no effect on the cell's membrane) or inhibitory/hyperpolarizing (makes the cell's membrane more negative) depends on the direction of the flow of chloride. When net chloride flows out of the cell, GABA is excitatory or depolarizing; when the net chloride flows into the cell, GABA is inhibitory or hyperpolarizing. When the net flow of chloride is close to zero, the action of GABA is shunting. Shunting inhibition has no direct effect on the membrane potential of the cell; however, it minimises the effect of any coincident synaptic input essentially by reducing the electrical resistance of the cell's membrane (in essence, equivalent to Ohm's law). A developmental switch in the molecular machinery controlling concentration of chloride inside the cell - and, hence, the direction of this ion flow - is responsible for the changes in the functional role of GABA between the neonatal and adult stages. That is to say, GABA's role changes from excitatory to inhibitory as the brain develops into adulthood. Brain development

For the past two decades, the theory of excitatory action of GABA early in development was unquestioned based on experiments in vitro, on brain slices. The main observation was that in the hippocampus and neocortex of the mammalian brain, GABA has primarily excitatory effects, and is in fact the major excitatory neurotransmitter in many regions of the brain before the maturation of glutamateergic synapses.

However, this theory has been questioned based on results showing that in brain slices of immature mice incubated in artificial cerebrospinal fluid (ACSF) (modified in a way that takes into account the normal composition of the neuronal milieu in sucklings by adding an energy substrate alternative to glucose, beta-hydroxybutyrate) GABA action shifts from excitatory to inhibitory mode. This effect has been later repeated when other energy substrates, pyruvate and lactate, supplemented glucose in the slices' media.

The effects of beta-hydroxybutyrate were later confirmed for pyruvate and for lactate. However it was argued that the concentrations of the alternative energy substrates used in these experiments were non-physiological and the GABA-shift was instead caused by changes in pH resulting from the substrates acting as 'weak acids'. These arguments were later rebutted by further findings showing that changes in pH even greater than that caused by energy substrates do not affect the GABA-shift described in the presence of energy substrate-fortified ACSF and that the mode of action of beta-hydroxybutyrate, pyruvate and lactate (assessed by measurement NAD(P)H and oxygen utilization) was energy metabolism-related.

In the developmental stages preceding the formation of synaptic contacts, GABA is synthesized by neurons and acts both as an autocrine (acting on the same cell) and paracrine (acting on nearby cells) signalling mediator.

GABA regulates the proliferation of neural progenitor cells the migration and differentiation the elongation of neurites and the formation of synapses.

GABA also regulates the growth of embryonic and neural stem cells. GABA can in?uence the development of neural progenitor cells via brain-derived neurotrophic factor (BDNF) expression. GABA activates the $GABA_A$ receptor, causing cell cycle arrest in the S-phase, limiting growth. Beyond the nervous system

GABAergic mechanisms have been demonstrated in various peripheral tissues and organs including, but not restricted to the intestine, stomach, pancreas, Fallopian tube, uterus, ovary, testis, kidney, urinary bladder, lung, and liver.

In 2007, an excitatory GABAergic system was described in the airway epithelium. The system activates following exposure to allergens and may participate in the mechanisms of asthma. GABAergic systems have also been found in the testis and in the eye lens. Structure and conformation

GABA is found mostly as a zwitterion, that is, with the carboxy group deprotonated and the amino group protonated. Its conformation depends on its environment. In the gas phase, a highly folded conformation is strongly favored because of the electrostatic attraction between the two functional groups. The stabilization is about 50 kcal/mol, according to quantum chemistry calculations. In the solid state, a more extended conformation is found, with a trans conformation at the amino end and a gauche conformation at the carboxyl end. This is due to the packing interactions with the neighboring molecules. In solution, five different conformations, some folded and some extended, are found as a result of solvation effects. The conformational flexibility of GABA is important for its biological function, as it has been found to bind to different receptors with different conformations. Many GABA analogues with pharmaceutical applications have more rigid structures in order to control the binding better. History

| | |
|---|---|
| Mental health | Mental health describes a level of psychological well-being, or an absence of a mental disorder. From the perspective of 'positive psychology' or 'holism', mental health may include an individual's ability to enjoy life, and create a balance between life activities and efforts to achieve psychological resilience. Mental health can also be defined as an expression of emotions, and as signifying a successful adaptation to a range of demands. |
| Personality test | A personality test is a questionnaire or other standardized instrument designed to reveal aspects of an individual's character or psychological makeup. The first personality tests were developed in the early 20th century and were intended to ease the process of personnel selection, particularly in the armed forces. Since these early efforts of these test, a wide variety of personality tests have been developed, notably the Myers Briggs Type Indicator (MBTI), the MMPI, and a number of tests based on the Five Factor Model of personality. |
| Rating scale | A rating scale is a set of categories designed to elicit information about a quantitative or a qualitative attribute. In the social sciences, common examples are the Likert scale and 1-10 rating scales in which a person selects the number which is considered to reflect the perceived quality of a product. <br><br> A rating scale is a method that requires the rater to assign a value, sometimes numeric, to the rated object, as a measure of some rated attribute. |
| Social worker | Social work is a professional and academic discipline that seeks to improve the quality of life and wellbeing of an individual, group, or community by intervening through research, policy, community organizing, direct practice, and teaching on behalf of those afflicted with poverty or any real or perceived social injustices and violations of their human rights. Research is often focused on areas such as human development, social policy, public administration, psychotherapy, program evaluation, and international and community development. Social workers are organized into local, national, continental and international professional bodies. |
| Psychoanalysis | Psychoanalysis is a body of ideas developed by Austrian neurologist Sigmund Freud and continued by others. It is primarily devoted to the study of human psychological functioning and behavior, although it can also be applied to societies. Psychoanalysis has three main components:•a method of investigation of the mind and the way one thinks;•a systematized set of theories about human behavior;•a method of treatment of psychological or emotional illness. <br><br> Under the broad umbrella of psychoanalysis, there are at least 22 theoretical orientations regarding human mentation and development. |
| Deese-Roediger-McDermott paradigm | The Deese-Roediger-McDermott (DRM) paradigm in cognitive psychology is an example of false memory. James Deese, an American psychologist and professor, first studied this paradigm in 1959. |

The DRM Paradigm refers to the tendency to falsely recall a target word from a set list of words centered around that target word. Henry L. Roediger III and Kathleen McDermott have done further research in more recent years to both confirm this phenomenon and find that it even extends into falsely recalling events, hence the name, the Deese-Roediger-McDermott paradigm.

| | |
|---|---|
| Personality Assessment Inventory | Personality Assessment Inventory PhD, is a multi-scale test of psychological functioning that assesses constructs relevant to personality and psychopathology evaluation (e.g., depression, anxiety, aggression) in various contexts including psychotherapy, crisis/evaluation, forensic, personnel selection, pain/medical, and child custody assessment. The PAI has 22 non-overlapping scales, providing a comprehensive overview of psychopathology in adults. The PAI contains four kinds of scales: 1) validity scales, which measure the respondent's approach to the test, including faking good or bad, exaggeration, or defensiveness; 2) clinical scales, which correspond to psychiatric diagnostic categories; 3) treatment consideration scales, which assess factors that may relate to treatment of clinical disorders or other risk factors but which are not captured in psychiatric diagnoses (e.g., suicidal ideation); and 4) interpersonal scales, which provide indicators of interpersonal dimensions of personality functioning. |
| Person-centered therapy | Person-centered therapy is also known as person-centered psychotherapy, person-centered counselling, client-centered therapy and Rogerian psychotherapy. Person centered therapy is a form of talk-psychotherapy developed by psychologist Carl Rogers in the 1940s and 1950s. It is one of the most widely used models in mental health and psychotherapy. |
| Unconditional positive regard | Unconditional positive regard, a term popularly believed to have been coined by the humanist Carl Rogers , is basic acceptance and support of a person regardless of what the person says or does. Rogers believes that unconditional positive regard is essential to healthy development. People who have not experienced it may come to see themselves in the negative ways that others have made them feel. |
| Ponzo illusion | The Ponzo illusion is a geometrical-optical illusion that was first demonstrated by the Italian psychologist Mario Ponzo (1882-1960) in 1913. He suggested that the human mind judges an object's size based on its background. He showed this by drawing two identical lines across a pair of converging lines, similar to railway tracks. The upper line looks longer because we interpret the converging sides according to linear perspective as parallel lines receding into the distance. |

# Chapter 15. Treatment of Psychological Disorders

| | |
|---|---|
| Positive psychology | Positive psychology is a recent branch of psychology whose purpose was summed up in 2000 by Martin Seligman and Mihaly Csikszentmihalyi: 'We believe that a psychology of positive human functioning will arise that achieves a scientific understanding and effective interventions to build thriving in individuals, families, and communities.' Positive psychologists seek 'to find and nurture genius and talent', and 'to make normal life more fulfilling', not simply to treat mental illness. The emerging field of Positive Psychology is intended to complement, not to replace traditional psychology.<br><br>By scientifically studying what has gone right, rather than wrong in both individuals and societies, Positive Psychology hopes to achieve a renaissance of sorts. |
| Positive Psychotherapy | Positive psychotherapy (since 1968) is the name of the method of the psychotherapeutic modality developed by Nossrat Peseschkian and co-workers. Prof. Peseschkian, MD, (1933-2010) was a specialist in neurology, psychiatry, psychotherapy and psychotherapeutic medicine. |
| Couples therapy | Relationship counseling is the process of counseling the parties of a relationship in an effort to recognize and to better manage or reconcile troublesome differences and repeating patterns of distress. The relationship involved may be between members of a family or a couple , employees or employers in a workplace, or between a professional and a client.<br><br>Couple therapy (or relationship therapy) is a related and different process. It may differ from relationship counseling in duration. Short term counseling may be between 1 to 3 sessions whereas long term couples therapy may be between 12 and 24 sessions. |
| Family therapy | Family therapy, also referred to as couple and family therapy, family systems therapy, and family counseling, is a branch of psychotherapy that works with families and couples in intimate relationships to nurture change and development. It tends to view change in terms of the systems of interaction between family members. It emphasizes family relationships as an important factor in psychological health. |
| Social skill | A social skill is any skill facilitating interaction and communication with others. Social rules and relations are created, communicated, and changed in verbal and nonverbal ways. The process of learning such skills is called socialization. |
| Behavior therapy | Behavior therapy is an approach to psychotherapy based on learning theory which aims to treat psychopathology through techniques designed to reinforce desired and eliminate undesired behaviors. |
| Behaviorism | Behaviorism also called the learning perspective (where any physical action is a behavior), is a philosophy of psychology based on the proposition that all things that organisms do--including acting, thinking and feeling--can and should be regarded as behaviors. |

The behaviorist school of thought maintains that behaviors as such can be described scientifically without recourse either to internal physiological events or to hypothetical constructs such as the mind. Behaviorism comprises the position that all theories should have observational correlates but that there are no philosophical differences between publicly observable processes (such as actions) and privately observable processes (such as thinking and feeling).

| | |
|---|---|
| Classical conditioning | Introduction<br><br>Classical conditioning is a form of learning in which one stimulus comes to signal the occurrence of a second stimulus. This is often brought about by pairing the two stimuli, as in Pavlov's classic experiments. Pavlov presented dogs with a ringing bell followed by food. |
| Systematics | Biological systematics is the study of the diversification of life on the planet Earth, both past and present, and the relationships among living things through time. Relationships are visualized as evolutionary trees . Phylogenies have two components, branching order (showing group relationships) and branch length (showing amount of evolution). |
| Systematic desensitization | Systematic desensitization is a type of behavioral therapy used in the field of psychology to help effectively overcome phobias and other anxiety disorders. More specifically, it is a type of Pavlovian therapy / classical conditioning therapy developed by a South African psychiatrist, Joseph Wolpe. To begin the process of systematic desensitization, one must first be taught relaxation skills in order to extinguish fear and anxiety responses to specific phobias. |
| Aversion therapy | Aversion therapy is a form of psychological treatment in which the patient is exposed to a stimulus while simultaneously being subjected to some form of discomfort. This conditioning is intended to cause the patient to associate the stimulus with unpleasant sensations in order to stop the specific behavior.<br><br>Aversion therapies can take many forms, for example: placing unpleasant-tasting substances on the fingernails to discourage nail-chewing; pairing the use of an emetic with the experience of alcohol; or pairing behavior with electric shocks of various intensities. |
| Electroconvulsive therapy | Electroconvulsive therapy formerly known as electroshock, is a psychiatric treatment in which seizures are electrically induced in anesthetized patients for therapeutic effect. Its mode of action is unknown. Today, ECT is most often recommended for use as a treatment for severe depression that has not responded to other treatment, and is also used in the treatment of mania and catatonia. |

# Chapter 15. Treatment of Psychological Disorders

| | |
|---|---|
| Exposure therapy | Exposure therapy is a technique in behavior therapy intended to treat anxiety disorders and involves the exposure to the feared object or context without any danger in order to overcome their anxiety. Procedurally it is similar to the fear extinction paradigm in rodent work. Numerous studies have demonstrated its effectiveness in the treatment of anxiety disorders such as PTSD and specific phobias. |
| Virtual reality | Virtual reality is a term that applies to computer-simulated environments that can simulate physical presence in places in the real world, as well as in imaginary worlds. Most current virtual reality environments are primarily visual experiences, displayed either on a computer screen or through special stereoscopic displays, but some simulations include additional sensory information, such as sound through speakers or headphones. Some advanced, haptic systems now include tactile information, generally known as force feedback, in medical and gaming applications. |
| Attention deficit disorder | Attention deficit disorder is one of the three subtypes of Attention-deficit hyperactivity disorder (ADHD). The term was formally changed in 1994 in the new Diagnostic and Statistical Manual of Mental Disorders, fourth edition (DSM-IV) to 'ADHD predominantly inattentive' (ADHD-PI or ADHD-I), though the term attention deficit disorder is still widely used. ADD is similar to the other subtypes of ADHD in that it is characterized primarily by inattention, easy distractibility, disorganization, procrastination, and forgetfulness; where it differs is in lethargy - fatigue, and having fewer or no symptoms of hyperactivity or impulsiveness typical of the other ADHD subtypes. |
| Behavior modification | Behavior modification is the use of empirically demonstrated behavior change techniques to increase or decrease the frequency of behaviors, such as altering an individual's behaviors and reactions to stimuli through positive and negative reinforcement of adaptive behavior and/or the reduction of behavior through its extinction, punishment and/or satiation. Most behavior modification programs currently used are those based on Applied behavior analysis (ABA), formerly known as the experimental analysis of behavior which was pioneered by B. F. Skinner. |
| Case study | A case study is a research method common in social science. It is based on an in-depth investigation of a single individual, group, or event. Case studies may be descriptive or explanatory. |
| Cognitive therapy | Cognitive therapy is a type of psychotherapy developed by American psychiatrist Aaron T. Beck. CT is one of the therapeutic approaches within the larger group of cognitive behavioral therapies (CBT) and was first expounded by Beck in the 1960s. Cognitive therapy seeks to help the patient overcome difficulties by identifying and changing dysfunctional thinking, behavior, and emotional responses. |
| Interpersonal skills | Interpersonal skills are sometimes also referred to as people skills or communication skills. |

Interpersonal skills involve using skills such as active listening, tone of voice, delegation, and leadership. It is how well you communicate with someone and how well you behave or carry yourself.

| | |
|---|---|
| Rational emotive behavior therapy | Rational emotive behavior therapy previously called rational therapy and rational emotive therapy, is a comprehensive, active-directive, philosophically and empirically based psychotherapy which focuses on resolving emotional and behavioral problems and disturbances and enabling people to lead happier and more fulfilling lives. REBT was created and developed by the American psychotherapist and psychologist Albert Ellis who was inspired by many of the teachings of Asian, Greek, Roman and modern philosophers. REBT is one form of cognitive behavior therapy (CBT) and was first expounded by Ellis in the mid-1950s; development continued until his death in 2007. |
| Social anxiety | Social anxiety is anxiety (emotional discomfort, fear, apprehension, or worry) about social situations, interactions with others, and being evaluated or scrutinized by other people. The difference between social anxiety and normal apprehension of social situations is that social anxiety involves an intense feeling of fear in social situations and especially situations that are unfamiliar or in which you will be watched or evaluated by others. The feeling of fear is so great that in these types of situations one may be so worried that they feel anxious just thinking about them and will go to great lengths to avoid them. |
| Mental disorder | A mental disorder is a psychological or behavioral pattern generally associated with subjective distress or disability that occurs in an individual, and which is not a part of normal development or culture. The recognition and understanding of mental health conditions has changed over time and across cultures, and there are still variations in the definition, assessment, and classification of mental disorders, although standard guideline criteria are widely accepted. A few mental disorders are diagnosed based on the harm to others, regardless of the subject's perception of distress. |
| Alprazolam | Alprazolam is a potent short-acting drug of the benzodiazepine class. It is primarily used to treat moderate to severe anxiety disorders (e.g., social anxiety disorder) and panic attacks, and is used as an adjunctive treatment for anxiety associated with moderate depression. It is available in an instant release and an extended-release (Xanax XR) preparation, both of which are available under several generic names. |
| Benzodiazepine | A benzodiazepine is a psychoactive drug whose core chemical structure is the fusion of a benzene ring and a diazepine ring. The first benzodiazepine, chlordiazepoxide (Librium), was discovered accidentally by Leo Sternbach in 1955, and made available in 1960 by Hoffmann-La Roche, which has also marketed diazepam (Valium) since 1963. |

# Chapter 15. Treatment of Psychological Disorders

| | |
|---|---|
| Chlorpromazine | Chlorpromazine is a typical antipsychotic. First synthesized on December 11, 1950, chlorpromazine was the first drug developed with specific antipsychotic action, and would serve as the prototype for the phenothiazine class of drugs, which later grew to comprise several other agents. The introduction of chlorpromazine into clinical use has been described as the single greatest advance in psychiatric care, dramatically improving the prognosis of patients in psychiatric hospitals worldwide; the availability of antipsychotic drugs curtailed indiscriminate use of electroconvulsive therapy and psychosurgery, and was one of the driving forces behind the deinstitutionalization movement. |
| Decision making | Decision making can be regarded as the mental processes (cognitive process) resulting in the selection of a course of action among several alternatives. Every decision making process produces a final choice. The output can be an action or an opinion of choice. |
| Diazepam | Diazepam first marketed as Valium by Hoffmann-La Roche, is a benzodiazepine drug. Diazepam is also marketed in Australia as Antenex. It is commonly used for treating anxiety, insomnia, seizures including status epilepticus, muscle spasms (such as in cases of tetanus), restless legs syndrome, alcohol withdrawal, benzodiazepine withdrawal and Ménière's disease. |
| Haloperidol | Haloperidol is a typical antipsychotic. It is in the butyrophenone class of antipsychotic medications and has pharmacological effects similar to the phenothiazines.<br><br>Haloperidol is an older antipsychotic used in the treatment of schizophrenia and acute psychotic states and delirium. |
| Problem solving | Problem solving is a mental process and is part of the larger problem process that includes problem finding and problem shaping. Considered the most complex of all intellectual functions, problem solving has been defined as higher-order cognitive process that requires the modulation and control of more routine or fundamental skills. Problem solving occurs when an organism or an artificial intelligence system needs to move from a given state to a desired goal state. |
| Schizophrenia | Schizophrenia is a mental disorder characterized by a disintegration of thought processes and of emotional responsiveness. It most commonly manifests as auditory hallucinations, paranoid or bizarre delusions, or disorganized speech and thinking, and it is accompanied by significant social or occupational dysfunction. The onset of symptoms typically occurs in young adulthood, with a global lifetime prevalence of about 0.3-0.7%. |
| Tranquilizer | A tranquilizer, is a drug that induces tranquillity in an individual. |

The term 'tranquilizer' is imprecise, and is usually qualified, or replaced with more precise terms:•minor tranquilizer usually refers to anxiolytic or antianxiety agent•major tranquilizer usually refers to antipsychotics

Antimanic agents can also be considered tranquilizing agents.

In music•'Tranquilizer' is a song written by Tom Stephan & Neil Tennant, from album Superchumbo 'WowieZowie' (2005).•Tranquilizer by Fat Jon The Ample Soul Physician, from album Repaint Tomorow.

| | |
|---|---|
| Atypical antipsychotic | The atypical antipsychotics (AAP) (also known as second generation antipsychotics) are a group of antipsychotic tranquilizing drugs used to treat psychiatric conditions. Some atypical antipsychotics are FDA approved for use in the treatment of schizophrenia. Some carry FDA approved indications for acute mania, bipolar depression, psychotic agitation, bipolar maintenance, and other indications. |
| Clozapine | Clozapine is an atypical antipsychotic medication used in the treatment of schizophrenia, and is also used off-label in the treatment of bipolar disorder. In 2005 three pharmaceutical companies marketed this drug: Novartis Pharmaceuticals (manufacturer), Mylan Laboratories and Ivax Pharmaceuticals (market generic clozapine). The first of the atypical antipsychotics to be developed, it was first introduced in Europe in 1971, but was voluntarily withdrawn by the manufacturer in 1975 after it was shown to cause agranulocytosis, a condition involving a dangerous decrease in the number of white blood cells, that led to death in some patients. |
| Fluoxetine | Fluoxetine is an antidepressant of the selective serotonin reuptake inhibitor (SSRI) class. It is manufactured and marketed by Eli Lilly and Company. In combination with olanzapine it is known as symbyax. Fluoxetine is approved for the treatment of major depression (including pediatric depression), obsessive-compulsive disorder (in both adult and pediatric populations), bulimia nervosa, panic disorder and premenstrual dysphoric disorder. |
| Fluphenazine | Fluphenazine is a typical antipsychotic drug used for the treatment of psychoses such as schizophrenia and acute manic phases of bipolar disorder. It belongs to the piperazine class of phenothiazines.

Its main use is as a long acting injection given once every two or three weeks to people with schizophrenia who suffer frequent relapses of illness. |
| Olanzapine | Olanzapine is an atypical antipsychotic, approved by the FDA for the treatment of schizophrenia and bipolar disorder. Olanzapine is structurally similar to clozapine, but is classified as a thienobenzodiazepine. |

# Chapter 15. Treatment of Psychological Disorders

|  |  |
|---|---|
|  | The olanzapine formulations are manufactured and marketed by the pharmaceutical company Eli Lilly and Company; the drug went generic in 2011. Sales of Zyprexa in 2008 were $2.2B in the US alone, and $4.7B in total. |
| Paroxetine | Paroxetine is an SSRI antidepressant. Marketing of the drug began in 1992 by the pharmaceutical company SmithKline Beecham, now GlaxoSmithKline. Paroxetine is used to treat major depression, obsessive-compulsive disorder, panic disorder, social anxiety, Posttraumatic stress disorder and generalized anxiety disorder in adult outpatients. |
| Quetiapine | Quetiapine (branded as Seroquel, Ketipinor), is an atypical antipsychotic approved for the treatment of schizophrenia, bipolar disorder and as an add-on to treat depression. |
|  | Annual sales are approximately $5.7 billion worldwide, and $2.9 billion in the United States. The U.S. patent, which was set to expire in 2011, received a pediatric exclusivity extension which pushed its expiration to March 26, 2012. The patent has already expired in Canada. |
| Reuptake | Reuptake, is the reabsorption of a neurotransmitter by a neurotransmitter transporter of a pre-synaptic neuron after it has performed its function of transmitting a neural impulse. |
|  | Reuptake is necessary for normal synaptic physiology because it allows for the recycling of neurotransmitters and regulates the level of neurotransmitter present in the synapse and controls how long a signal resulting from neurotransmitter release lasts. Because neurotransmitters are too large and hydrophilic to diffuse through the membrane, specific transport proteins are necessary for the reabsorption of neurotransmitters. |
| Selective serotonin reuptake inhibitor | Selective serotonin reuptake inhibitors or serotonin-specific reuptake inhibitor are a class of compounds typically used as antidepressants in the treatment of depression, anxiety disorders, and some personality disorders. The efficacy of Selective serotonin reuptake inhibitors is disputed. A 2010 meta-analysis states that 'The magnitude of benefit of antidepressant medication compared with placebo ... may be minimal or nonexistent, on average, in patients with mild or moderate symptoms. |
| Serotonin | Serotonin is a monoamine neurotransmitter. Biochemically derived from tryptophan, serotonin is primarily found in the gastrointestinal (GI) tract, platelets, and in the central nervous system (CNS) of animals including humans. It is a well-known contributor to feelings of well-being; therefore it is also known as a 'happiness hormone' despite not being a hormone. |
| Sertraline | Sertraline hydrochloride (trademark names Zoloft and Lustral) is an antidepressant of the selective serotonin reuptake inhibitor (SSRI) class. It was introduced to the market by Pfizer in 1991. Sertraline is primarily used to treat major depression in adult outpatients as well as obsessive-compulsive, panic, and social anxiety disorders in both adults and children. |

| | |
|---|---|
| | In 2007, it was the most prescribed antidepressant on the U.S. retail market, with 29,652,000 prescriptions. |
| Tardive dyskinesia | Tardive dyskinesia is a difficult-to-treat form of dyskinesia (disorder resulting in involuntary, repetitive body movements) that can be tardive (having a slow or belated onset). It frequently appears after long-term or high-dose use of antipsychotic drugs, or in children and infants as a side effect from usage of drugs for gastrointestinal disorders prevention.<br><br>Tardive dyskinesia is characterized by repetitive, involuntary, purposeless movements, such as grimacing, tongue protrusion, lip smacking, puckering and pursing of the lips, and rapid eye blinking. |
| Norepinephrine | Norepinephrine is a catecholamine with multiple roles including as a hormone and a neurotransmitter.<br><br>As a stress hormone, norepinephrine affects parts of the brain, such as the amygdala, where attention and responses are controlled. Along with epinephrine, norepinephrine also underlies the fight-or-flight response, directly increasing heart rate, triggering the release of glucose from energy stores, and increasing blood flow to skeletal muscle. It increases the brain's oxygen supply. Norepinephrine can also suppress neuroinflammation when released diffusely in the brain from the locus ceruleus. |
| Mood stabilizer | A mood stabilizer is a psychiatric medication used to treat mood disorders characterized by intense and sustained mood shifts, typically bipolar disorder.<br><br>Used to treat bipolar disorder, mood stabilizers suppress swings between mania and depression. Mood-stabilizing drugs are also used in borderline personality disorder and Schizoaffective disorder. |
| Parkinsonism | Parkinsonism is a neurological syndrome characterized by tremor, hypokinesia, rigidity, and postural instability. The underlying causes of parkinsonism are numerous, and diagnosis can be complex. While the neurodegenerative condition Parkinson's disease (PD) is the most common cause of parkinsonism, a wide-range of other etiologies may lead to a similar set of symptoms, including some toxins, a few metabolic diseases, and a handful of non-PD neurological conditions. |
| Prefrontal cortex | The prefrontal cortex. is the anterior part of the frontal lobes of the brain, lying in front of the motor and premotor areas. |

# Chapter 15. Treatment of Psychological Disorders

| | |
|---|---|
| Transcranial magnetic stimulation | Transcranial magnetic stimulation is a noninvasive method to cause depolarization or hyperpolarization in the neurons of the brain. Transcranial magnetic stimulation uses electromagnetic induction to induce weak electric currents using a rapidly changing magnetic field; this can cause activity in specific or general parts of the brain with minimal discomfort, allowing the functioning and interconnections of the brain to be studied. A variant of Transcranial magnetic stimulation, repetitive transcranial magnetic stimulation has been tested as a treatment tool for various neurological and psychiatric disorders including migraines, strokes, Parkinson's disease, dystonia, tinnitus, depression and auditory hallucinations. |
| Geriatrics | Geriatrics is a sub-specialty of internal medicine that focuses on health care of elderly people. It aims to promote health by preventing and treating diseases and disabilities in older adults. There is no set age at which patients may be under the care of a geriatrician, or physician who specializes in the care of elderly people. |
| Interpersonal psychotherapy | Interpersonal Psychotherapy is a time-limited treatment that encourages the patient to regain control of mood and functioning typically lasting 12-16 weeks. IPT is based on the common factors of psychotherapy: a 'treatment alliance in which the therapist empathically engages the patient, helps the patient to feel understood, arouses affect, presents a clear rationale and treatment ritual, and yields success experiences.'. Interpersonal Psychotherapy of Depression was developed in the New Haven-Boston Collaborative Depression Research Project by Gerald Klerman, MD, Myrna Weissman, PhD, and their colleagues for the treatment of ambulatory depressed, nonpsychotic, nonbipolar patients. |
| Cognitive behavioral therapy | Cognitive behavioral therapy is a psychotherapeutic approach that addresses dysfunctional emotions, behaviors, and cognitions through a goal-oriented, systematic process. The name refers to behavior therapy, cognitive therapy, and to therapy based upon a combination of basic behavioral and cognitive research. CBT is effective for the treatment of a variety of conditions, including mood, anxiety, personality, eating, substance abuse, tic, and psychotic disorders. |
| Halfway house | The purpose of a halfway house is generally to allow people to begin the process of reintegration with society while still providing monitoring and support; this is generally believed to reduce the risk of recidivism or relapse when compared to a release directly into society. Some halfway houses are meant solely for reintegration of persons who have been recently released from prison or jail, others are meant for people with chronic mental health disorders, and most others are for people with substance abuse issues. These sober halfway houses are many times voluntary places of residence and many of the residents may have no criminal record whatsoever. |

| Human services | Human services refers to a variety of delivery systems such as social welfare services, education, mental health services, and other forms of healthcare. Human services professionals may provide services directly to clients or help clients access services. Human services professionals also manage agencies that provide these services. |
| --- | --- |
| Multimodal therapy | Multimodal therapy is approach to psychotherapy founded by Arnold Lazarus. It is based on the idea that humans are biological beings that think, feel, act, sense, imagine, and interact; and that each of these 'modalities' should be addressed in psychological treatment. Multimodal assessment and treatment which follows BASIC I.D.: (i.e., seven interactive and reciprocally influential dimensions of personality/psychology or 'modalities' which are Behavior, Affect, Sensation, Imagery, Cognition, Interpersonal relationships, and Drugs/biology, respectively). |
| Regression toward the mean | In statistics, regression toward the mean is the phenomenon that if a variable is extreme on its first measurement, it will tend to be closer to the average on a second measurement, and--a fact that may superficially seem paradoxical--if it is extreme on a second measurement, will tend to have been closer to the average on the first measurement. To avoid making wrong inferences, the possibility of regression toward the mean must be considered when designing experiments and interpreting experimental, survey, and other empirical data in the physical, life, behavioral and social sciences.<br><br>The conditions under which regression toward the mean occurs depend on the way the term is mathematically defined. |
| Quackery | Quackery is a derogatory term used to describe the promotion of unproven or fraudulent medical practices. Random House Dictionary describes a 'quack' as a 'fraudulent or ignorant pretender to medical skill' or 'a person who pretends, professionally or publicly, to have skill, knowledge, or qualifications he or she does not possess; a charlatan.' In the Middle Ages the word quack meant 'shouting'. The quacksalvers sold their wares on the market shouting in a loud voice. |
| Prenatal development | Prenatal development is the process in which a human embryo or fetus (or foetus) gestates during pregnancy, from fertilization until birth. Often, the terms fetal development, foetal development, or embryology are used in a similar sense. |
| Insomnia | Insomnia is most often defined by an individual's report of sleeping difficulties. While the term is sometimes used in sleep literature to describe a disorder demonstrated by polysomnographic evidence of disturbed sleep, insomnia is often defined as a positive response to either of two questions: 'Do you experience difficulty sleeping?' or 'Do you have difficulty falling or staying asleep?' |

# Chapter 15. Treatment of Psychological Disorders

Thus, insomnia is most often thought of as both a sign and a symptom that can accompany several sleep, medical, and psychiatric disorders, characterized by persistent difficulty falling asleep and/or staying asleep or sleep of poor quality. Insomnia is typically followed by functional impairment while awake.

1. _____ is a psychotherapeutic approach that addresses dysfunctional emotions, behaviors, and cognitions through a goal-oriented, systematic process. The name refers to behavior therapy, cognitive therapy, and to therapy based upon a combination of basic behavioral and cognitive research.

   CBT is effective for the treatment of a variety of conditions, including mood, anxiety, personality, eating, substance abuse, tic, and psychotic disorders.

   a. Cognitive behavioral therapy
   b. Cognitive restructuring
   c. Cognitive therapy
   d. Coherence therapy

2. _____ is a typical antipsychotic drug used for the treatment of psychoses such as schizophrenia and acute manic phases of bipolar disorder. It belongs to the piperazine class of phenothiazines.

   Its main use is as a long acting injection given once every two or three weeks to people with schizophrenia who suffer frequent relapses of illness.

   a. Haloperidol
   b. Hydroxyzine
   c. Fluphenazine
   d. Lorazepam

3. . A _____, is a drug that induces tranquillity in an individual.

   The term '_____' is imprecise, and is usually qualified, or replaced with more precise terms:•minor _____ usually refers to anxiolytic or antianxiety agent•major _____ usually refers to antipsychotics

   Antimanic agents can also be considered tranquilizing agents.

   In music•'_____' is a song written by Tom Stephan & Neil Tennant, from album Superchumbo 'WowieZowie' (2005).•_____ by Fat Jon The Ample Soul Physician, from album Repaint Tomorow.

a. Vesparax
b. Chemical imbalance
c. Medication phobia
d. Tranquilizer

4. In statistics, _____ is the phenomenon that if a variable is extreme on its first measurement, it will tend to be closer to the average on a second measurement, and--a fact that may superficially seem paradoxical--if it is extreme on a second measurement, will tend to have been closer to the average on the first measurement. To avoid making wrong inferences, the possibility of _____ must be considered when designing experiments and interpreting experimental, survey, and other empirical data in the physical, life, behavioral and social sciences.

The conditions under which _____ occurs depend on the way the term is mathematically defined.

a. Robust regression
b. Regression toward the mean
c. Simple linear regression
d. Sinusoidal model

5. _____ describes a level of psychological well-being, or an absence of a mental disorder. From the perspective of 'positive psychology' or 'holism', _____ may include an individual's ability to enjoy life, and create a balance between life activities and efforts to achieve psychological resilience. _____ can also be defined as an expression of emotions, and as signifying a successful adaptation to a range of demands.

a. Behavioral health
b. Mental health
c. Biological psychopathology
d. Body psychotherapy

1. a
2. c
3. d
4. b
5. b

---

## You can take the complete Chapter Practice Test

**for Chapter 15. Treatment of Psychological Disorders**
on all key terms, persons, places, and concepts.

## Online 99 Cents

## http://www.epub3.2.20111.15.cram101.com/

**Use www.Cram101.com for all your study needs**

**including Cram101's online interactive problem solving labs in**

**chemistry, statistics, mathematics, and more.**

**Want More?**
**Cram101.com...**

Cram101.com provides the outlines and highlights of your textbooks, just like this e-StudyGuide, but also gives you the **PRACTICE TESTS**, and other exclusive study tools for all of your textbooks.

**Learn More.** *Just click*
*http://www.cram101.com/*